FREE Test Taking Tips DVD Offer

To help us better serve you, we have developed a Test Taking Tips DVD that we would like to give you for FREE. **This DVD covers world-class test taking tips that you can use to be even more successful when you are taking your test.**

All that we ask is that you email us your feedback about your study guide. Please let us know what you thought about it – whether that is good, bad or indifferent.

To get your **FREE Test Taking Tips DVD**, email freedvd@studyguideteam.com with "FREE DVD" in the subject line and the following information in the body of the email:

a. The title of your study guide.

b. Your product rating on a scale of 1-5, with 5 being the highest rating.

c. Your feedback about the study guide. What did you think of it?

d. Your full name and shipping address to send your free DVD.

If you have any questions or concerns, please don't hesitate to contact us at freedvd@studyguideteam.com.

Thanks again!

Praxis II Social Studies Content Knowledge 5081 Study Guide

Test Prep & Practice Test Questions for the Praxis 2 Social Studies Exam

Test Prep Books Teaching Study Guide Team

Table of Contents

Quick Overview

As you draw closer to taking your exam, effective preparation becomes more and more important. Thankfully, you have this study guide to help you get ready. Use this guide to help keep your studying on track and refer to it often.

This study guide contains several key sections that will help you be successful on your exam. The guide contains tips for what you should do the night before and the day of the test. Also included are test-taking tips. Knowing the right information is not always enough. Many well-prepared test takers struggle with exams. These tips will help equip you to accurately read, assess, and answer test questions.

A large part of the guide is devoted to showing you what content to expect on the exam and to helping you better understand that content. Near the end of this guide is a practice test so that you can see how well you have grasped the content. Then, answer explanations are provided so that you can understand why you missed certain questions.

Don't try to cram the night before you take your exam. This is not a wise strategy for a few reasons. First, your retention of the information will be low. Your time would be better used by reviewing information you already know rather than trying to learn a lot of new information. Second, you will likely become stressed as you try to gain a large amount of knowledge in a short amount of time. Third, you will be depriving yourself of sleep. So be sure to go to bed at a reasonable time the night before. Being well-rested helps you focus and remain calm.

Be sure to eat a substantial breakfast the morning of the exam. If you are taking the exam in the afternoon, be sure to have a good lunch as well. Being hungry is distracting and can make it difficult to focus. You have hopefully spent lots of time preparing for the exam. Don't let an empty stomach get in the way of success!

When travelling to the testing center, leave earlier than needed. That way, you have a buffer in case you experience any delays. This will help you remain calm and will keep you from missing your appointment time at the testing center.

Be sure to pace yourself during the exam. Don't try to rush through the exam. There is no need to risk performing poorly on the exam just so you can leave the testing center early. Allow yourself to use all of the allotted time if needed.

Remain positive while taking the exam even if you feel like you are performing poorly. Thinking about the content you should have mastered will not help you perform better on the exam.

Once the exam is complete, take some time to relax. Even if you feel that you need to take the exam again, you will be well served by some down time before you begin studying again. It's often easier to convince yourself to study if you know that it will come with a reward!

Test-Taking Strategies

1. Predicting the Answer

When you feel confident in your preparation for a multiple-choice test, try predicting the answer before reading the answer choices. This is especially useful on questions that test objective factual knowledge or that ask you to fill in a blank. By predicting the answer before reading the available choices, you eliminate the possibility that you will be distracted or led astray by an incorrect answer choice. You will feel more confident in your selection if you read the question, predict the answer, and then find your prediction among the answer choices. After using this strategy, be sure to still read all of the answer choices carefully and completely. If you feel unprepared, you should not attempt to predict the answers. This would be a waste of time and an opportunity for your mind to wander in the wrong direction.

2. Reading the Whole Question

Too often, test takers scan a multiple-choice question, recognize a few familiar words, and immediately jump to the answer choices. Test authors are aware of this common impatience, and they will sometimes prey upon it. For instance, a test author might subtly turn the question into a negative, or he or she might redirect the focus of the question right at the end. The only way to avoid falling into these traps is to read the entirety of the question carefully before reading the answer choices.

3. Looking for Wrong Answers

Long and complicated multiple-choice questions can be intimidating. One way to simplify a difficult multiple-choice question is to eliminate all of the answer choices that are clearly wrong. In most sets of answers, there will be at least one selection that can be dismissed right away. If the test is administered on paper, the test taker could draw a line through it to indicate that it may be ignored; otherwise, the test taker will have to perform this operation mentally or on scratch paper. In either case, once the obviously incorrect answers have been eliminated, the remaining choices may be considered. Sometimes identifying the clearly wrong answers will give the test taker some information about the correct answer. For instance, if one of the remaining answer choices is a direct opposite of one of the eliminated answer choices, it may well be the correct answer. The opposite of obviously wrong is obviously right! Of course, this is not always the case. Some answers are obviously incorrect simply because they are irrelevant to the question being asked. Still, identifying and eliminating some incorrect answer choices is a good way to simplify a multiple-choice question.

4. Don't Overanalyze

Anxious test takers often overanalyze questions. When you are nervous, your brain will often run wild, causing you to make associations and discover clues that don't actually exist. If you feel that this may be a problem for you, do whatever you can to slow down during the test. Try taking a deep breath or counting to ten. As you read and consider the question, restrict yourself to the particular words used by the author. Avoid thought tangents about what the author *really* meant, or what he or she was *trying* to say. The only things that matter on a multiple-choice test are the words that are actually in the question. You must avoid reading too much into a multiple-choice question, or supposing that the writer meant something other than what he or she wrote.

5. No Need for Panic

It is wise to learn as many strategies as possible before taking a multiple-choice test, but it is likely that you will come across a few questions for which you simply don't know the answer. In this situation, avoid panicking. Because most multiple-choice tests include dozens of questions, the relative value of a single wrong answer is small. Moreover, your failure on one question has no effect on your success elsewhere on the test. As much as possible, you should compartmentalize each question on a multiple-choice test. In other words, you should not allow your feelings about one question to affect your success on the others. When you find a question that you either don't understand or don't know how to answer, just take a deep breath and do your best. Read the entire question slowly and carefully. Try rephrasing the question a couple of different ways. Then, read all of the answer choices carefully. After eliminating obviously wrong answers, make a selection and move on to the next question.

6. Confusing Answer Choices

When working on a difficult multiple-choice question, there may be a tendency to focus on the answer choices that are the easiest to understand. Many people, whether consciously or not, gravitate to the answer choices that require the least concentration, knowledge, and memory. This is a mistake. When you come across an answer choice that is confusing, you should give it extra attention. A question might be confusing because you do not know the subject matter to which it refers. If this is the case, don't eliminate the answer before you have affirmatively settled on another. When you come across an answer choice of this type, set it aside as you look at the remaining choices. If you can confidently assert that one of the other choices is correct, you can leave the confusing answer aside. Otherwise, you will need to take a moment to try to better understand the confusing answer choice. Rephrasing is one way to tease out the sense of a confusing answer choice.

7. Your First Instinct

Many people struggle with multiple-choice tests because they overthink the questions. If you have studied sufficiently for the test, you should be prepared to trust your first instinct once you have carefully and completely read the question and all of the answer choices. There is a great deal of research suggesting that the mind can come to the correct conclusion very quickly once it has obtained all of the relevant information. At times, it may seem to you as if your intuition is working faster even than your reasoning mind. This may in fact be true. The knowledge you obtain while studying may be retrieved from your subconscious before you have a chance to work out the associations that support it. Verify your instinct by working out the reasons that it should be trusted.

8. Key Words

Many test takers struggle with multiple-choice questions because they have poor reading comprehension skills. Quickly reading and understanding a multiple-choice question requires a mixture of skill and experience. To help with this, try jotting down a few key words and phrases on a piece of scrap paper. Doing this concentrates the process of reading and forces the mind to weigh the relative importance of the question's parts. In selecting words and phrases to write down, the test taker thinks about the question more deeply and carefully. This is especially true for multiple-choice questions that are preceded by a long prompt.

9. Subtle Negatives

One of the oldest tricks in the multiple-choice test writer's book is to subtly reverse the meaning of a question with a word like *not* or *except*. If you are not paying attention to each word in the question, you can easily be led astray by this trick. For instance, a common question format is, "Which of the following is...?" Obviously, if the question instead is, "Which of the following is not...?," then the answer will be quite different. Even worse, the test makers are aware of the potential for this mistake and will include one answer choice that would be correct if the question were not negated or reversed. A test taker who misses the reversal will find what he or she believes to be a correct answer and will be so confident that he or she will fail to reread the question and discover the original error. The only way to avoid this is to practice a wide variety of multiple-choice questions and to pay close attention to each and every word.

10. Reading Every Answer Choice

It may seem obvious, but you should always read every one of the answer choices! Too many test takers fall into the habit of scanning the question and assuming that they understand the question because they recognize a few key words. From there, they pick the first answer choice that answers the question they believe they have read. Test takers who read all of the answer choices might discover that one of the latter answer choices is actually *more* correct. Moreover, reading all of the answer choices can remind you of facts related to the question that can help you arrive at the correct answer. Sometimes, a misstatement or incorrect detail in one of the latter answer choices will trigger your memory of the subject and will enable you to find the right answer. Failing to read all of the answer choices is like not reading all of the items on a restaurant menu: you might miss out on the perfect choice.

11. Spot the Hedges

One of the keys to success on multiple-choice tests is paying close attention to every word. This is never more true than with words like *almost*, *most*, *some*, and *sometimes*. These words are called "hedges" because they indicate that a statement is not totally true or not true in every place and time. An absolute statement will contain no hedges, but in many subjects, like literature and history, the answers are not always straightforward or absolute. There are always exceptions to the rules in these subjects. For this reason, you should favor those multiple-choice questions that contain hedging language. The presence of qualifying words indicates that the author is taking special care with his or her words, which is certainly important when composing the right answer. After all, there are many ways to be wrong, but there is only one way to be right! For this reason, it is wise to avoid answers that are absolute when taking a multiple-choice test. An absolute answer is one that says things are either all one way or all another. They often include words like *every*, *always*, *best*, and *never*. If you are taking a multiple-choice test in a subject that doesn't lend itself to absolute answers, be on your guard if you see any of these words.

12. Long Answers

In many subject areas, the answers are not simple. As already mentioned, the right answer often requires hedges. Another common feature of the answers to a complex or subjective question are qualifying clauses, which are groups of words that subtly modify the meaning of the sentence. If the question or answer choice describes a rule to which there are exceptions or the subject matter is complicated, ambiguous, or confusing, the correct answer will require many words in order to be expressed clearly and accurately. In essence, you should not be deterred by answer choices that seem excessively long. Oftentimes, the author of the text will not be able to write the correct answer without offering some qualifications and modifications. Your job is to read the answer choices thoroughly and completely and to select the one that most accurately and precisely answers the question.

13. Restating to Understand

Sometimes, a question on a multiple-choice test is difficult not because of what it asks but because of how it is written. If this is the case, restate the question or answer choice in different words. This process serves a couple of important purposes. First, it forces you to concentrate on the core of the question. In order to rephrase the question accurately, you have to understand it well. Rephrasing the question will concentrate your mind on the key words and ideas. Second, it will present the information to your mind in a fresh way. This process may trigger your memory and render some useful scrap of information picked up while studying.

14. True Statements

Sometimes an answer choice will be true in itself, but it does not answer the question. This is one of the main reasons why it is essential to read the question carefully and completely before proceeding to the answer choices. Too often, test takers skip ahead to the answer choices and look for true statements. Having found one of these, they are content to select it without reference to the question above. Obviously, this provides an easy way for test makers to play tricks. The savvy test taker will always read the entire question before turning to the answer choices. Then, having settled on a correct answer choice, he or she will refer to the original question and ensure that the selected answer is relevant. The mistake of choosing a correct-but-irrelevant answer choice is especially common on questions related to specific pieces of objective knowledge, like historical or scientific facts. A prepared test taker will have a wealth of factual knowledge at his or her disposal, and should not be careless in its application.

15. No Patterns

One of the more dangerous ideas that circulates about multiple-choice tests is that the correct answers tend to fall into patterns. These erroneous ideas range from a belief that B and C are the most common right answers, to the idea that an unprepared test-taker should answer "A-B-A-C-A-D-A-B-A." It cannot be emphasized enough that pattern-seeking of this type is exactly the WRONG way to approach a multiple-choice test. To begin with, it is highly unlikely that the test maker will plot the correct answers according to some predetermined pattern. The questions are scrambled and delivered in a random order. Furthermore, even if the test maker was following a pattern in the assignation of correct answers, there is no reason why the test taker would know which pattern he or she was using. Any attempt to discern a pattern in the answer choices is a waste of time and a distraction from the real work of taking the test. A test taker would be much better served by extra preparation before the test than by reliance on a pattern in the answers.

FREE DVD OFFER

Don't forget that doing well on your exam includes both understanding the test content and understanding how to use what you know to do well on the test. We offer a completely FREE Test Taking Tips DVD that covers world class test taking tips that you can use to be even more successful when you are taking your test.

All that we ask is that you email us your feedback about your study guide. To get your **FREE Test Taking Tips DVD**, email freedvd@studyguideteam.com with "FREE DVD" in the subject line and the following information in the body of the email:

- The title of your study guide.
- Your product rating on a scale of 1-5, with 5 being the highest rating.
- Your feedback about the study guide. What did you think of it?
- Your full name and shipping address to send your free DVD.

Introduction to the Praxis II Social Studies Test

Function of the Test

The Praxis II Social Studies Content Knowledge exam is one of the Educational Testing Service's (ETS's) Subject Assessment tests. The Subject Assessment tests are intended to measure knowledge in more than ninety specific subjects taught by educators in kindergarten through 12th grade classrooms, as well as teaching skills and knowledge in those subject areas. The tests are offered worldwide, but are primarily used in the United States, most often as a required part of the certification and licensing procedure in certain individual states. They are also used as part of the licensing process by some professional associations and organizations.

The Social Studies Content Knowledge exam is designed to evaluate the knowledge and skills of prospective secondary school social studies teachers to determine whether they are of a sufficient level to be a beginning teacher. Individuals taking the test are usually teachers beginning their careers, either freshly out of college, having recently decided to seek a particular license or certification, or having recently moved to a state where the test is required or preferred.

Test Administration

The test is administered by computer through an international network of testing centers, including Prometric testing centers, some colleges and universities, as well as a variety of other locations. Although it is primarily used in the United States, the test is available at locations throughout the world. However, the test is not available at all times. Instead, the test is offered during a window of about two weeks per month.

Accommodations for test takers meeting the requirements of the Americans with Disabilities Act include extended testing time, additional rest breaks, a separate testing room, a writer/recorder of answers, a test reader, and tests in sign language, Braille, large print, or audio. Test takers may opt to retake the test at any time after twenty-one days from the initial attempt.

Test Format

The test addresses a wide range of social studies topics, including United States history, world history, government/civics/political science, geography, economics, sociology, anthropology, and psychology. It also includes interdisciplinary questions, which reflect relationships between these fields. In total, the test is comprised of 130 selected-response questions in which the test-taker chooses from multiple choice options or chooses a particular word, sentence, or part of a graphic. A maximum of 60% of the questions are knowledge recall questions, and the remainder are higher-order thinking questions. Some questions require test takers to interpret material such as written passages, maps, charts, or graphs. Between 10 and 15 percent of the test pertains to diversity of gender, culture, race, and/or content relating to Latin America, Africa, Asia, or Oceania.

The approximate breakdown of the questions by subject area is as follows:

Content Category	# of Questions	Percentage of Exam
United States History	26	20%
World History	26	20%
Government/Civics/Political Science	26	20%
Geography	19	15%
Economics	19	15%
Behavioral Sciences	14	10%

Scoring

Raw scores are based on the number of correct responses, with no penalty for incorrect answers. The raw scores are then converted to a scaled score, which ranges from 100 to 200. The required passing scaled score varies from state to state, from a low of 146 in South Dakota to a high of 162 in Rhode Island and Connecticut. The median score in 2015 was 166, with the average performance ranging from 156 to 176.

ETS also offers a "Recognition of Excellence" to test takers who perform exceptionally well on the exam. The award is typically given to test takers whose scores fall in the top fifteen percent of scores on the exam; in 2015, the required score was 184.

United States History

North American Geography, Peoples, and Cultures Prior to European Colonization

During the last Ice Age, large glaciers covered much of North America, trapping seawater and lowering the sea level. This exposed a land bridge between northwest Asia and North America that has been named Beringia. Nomadic peoples from Siberia used the Beringia land bridge to cross into North America. When the Ice Age ended a few thousand years later, the glaciers melted, the sea level rose, and Beringia disappeared beneath the ocean. The nomads who had crossed into North America before the Ice Age ended were searching for prey such as mastodons and wooly mammoths. These nomadic peoples lived in small groups and slowly spread out across North and South America during the next several millennia.

Several thousand years ago, the Neolithic Revolution occurred. This event occurred at different times in different places around the world, but it marked an important turning point in human history. The Neolithic Revolution included the development of agriculture and the domestication of animals. In North America, the primary crops were maize (corn), tomatoes, pumpkins, chilies, potatoes, and beans. There were only a few animals for Native Americans to domesticate, including the dog (in North America) and the llama (in Central America). Dogs were used to guard and hunt, and llamas produced wool and also transported goods.

The development of agriculture and domesticated animals led to a major change in North American societies: instead of small nomadic bands of hunter-gatherers, many native peoples became semi-sedentary. They began to form settlements, create social hierarchies, and develop new religious beliefs. However, many Native Americans remained semi-nomadic and lived in villages for only part of the year. Most Native American villages engaged in long distance trade with other groups. In general, most Native American peoples practiced animist beliefs—in other words, they thought that everything in the natural world had some spiritual power, including plants, animals, and rocks. In most Native American societies, women were responsible for farming while men hunted and fished.

Although most Native Americans continued to live in small villages, some larger settlements eventually developed. In Central America in 1325 A.D., the Aztec built the city of Tenochtitlan, located on the site of present day Mexico City, which was thought to contain more than 200,000 inhabitants. This meant it could have been one of the largest cities in the world before Spanish conquistadors destroyed it in 1521. In North America, Native Americans built the city of Cahokia (near the modern city of St. Louis), which may have had up to 40,000 residents before it was abandoned sometime around 1300. Cahokia also included a large circle of timber posts that may have had been used for astronomical predictions, similar to Stonehenge in Britain.

North and South America were rich in natural resources and also featured a variety of climates and geographies. This led to the development of various Native American societies before European colonists arrived.

The Iroquois and Algonquians were the major tribes in the eastern part of North America. They spoke different languages and frequently fought each other. The vast forests, especially in the Northeast, Midwest, and Southeast, provided wood for building wigwams and longhouses, as well as tools and weapons. Native Americans also used major waterways such as the Ohio and Mississippi Rivers to engage in trade, participate in small- and large-scale fishing activities, and launch raids against each other.

Several different tribes also lived between the Mississippi River and the Rocky Mountains—an area later known as the Great Plains. The Sioux, Comanche, Blackfoot, and Cheyenne were among these more nomadic peoples who hunted buffalo. They lived in teepees that were easy to take apart and rebuild in a new location as the tribe moved across the vast prairies. Native Americans sometimes set fire to the grasslands in order to control vegetation and improve grazing conditions.

The Pueblo people—including the Zuni, Hope, and Acoma tribes—lived in the deserts of the southwest. They used clay bricks to build large apartment complexes called pueblos, digging into the side of cliffs to create shelter. Since the environment was so dry, they had to build complex irrigation systems in order to grow crops.

The Tlingit, Chinook, and Salish people lived on the Pacific coast where they survived by hunting and fishing. Salmon were a staple of their diet and culture, playing an important part in their eating habits as well as their religious beliefs. The tribes developed techniques to create waterproof baskets and woven raincoats due to the wet climate of the Pacific Northwest.

The Aleuts and Inuit lived in the arctic and subarctic regions of North America where they hunted seals and whales. Because of the harsh conditions, they built semi-subterranean shelters that were insulated against the cold.

Founding and Development of European Colonies in North America

European monarchs began dispatching naval expeditions in the 15th century in an effort to bypass Muslim powers in the Middle East, such as the Ottoman Empire, which controlled the overland trade routes that led to Asia. European nation-states were competing against each other for wealth and power and wanted to have direct contact with Asia. The spice trade was especially lucrative, but Europeans also sought to spread Christianity and earn a reputation for making exciting discoveries. Several technological improvements helped European explorers establish trading outposts in Africa, Asia, and the Americas. Tools such as the astrolabe and quadrant allowed sailors to navigate more accurately, and the Portuguese built a new ship called a caravel that was faster and more maneuverable.

Europeans had discovered a route around the southern tip of Africa that led to Asia. However, the journey was long and dangerous. Christopher Columbus, a Genoese sailor, lobbied several European monarchs and sought financial support for an expedition across the Atlantic Ocean. He mistakenly believed he could reach Asia much more quickly via a western route across the Atlantic and was unaware that his path was blocked. Eventually, King Ferdinand and Queen Isabella of Castile accepted his proposal and provided funding for three ships as well as sailors and provisions. They agreed to appoint Columbus governor of any territory he discovered and granted him ten percent of the revenue from the new lands. After five weeks at sea, Columbus landed on San Salvador and explored the Caribbean islands for about three months before returning home.

Interaction of European, Native American, and African Peoples During the Colonial Period

News of his success sparked a number of other expeditions and the British, French, Dutch, Spanish, and Portuguese all eventually laid claim to lands in the New World. Columbus himself made three more voyages to the Americas. The French and Dutch focused mostly on the lucrative fur trade in North America. The Spanish and Portuguese sought gold in Central and South America but also tried to convert Native Americans to Christianity. British settlers also sought economic opportunity and created the first British colony at Jamestown, Virginia, in 1607. However, the Puritans who landed at Plymouth Rock in 1620 left for the New World in order to establish their ideal religious community.

Connecticut, New Hampshire, Massachusetts, and Rhode Island were considered the "New England colonies." The settlements in New England were based around an economy focused on fishing and lumber. These colonies maintained puritanical and Congregationalist religious beliefs. While English Puritans mostly settled in New England, a wide variety of colonists settled in the mid-Atlantic region. English, Scottish, Dutch, and Swedish settlers came to Delaware, New York, New Jersey, and Pennsylvania. As a result, the mid-Atlantic colonies were more religiously diverse and tolerant than the settlements in New England. Agriculture was the foundation of the economy in mid-Atlantic colonies. This meant that settlements were more dispersed. Government and administration were based on counties instead of towns.

The southern colonies, including Virginia, Maryland, the Carolinas, and Georgia, were also organized by county. The southern economy focused on labor-intensive crops such as tobacco and rice, and as a result, landowners relied on indentured servants and African slaves. Slaves were present in most colonies, but were more common in the south.

Political power was also distributed differently among the colonies. Some colonies, such as New York and Virginia, were royal colonies ruled directly by the king. Pennsylvania was a proprietary colony—the king allowed William Penn to appoint officials and govern the colony as he saw fit. Corporate colonies, such as Rhode Island and Connecticut, were administered by a group of investors. But, by the early 1700s, the king had revoked the charters of most proprietary and corporate colonies and assumed direct control himself.

Native Americans continued to play an important role in the early history of Britain's North American colonies. Squanto was an Algonquian Indian who helped English settlers in Massachusetts survive by teaching them how to plant native crops. Some Native American tribes were friendly towards the colonists and traded with them.

However, Native Americans and Europeans often came into conflict, frequently over land disputes. The Native Americans and Europeans had very different concepts of land use and ownership. Native Americans did not understand the concept of landownership or sale. When they entered into agreements with the colonists, Native Americans thought they were allowing the settlers to farm the land temporarily, rather than retain it in perpetuity. On the other hand, colonists were frustrated when Native Americans continued to hunt and fish on lands they had "sold." These, and other disagreements, eventually led to bloody conflicts that gradually weakened Native American tribes.

Native Americans were also vulnerable to diseases to which the Europeans had developed immunity. These diseases included bubonic plague, cholera, chicken pox, pneumonic plague, influenza, measles, scarlet fever, typhus, smallpox, and tuberculosis. These diseases killed millions of Native Americans and were sometimes used as a biological weapon. Historians estimate that as much as 80 percent of the Native American population died through disease and warfare.

Origins of the American Revolution and Founding of the United States

The French colonies in Canada also threatened the British settlements. France and Britain had been enemies for centuries. Religious differences reinforced their hostility; the British were Protestant and the French were mostly Catholic. Far fewer colonists settled in "New France," but they often clashed with the British, especially over the lucrative fur trade. Both the British and French sought to dominate the trade in beaver pelts, which were used to make hats in Europe. The British and French fought a series of colonial wars between 1689 and 1748 that failed to resolve the struggle for dominance in North America.

Eventually, the contest culminated in the French and Indian War (also known as the Seven Years' War), which ended in 1763. The French initially enjoyed the upper hand because they were able to persuade more Native American tribes to support them. The Native Americans felt the French were less likely to encroach on their territory than the land-hungry British. The Native Americans launched devastating raids along the British colonial frontier. However, the British eventually emerged victorious after they blockaded the French colonies in Canada. This prevented the French from bringing in reinforcements or from resupplying their Native American allies with gunpowder and ammunition. Native American raids subsided and eventually the French surrendered almost all of their colonial possessions in North America. Some historians consider this war the first global conflict because battles were also fought in Europe, Asia, and Africa.

The French defeat radically altered the balance of power in North America. Previously, Native Americans had been able to play the French and British against each other, but now they were without many of their French allies. In addition, the French and Indian War also set the stage for the American Revolution. Although victorious, the British monarchy spent an enormous amount of money and the war doubled the national debt. In order to pay off the debts, King George III began imposing taxes upon the North American colonies, which eventually led to revolution.

Since 1651, the British crown had tried to control trade within its empire, which eventually led to tension and discontent in the North American colonies. That year, the monarchy introduced the Navigation Acts, which prevented the North American colonies from trading directly with other European powers—all goods had to be shipped to Britain first. This was an attempt to keep wealth within the British Empire and to prevent other empires from profiting from their colonies. This was an example of mercantilism—an economic policy that formed the foundation of Britain's empire. Mercantilism called for government regulation in the form of tariffs, a tax on imports from other countries. This raised prices on foreign goods and encouraged British imperial subjects to purchase goods made in Britain or the colonies. This reduced imports and maximized exports, thus enriching the British Empire.

The Molasses Act in 1731 was another outgrowth of mercantilism. This law imposed a higher tax on the molasses that colonists purchased from the Dutch, French, or Spanish colonies. The tax was unpopular with the colonists and British imperial officials eventually decided not to enforce the tax. The Molasses Act had threatened to disrupt the pattern of triangular trade that had emerged in the Atlantic world. First, ships from Britain's North American colonies carried rum to Africa where it was traded for slaves and gold. Then, the ships took the slaves to French and Spanish colonies in the Caribbean and exchanged them for sugar or molasses. In the last part of the triangular trade system, merchants sailed back to North America where the sugar and molasses was used to make rum, and the cycle could start over again.

In addition to economic connections, many other bonds also bridged the Atlantic Ocean. Most colonists shared a common language, common religion, and common culture. However, as the colonies grew in population, they began to develop local institutions and a separate sense of identity. For example, it became common for ministers to receive their education at seminaries in North America rather than Britain. Newspapers also began to focus on printing more local news as well. Perhaps most importantly, the colonies began to exercise more control over their own political affairs. The British government retained control over international issues, such as war and trade, but the colonists controlled their own domestic affairs. Colonies began to form their own political assemblies and elect landowners who represented local districts. In addition, communications between the colonies and Britain were very slow because it took months for a ship to cross the Atlantic and return with a response.

A number of political acts by the British monarchy also led to more discontent among the colonies. After the French and Indian War ended in 1763, the king declared that the colonists could not settle west of the Appalachian Mountains. This was known as the Proclamation of 1763. Many colonists were frustrated because they had expected this territory would be open for expansion after the French had been defeated.

Additionally, taxes were imposed in an effort to help reduce the debt Britain amassed during the French and Indian War. In 1764, Parliament passed the Sugar Act, which reduced the tax on molasses but also provided for greater enforcement powers. Some colonists protested by organizing boycotts on British goods. One year later, in 1765, Parliament passed the Quartering Act, which required colonists to provide housing and food to British troops. This law was also very unpopular and led to protests in the North American colonies.

The Stamp Act of 1765 required the colonists to pay a tax on legal documents, newspapers, magazines and other printed materials. Colonial assemblies protested the tax and petitioned the British government in order to have it repealed. Merchants also organized boycotts and established correspondence committees in order to share information. Eventually, Parliament repealed the Stamp Act but simultaneously reaffirmed the Crown's right to tax the colonies.

In 1767, Parliament introduced the Townshend Acts, which imposed a tax on goods the colonies imported from Britain, such as tea, lead, paint, glass, and paper. The colonies protested again and British imperial officials were assaulted in some cases. The British government sent additional troops to North America to restore order. The arrival of troops in Boston only led to more tension that eventually culminated in the Boston Massacre in 1770, where five colonists were killed and eight were wounded. Except for the duty on tea, most of Townshend Act taxes were repealed after the Boston Massacre.

Parliament passed the Tea Act in 1773 and, although it actually reduced the tax on tea, it was another unpopular piece of legislation. The Tea Act allowed the British East India Company to sell its products directly, effectively cutting out colonial merchants and stirring more Anglo-American anger and resentment. This resulted in the Boston Tea Party in 1773, an incident in which colonial tea merchants disguised themselves as Indians before storming several British ships that were anchored in Boston harbor. Once aboard, the disguised colonists dumped more than 300 chests of tea into the water.

Because the British government was unable to identify the perpetrators, Parliament passed a series of laws that punished the entire colony of Massachusetts. These acts were known as the Coercive or Intolerable Acts. The first law closed the port of Boston until the tea had been paid for (an estimated $1.7 million in today's currency). The second act curtailed the authority of Massachusetts' colonial government. Instead of being elected by colonists, most government officials were now appointed by the king. In addition, the act restricted town meetings, the basic form of government in Massachusetts, and limited most villages to one meeting per year. This act angered colonists throughout the thirteen colonies because they feared their rights could be stripped away as well. A third act allowed for British soldiers to be tried in Britain if they were accused of a crime. The fourth act once again required colonists to provide food and shelter to British soldiers.

Colonists responded by forming the First Continental Congress in 1774, and all the colonies except for Georgia sent delegates. The delegates sought a compromise with the British government instead of launching an armed revolt. The First Continental Congress sent a petition to King George III affirming their loyalty but demanding the repeal of the Intolerable Acts. The delegates organized a boycott of imports from and exports to Britain until their demands were met.

The colonists began to form militias and gather weapons and ammunition. The first battle of the revolution began at Lexington and Concord in April 1775 when British troops tried to seize a supply of gunpowder and were confronted by about eighty Minutemen. A brief skirmish left eight colonists dead and ten wounded. Colonial reinforcements poured in and harassed the British force as they retreated to Boston. Although the battle did not result in many casualties, it marked the beginning of war.

A month later, the Second Continental Congress convened in Philadelphia. The delegates formed an army and appointed George Washington as commander in chief. Delegates were still reluctant to repudiate their allegiance to King George III and did not do so until they issued the Declaration of Independence on July 4, 1776. The Declaration drew on the ideas of the Enlightenment and declared that the colonists had the right to life, liberty, and the pursuit of happiness. The Declaration stated that the colonists had to break away from Britain because King George III had violated their rights.

After the Battle of Lexington and Concord, British troops retreated to Boston and the colonial militias laid siege to the city. Colonists built fortifications on Bunker Hill outside the city and British troops attacked the position in June 1775. The colonists inflicted heavy casualties on the British and killed a number of officers. However, the defenders ran out of ammunition and British troops captured Bunker Hill on the third assault. Although it was a defeat for the colonists, the Battle of Bunker Hill demonstrated that they could stand and fight against the disciplined and professional British army.

The British army initially had the upper hand and defeated colonial forces in a number of engagements. The Americans did not achieve a victory until the Battle of Trenton in December 1776. Washington famously crossed the Delaware River on Christmas Day and launched a surprise attack against Hessian mercenaries. They captured more than 1,000 soldiers and suffered very minimal casualties. The victory at Trenton bolstered American morale and showed that they could defeat professional European soldiers.

The Battle of Saratoga in New York in the fall of 1777 was an important turning point in the American War for Independence. American troops surrounded and captured more than 6,000 British soldiers. This victory convinced the French king to support the revolutionaries by sending troops, money, weapons, and ships to the American continent. French officers who fought alongside the Patriots brought back many ideas with them that eventually sparked a revolution in France in 1789.

French support was very important in the last major battle of the revolution at Yorktown, Virginia, in 1781. American troops laid siege to General Cornwallis's British forces at Yorktown. The French fleet defeated a British naval squadron sent to relieve Cornwallis. French and American troops began attacking the British fortifications in Yorktown; a sustained artillery bombardment by American guns eventually forced Cornwallis to surrender. This ended the Revolutionary War, and in 1783 the British signed the Treaty of Paris. Britain recognized the United States as an independent country and set the Mississippi River as the nation's western border. However, British troops continued to occupy several forts in the Great Lakes region.

In addition, tens of thousands of colonists who remained loyal to the British Empire fled the United States after the war. They were known as loyalists and many thousands had joined militias and fought against the patriots. Some loyalists fled to Canada or Britain but many remained in the United States. Many Native American tribes had sided with the British as well in an attempt to curb western expansion. No Native American leaders signed the Treaty of Paris and they refused to give up their territories, which led to further conflict as the new American nation began to expand westward.

Adoption of the Constitution and Bill of Rights and Their Impact on the Political Development of the Early United States

America's first system of government was actually laid out in the Articles of Confederation, and not the Constitution. The Articles of Confederation were ratified during the Revolutionary War and went into effect in 1781. The Articles of Confederation created a relatively weak central government and allowed individual states to retain most of the power. Under this system, the national government did not have a president or judiciary. Each state had only one vote in the Confederation Congress and most major decisions required unanimous approval by all thirteen states. Despite this requirement, the Confederation Congress did pass some important legislation, including the Northwest Ordinance, which organized the land west of Appalachian Mountains. The territories eventually became the states of Ohio, Indiana, Michigan, Illinois, Wisconsin, and Minnesota. However, Congress did not have the power to tax and could only request money from the states without any way to enforce its demands. A Revolutionary War veteran named Daniel Shays led an armed insurrection in western Massachusetts in 1787. Although Shay's Rebellion was defeated, it drew attention to the weaknesses of the Articles of Confederation.

The Constitutional Convention met in Philadelphia a few months after the rebellion in order to create a stronger federal government. However, delegates disagreed over how to structure the new system. The Virginia Plan was one proposal that included a bicameral legislature where states were awarded representation based on their population size. This would benefit more populous states at the expense of smaller states. The other main proposal was the New Jersey Plan, which retained many elements of the Articles of Confederation, including a unicameral legislature with one vote per state. This plan would put states on an equal footing regardless of population.

Eventually, delegates agreed to support the Connecticut Compromise (also known as the Great Compromise), which incorporated elements from both the Virginia and New Jersey Plans. Under the new Constitution, Congress would be a bicameral body. In the House of Representatives, states would be allocated seats based on population, but in the Senate each state would have two votes. The Constitution also included a president and judiciary that would each serve to check the power of other branches of government. In addition, Congress had the power to tax and had more enforcement powers.

Slavery was another contentious issue during the Constitutional Convention. Slavery was more common in the Southern states and less common in the North. The Southern states wanted slaves to be counted when calculating representation in Congress but not when it came to assessing taxes. Northern states wanted the opposite and eventually the two sides agreed to the Three-Fifths Compromise where slaves were counted as three-fifths of a person for the purposes of both taxation and representation. The Constitution also included a provision that allowed slave owners to recover slaves who had escaped and permitted the international slave trade to continue until 1808.

Once the Constitution had been drafted, nine of the thirteen states had to ratify it. Vigorous debate erupted over whether or not the Constitution should be approved. Two different political factions emerged. The Federalists supported the Constitution because they felt a stronger central government was necessary in order to promote economic growth and improve national security. Several leading federalists, including Alexander Hamilton, John Jay, and James Madison, published a series of articles urging voters to support the Constitution. However, the Anti-Federalists, including Thomas Jefferson and Patrick Henry, felt that the Constitution took too much power away from the states and gave it to the national government. They also thought there weren't enough protections for individual rights and lobbied for the addition of a Bill of Rights that guaranteed basic liberties. Ultimately, the Constitution was ratified in 1788 and the Bill of Rights was approved a year later.

The Electoral College unanimously elected George Washington as the nation's first president in 1789. Despite this appearance of unity, deep political divisions led to the formation of the nation's first party system. Washington supported the Federalist ideology and appointed several Federalists to his cabinet, including Alexander Hamilton as secretary of the treasury. The Anti-Federalist faction evolved into the Democratic-Republican Party and favored stronger state governments instead of a powerful federal government. As settlers moved into the new Northwest Territories, Washington helped pacify Indians who opposed further expansion. He also successfully put down a rebellion in western Pennsylvania by farmers opposed to a federal tax on whiskey.

A number of different issues divided the Federalists and the Democratic-Republicans, including the French Revolution, which began in 1789. Initially, many Americans supported the French effort to replace their monarchy and create a republican government. However, the French Revolution quickly became more violent, as thousands of suspected opponents of the revolution were executed during the Reign of Terror. The Federalists, including Washington, were horrified by the violence, while Jefferson and the Democratic-Republicans thought the United States should help its former ally. Washington ensured that the country remain officially neutral.

Washington declined to seek a third term and another Federalist, John Adams, became our second president. Adams signed the Alien and Sedition Acts, which made it a criminal offense to criticize the government, and allowed the president to deport aliens suspected of treason. Adams and the Federalists argued that the laws were necessary in order to improve security as Europe became embroiled in a war against the new French republic. Jefferson and the Democratic-Republicans said the laws restricted free speech. Jefferson made the acts an important topic in 1800 when he successfully ran for president.

Jefferson's victory marked a turning point in the political system because the Democratic-Republicans gained more power while the Federalists went into decline. He repealed the Alien and Sedition Acts when he was elected. The Federalists were further weakened when Hamilton was killed in a duel in 1804.

Jefferson accomplished several significant achievements during his presidency, and one of the most important was the Louisiana Purchase in 1803. For $15 million, Jefferson bought French territory west of the Mississippi River that doubled the size of the United States. He then appointed Meriwether Lewis and William Clark to lead an expedition to explore the vast new territory and study its geography, vegetation, and plant life. Clark also brought his African-American slave, York, on the journey. York helped hunt and even saved Clark's life during a flood. The expedition was also aided by Sacagawea, a Shoshone woman, who acted as a guide and interpreter. The explorers also established relations with Native American tribes and set the stage for further western expansion in the 1800s.

Several key Supreme Court decisions were also issued during this time. The case of *Marbury vs. Madison* established the policy of judicial review, which declared that the Supreme Court could rule whether or not an act of Congress was constitutional. The case of *McCullough vs. Maryland* affirmed that Congress had the power to pass laws that were "necessary and proper" in order to carry out its other duties. The case also upheld the supremacy of federal laws over state laws when they came into conflict.

War between the United States and Britain broke out in 1812 because the United States was drawn into a conflict between Britain and France. Britain refused to stop interfering with American ships bound for

France and had begun forcibly recruiting American citizens into the British navy. Furthermore, the British still occupied several forts near the Great Lakes and continued to encourage Indians to attack American settlements in the Northwest Territories.

This led to war in 1812, and many Native American leaders allied themselves with the British, including the Shawnee warrior Tecumseh. Tecumseh temporarily united several tribes but his confederacy fell apart when he was killed in battle. This further weakened Native American resistance and facilitated American settlement in the Northwest Territory after the war.

The United States also achieved a victory at the Battle of Lake Erie where several American ships routed a British squadron. However, an American attempt to invade Canada failed, and the British humiliated the nation by invading Washington D.C. and burning down several public buildings, including the White House. The United States did achieve another victory after hostilities had ceased when future president Andrew Jackson repulsed a British attack at New Orleans. The war did not result in any major territorial gains or losses, but it did reaffirm American independence and gave America its national anthem, the "Star Spangled Banner." It also led to the collapse of the Federalist Party, which had opposed the war. The Democratic-Republicans dominated politics for the next decade, which was known as the "Era of Good Feelings," thus marking the end of the first party system.

Causes and Consequences of Territorial Expansion

Constant immigration meant that land prices in the eastern United States rose, and people sought new economic opportunities on the frontier where land was cheaper. The United States government tried purchasing land from Native Americans, but most refused to relinquish their territories. Native Americans continued to defend their land until Tecumseh was defeated in the War of 1812. This defeat helped secure the Northwest Territory, and more settlers began pouring in. After the Louisiana Purchase, Lewis and Clark paved the way for expansion into the Great Plains and further west.

The Cherokee, Chickasaw, Choctaw, Creek, and Seminole tribes of the Southeastern United States were known as the "Five Civilized Tribes" because they had developed a written language and many members had become Christians. Nevertheless, Andrew Jackson signed the Indian Removal Act of 1830, which gave him the power to continue buying land from various tribes. The Cherokee filed a lawsuit to protect their territory and won their arguments before the Supreme Court. However, President Andrew Jackson ignored the ruling and eventually used troops to force many tribes off their land and sent them west to Oklahoma during the 1830s. This was known as the "Trail of Tears" because thousands of Native Americans died from starvation, exposure, and disease along the way.

Furthermore, the concept of Manifest Density emerged during the 1800s and introduced the idea that God wanted Americans to civilize and control the entire continent. This led to conflict when the province of Texas declared its independence from Mexico and asked to be annexed by the United States. President James K. Polk tried to buy Texas, but when Mexico refused, he sent troops into the disputed territory. Mexican troops responding by attacking an American unit, which led to war in 1846.

In the Mexican-American War, American troops won several battles although the Mexican army usually outnumbered them. The Mexican troops were poorly armed and trained, but, on the other hand, the Americans made use of their highly skilled artillery force. They eventually captured Mexico City and forced the Mexican government to sign the Treaty of Guadalupe-Hidalgo in 1848. The treaty recognized American control over Texas and also ceded California, Utah, Colorado, Arizona, New Mexico, and Nevada in exchange for $15 million. Tens of thousands of prospectors flooded into California when gold was discovered there in 1849. The prospectors often encroached on Native American lands, which led to further conflict. In 1854, the United States also acquired additional territories as part of the Gadsden Purchase. The acquisition of so much new territory sparked a debate over whether the land would be open or closed to slavery.

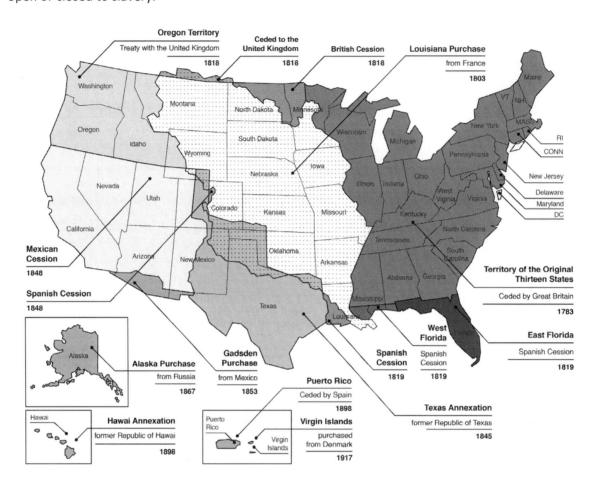

Manifest Destiny also sparked a desire to expand American influence into Central and South America. Adventurers launched several unsuccessful attempts to invade Nicaragua and Cuba.

Several important laws also stimulated western expansion during the second half of the 19th century. Congress passed the Homestead Act in 1862, which allowed citizens to claim 160 acres for only $1.25 per acre. The settler also had to live on the land for five years and make improvements. That same year, Congress also passed the Pacific Railroad Act, which supported the construction of a transcontinental railroad. The United States government provided land and financial support to railroad companies and the first transcontinental link was established in 1869. This facilitated trade and communication between the eastern and western United States.

As Americans poured westward, conflict again broke out between settlers and Native Americans. The discovery of gold in the Black Hills of South Dakota caused prospectors to flood into the area although the U.S. government had recognized the territory belonged to the Sioux. General George Armstrong Custer brought in troops to try and take possession of the Black Hills. This led to disaster when Custer and more than 250 soldiers died at the Battle of Little Big Horn in 1876.

The U.S. government continued its efforts to control Native American tribes. The Dawes Act of 1887 encouraged Native Americans to settle on reservations and become farmers in exchange for U.S. citizenship. Chief Joseph was a leader of the Nez Perce tribe who refused to live on a reservation and tried to flee to Canada. However, the U.S. captured Chief Joseph and his tribe and forced them onto a reservation. Reformers also required Native Americans to send their children to boarding schools where they had to speak English and dress like Caucasians instead of maintaining their traditional culture. The schools were often crowded, and students were also subjected to physical and sexual abuse.

In 1890, the Lakota Indians tried to preserve their traditional beliefs by performing a special ceremony called a Ghost Dance. U.S. government officials felt threatened and sent soldiers to try and disarm the Lakota. This led to the Massacre at Wounded Knee in 1890 where at least 150 Lakota, including many women and children, were slaughtered. It was the last major conflict between Native Americans and U.S. forces.

The United States purchased Alaska from Russia in 1867 for $7.2 million. At the time, the purchase was unpopular with the public, but seal hunting became very profitable and gold was discovered in 1896. Alaska became a state in 1959.

In 1893, American businessmen launched an armed coup, overthrew the queen of Hawaii, and asked Congress to annex Hawaii. The businessmen owned sugar plantations and feared the queen's attempts to enact reform would threaten their political influence. Hawaii became a U.S. territory in 1898 and a state in 1959.

The last phase of American territorial expansion occurred as a result of the Spanish-American War in 1898. New ideas arose in the late 19th century that helped justify further expansion. Some intellectuals applied Charles Darwin's ideas of "survival of the fittest" to the human race and called this new concept Social Darwinism. They used this idea to justify why stronger groups of people colonized and exploited weaker groups. In addition, imperialists also used the idea of the White Man's Burden to justify further expansion. They claimed that Caucasians were obligated to civilize and govern groups thought to be less advanced.

These ideas were used to justify America's new status as a colonial power as a result of the Spanish-American War. Although Spain had once been a powerful empire, it had been in decline. The United States went to war against Spain in 1898 when the American battleship USS Maine exploded in Havana Harbor and killed more than 250 sailors. The U.S. Navy defeated the Spanish fleet in several engagements and then the Army followed up with a victory at San Juan Hill, which included the famous charge by Teddy Roosevelt and the Rough Riders.

The war lasted less than four months and made the United States a world power. The U.S. also acquired several Spanish colonies, including Puerto Rico, Guam, and the Philippines. Guam became an important refueling station for American naval forces in the Pacific and remains a U.S. territory today, along with Puerto Rico. When the United States occupied the Philippines, the Filipino people launched a rebellion in order to obtain their independence. The U.S. Army put down the insurrection, but in doing so, they committed many atrocities against the Filipino people. The Philippines would remain an American territory until 1946.

Causes and Consequences of 19th-Century Sectionalism, the Civil War, and Reconstruction

In the early 1800s, political and economic differences between the North and South became more apparent. Politically, a small but vocal group of abolitionists emerged in the North who demanded a complete end to slavery throughout the United States. William Lloyd Garrison edited the abolitionist newspaper *The Liberator* and vehemently denounced the brutality of slavery. His criticism was so vicious that the legislature of Georgia offered a $5,000 bounty to anyone who could capture Garrison and deliver him to state authorities. Other activists participated in the Underground Railroad—a network that helped fugitive slaves escape to the Northern United States or Canada.

Economic differences emerged as the North began to industrialize, especially in the textile industry where factories increased productivity. However, the Southern economy remained largely agricultural and focused on labor-intensive crops such as tobacco and cotton. This meant that slavery remained an essential part of the Southern economy. In addition, the North built more roads, railroads, and canals, while the Southern transportation system lagged behind. The Northern economy was also based on cash, while many Southerners still bartered for goods and services. This led to growing sectional tension between the North and South as their economies began to diverge further apart.

These economic differences led to political tension as well, especially over the debate about the expansion of slavery. This debate became more important as the United States expanded westward into the Louisiana Purchase and acquired more land after the Mexican-American War. Most Northerners were not abolitionists. However, many opposed the expansion of slavery into the western territories because it would limit their economic opportunities. If a territory was open to slavery, it would be more attractive to wealthy slave owners who could afford to buy up the best land. In addition, the presence of slave labor would make it hard for independent farmers, artisans, and craftsman to make a living, because they would have to compete against slaves who did not earn any wages. For their part, Southerners felt it was essential to continue expanding in order to strengthen the southern economy and ensure that the Southern way of life survived. As intensive farming depleted the soil of nutrients, Southern slave owners sought more fertile land in the west.

Both the North and South also feared losing political power as more states were admitted to the nation. For example, neither side wanted to lose influence in the United States senate if the careful balance of free and slave state representation was disrupted. Several compromises were negotiated in Congress, but they only temporarily quieted debate. The first such effort, called the Missouri Compromise, was passed in 1820, and it maintained political parity in the U.S. Senate by admitting Missouri as a slave state and Maine as a free state. The Missouri Compromise banned slavery in the portion of the Louisiana Purchase that was north of the 36°30' parallel and permitted slavery in the portion south of that line as well as Missouri.

However, the slavery debate erupted again after the acquisition of new territory during the Mexican-American War. The Compromise of 1850 admitted California as a free state and ended the slave trade, but not slavery itself, in Washington D.C., in order to please Northern politicians. In return, Southern politicians were able to pass a stronger fugitive slave law and demanded that New Mexico and Utah be allowed to vote on whether or not slavery would be permitted in their state constitutions. This introduced the idea of popular sovereignty where the residents of each new territory, and not the federal government, could decide whether or not they would become a slave state or a free state. This essentially negated the Missouri Compromise of 1820. The enhanced fugitive slave law also angered many Northerners, because it empowered federal marshals to deputize anyone, even residents of a free state, and force them to help recapture escaped slaves. Anyone who refused would be subject to a $1,000 fine (equivalent to more than $28,000 in 2015).

The debate over slavery erupted again only a few years later when the territories of Kansas and Nebraska were created in 1854. The application of popular sovereignty meant that pro- and anti-slavery settlers flooded into these two territories to ensure that their faction would have a majority when it came time to vote on the state constitution. Tension between pro- and anti-slavery forces in Kansas led to an armed conflict known as "Bleeding Kansas."

John Brown was a militant abolitionist who fought in "Bleeding Kansas" and murdered five pro-slavery settlers there in 1856. He returned to the eastern United States and attacked the federal arsenal at Harper's Ferry, Virginia, in 1859. He hoped to seize the weapons there and launch a slave rebellion, but federal troops killed or captured most of Brown's accomplices and Brown was executed. The attack terrified Southerners and reflected the increasing hostility between North and South.

The sectional differences that emerged in the last several decades culminated in the presidential election of 1860. Abraham Lincoln led the new Republican Party, which opposed slavery on moral and economic grounds. The question of how best to expand slavery into new territories split the Democratic Party into two different factions that each nominated a presidential candidate. A fourth candidate also ran on a platform of preserving the union by trying to ignore the slavery controversy.

Lincoln found little support outside of the North but managed to win the White House since the Democratic Party was divided. Southern states felt threatened by Lincoln's anti-slavery stance and feared he would abolish slavery throughout the country. South Carolina was the first Southern state to secede from the Union and ten more eventually followed. Lincoln declared that the Union could not be dissolved and swore to defend federal installations. The Civil War began when Confederate troops fired on Fort Sumter in Charleston in 1861.

The Civil War

The First Battle of Bull Run (also known as the First Battle of Manassas) in 1861 was the first major infantry engagement of the Civil War. Both the Northern and Southern troops were inexperienced and although they had equal numbers, the Confederates emerged victorious. Many had thought the war would be short, but it continued for another four years.

The Union navy imposed a blockade on the Confederacy and captured the port of New Orleans in 1862. The Union navy was much stronger than the Confederate fleet and prevented the Southern states from selling cotton to foreign countries or buying weapons.

In 1862, Union forces thwarted a Confederate invasion of Maryland at the Battle of Antietam. This engagement was the single bloodiest day of the war and more than 23,000 men on both sides were killed or wounded. Union troops forced the Confederates to retreat, and that gave Lincoln the political capital he needed to issue the Emancipation Proclamation in 1863. This declaration did not abolish slavery, but it did free slaves in Southern territory. It also allowed African Americans to join the Union navy and about 200,000 did so. The 54th Massachusetts Infantry was a famous unit of African American soldiers who led an assault on Fort Wagner in South Carolina in 1863. Although the attack failed, the 54th Massachusetts witnessed African American troops fighting bravely under fire.

The Siege of Vicksburg in 1863 was a major Union victory because they gained control of the Mississippi River and cut the Confederacy in half. This made it difficult the Confederacy to move troops around and communicate with their forces. Grant commanded the Northern forces in the siege and eventually became the Union army's top general.

The Battle of Gettysburg in 1863 marked the turning point of the Civil War. Robert E. Lee led Confederate troops into Pennsylvania, but in three days of heavy fighting, the Union army forced them to retreat. The victory bolstered Northern morale and weakened Southern resolve. Never again would Confederate forces threaten Northern territory.

In 1864, Union general William T. Sherman captured Atlanta and then marched more than 200 miles to Savannah. Along the way, he destroyed anything that could support the Southern war effort, such as railroads and cotton mills. At this point, the Southern economy was beginning to collapse. The North had more manpower than the South and could afford to sustain more casualties. The North also had more industrial capacity to produce weapons and supplies and more railroads to transport men and equipment.

Eventually, Robert E. Lee surrendered to Ulysses S. Grant at Appomattox, Virginia, on April 9, 1865. Five days later, John Wilkes Booth assassinated Lincoln in Washington D.C. Vice President Andrew Johnson, a Democrat, succeeded him and soon came into conflict with Republicans in Congress about how to reintegrate Southern states into the nation. This process was known as Reconstruction and lasted from 1865 to 1877.

Reconstruction

Johnson opposed equal rights for African Americans and pardoned many Confederate leaders. However, many Congressional Republicans wanted to harshly punish Southerners for their attempts to secede from the Union. They were known as Radical Republicans because they also wanted to give former slaves equal rights.

Johnson vetoed bills that were designed to protect the rights of freed slaves, but Congress overrode his vetoes. This led to increasing conflict between Johnson and Congress, which eventually caused Radical Republicans to impeach him. Although Johnson was acquitted in 1868, he had very little power, and Radical Republicans took control of the Reconstruction process.

Republicans passed three important constitutional amendments as part of the Reconstruction process. The 13th amendment was ratified in 1865, and it abolished slavery throughout the country. The 14th Amendment was ratified in 1868 and gave equal rights to all citizens. The 15th Amendment was ratified in 1870 and specifically granted all men the right to vote regardless of race.

Southerners resisted these demands and passed laws that prohibited freed slaves from owning weapons or testifying against whites. They also formed militias and vigilante groups, such as the Ku Klux Klan, in order to intimidate African Americans who tried to vote. Congress sent federal troops into Southern states in order to enforce the law and prevent vigilante violence.

After the much-disputed election of 1876, the Democrats offered to let the Republicans have the White House if they agreed to end Reconstruction. After the Republicans agreed, federal troops were withdrawn and African Americans in the South were subjected to discrimination until the Civil Rights movement of the 1960s. Scholars often consider the Reconstruction era the beginning of Jim Crow and a transition into a new form of "institutionalized racism" that still pervades much of modern U.S. society.

Relationships Among Industrialization, Urbanization, and Immigration in the Late 19th and Early 20th Centuries

After the end of the Civil War, America experienced a period of intense industrialization, immigration, and urbanization, and all three trends were interrelated. The process of industrialization had begun before the Civil War but expanded into more sectors of the economy in the later part of the century.

This era is often called the Second Industrial Revolution and included growth in the chemical, petroleum, iron, steel, and telecommunications industries. For example, the Bessemer process made it much easier to produce high quality steel by removing impurities during the smelting process.

The writer Mark Twain called the late 19th century the Gilded Age because the era was also one of extreme social inequality. Some corporations expanded and began to control entire industries. For example, by 1890, the Standard Oil Company produced 88 percent of all the refined oil in the nation. This made a few individuals, such as John D. Rockefeller who owned Standard Oil, extremely wealthy. On the other hand, many workers earned low wages and began to form labor unions, such as the American Federation of Labor in 1886, in order to demand better working conditions and higher pay. Strikes were one of the most common ways workers could express their dissatisfaction, and the Pullman Strike of 1894 was one of the largest such incidents in the 19th century. Workers went on strike after the Pullman Company, which manufactured railroad cars, cut wages by about 25 percent. More than 125,000 workers around the country walked off the job and attacked workers hired to replace them. Federal troops were sent in to end the strike, and more than eighty workers were killed or wounded during confrontations. The strike was unsuccessful, but Congress passed a law making Labor Day a federal holiday in order to placate union members.

Immigration also played an important part in the economic and social changes that occurred during the late 19th century. Immigration patterns changed during this time and immigrants from Southern and Eastern Europe, such as Italy and Poland, began to surpass the number of arrivals from Northern and Western Europe. The immigrants sought economic opportunity in the United States because wages for unskilled workers were higher than in their home countries. Some Americans resented the influx of immigrants because they spoke different languages and practiced Catholicism. In 1924, Congress passed a law that restricted immigration from Southern and Eastern Europe.

Increased urbanization was the last factor that contributed to the rapid changes of the Gilded Age. Factories were located near cities in order to draw upon a large pool of potential employees. Immigrants flooded into cities in search of work, and new arrivals often settled in the same neighborhoods where their compatriots lived. Between 1860 and 1890, the urbanization rate increased from about 20 percent to 35 percent. Cities struggled to keep up with growing populations, and services such as sanitation and water often lagged behind demand. Immigrants often lived in crowded living conditions that facilitated the spread of diseases.

Political, Economic, Social, and Cultural Developments from the Progressive Era Through the New Deal

The social inequalities and economic abuses of the Gilded Age did not go unnoticed, and in the 1890s many reformers began to demand change. This period was called the Progressive Era and included activists in both the Democratic and Republican parties. The Progressives wanted to use scientific methods and government regulation to improve society. For example, they advocated the use of initiative, referendum, and recall to make government more responsive to its citizens. Progressives also argued that it was necessary to breakup large monopolies (known as trust busting) in order to promote equal economic competition. In 1911, Rockefeller's Standard Oil was split up into thirty-four different companies in order to promote competition, and the Federal Trade Commission was established in 1914 in order to prevent other monopolies from forming. Many Progressives also supported several constitutional amendments that were ratified in early 20th century, including the 17th amendment, which established the direct election of U.S. Senators in 1913 (previously state legislatures had elected senators). They also favored the Prohibition of alcohol that went into effect with the 18th Amendment in

1919. Progressives also advocated for women's rights and backed the 19th Amendment, which gave women the right to vote in 1920.

Many journalists who supported the reform movement of the Progressives were known as Muckrackers because they helped expose political corruption and social inequality. Upton Sinclair wrote a novel in 1906 called "The Jungle," which exposed poor working conditions and health violations in the Chicago meatpacking industry. His exposé led to the passages of the Pure Food and Drug Act in 1906, which authorized the federal government to inspect the purity of foodstuffs and medicines. Jacob Riis was a photographer who documented the crowded and unhealthy living conditions that many immigrants and poor workers endured.

World War I, from 1914 to 1918, led to a communist revolution in Russia in 1917. Many Americans wanted to prevent political radicals from gaining influence in the United States. A number of strikes and bombings around the country led the federal government to crack down on anarchists, socialists, and communists in an event known as the First Red Scare. In 1919, U.S. Attorney General A. Mitchell Palmer launched a series of raids and arrested resident aliens suspected of belonging to radical groups. About 500 resident aliens were eventually deported.

In 1933, President Franklin D. Roosevelt introduced the New Deal, which was a series of executive orders and laws passed by Congress in response to the Great Depression. The programs focused on relief, recovery, and reform, and were enacted until 1938. The second New Deal from 1935-1938 promoted the Social Security Act, labor unions, and aided tenant farmers and migrant workers who were struggling from the economic devastation of the Great Depression.

Social Developments
With the ratification of the 19th Amendment in 1920, women obtained the right to vote. This achievement was partly due to women's contributions on the home front during World War I. Women served as Army nurses and worked in factories to help produce weapons, ammunition, and equipment. As more women entered the workforce, they became more financially independent and began to socialize without being supervised by a chaperone, as was the norm during the 19th century. Overall, women during this period, known as "New Women," took on a more active role in public life, pursued higher education in greater numbers, and sought more sexual freedom. During the 1920s, women, known as "flappers," began to flaunt social conventions by wearing short skirts, bobbing hair, smoking cigarettes, and driving automobiles. Nevertheless, a "glass ceiling" still remains in place decades after women's suffrage in regards to a gender wage gap.

Millions of African Americans also moved north during and after World War I in search of work in a phenomenon known as the Great Migration. This led to increased racial tension as whites and blacks competed for jobs and housing. This culminated in a wave of race riots that swept across the country in the summer of 1919. In Chicago, conflict broke out between whites and blacks at a segregated beach, which led to five days of violence during which thirty-eight people were killed and more than 500 injured. The impact of the Great Migration can still be seen in contemporary, heavily segregated Rust Belt cities such as Gary, IN and Milwaukee, WI.

The invention of the automobile also contributed to social change. Henry Ford applied the method of assembly line construction and scientific management to the automobile manufacturing industry. This made it much cheaper to manufacture cars and allowed more people to purchase them. Automobiles allowed young men and women to socialize and date without adult supervision. Automobiles also improved transportation, increased mobility, and spawned the first suburbs.

Cultural Developments

Motion picture cameras were invented in the late 19th century, and the film industry experienced significant growth in the early 20th century. Because the first movies were silent, dialogue was displayed on intertitles and a live orchestra usually performed during a screening. "Birth of a Nation," by D.W. Griffith, was one of the first major cinema blockbusters, and it portrayed the Ku Klux Klan in a heroic light. Millions of Americans saw the film, which helped the Klan spread throughout the Northern and Western United States.

The Great Migration also led to cultural changes during the 1920s known as the Harlem Renaissance. The movement was based in the neighborhood of Harlem and led to a rebirth of black literature, art, music, and fashion. Jazz was an important feature of the Harlem Renaissance and challenged musical conventions by emphasizing improvisation and spontaneity. Jazz became very popular with both whites and blacks during the 1920s. Langston Hughes was a poet of the Harlem Renaissance who encouraged his readers to take pride in their black identity.

Economic Developments

The Panic of 1893 was a worldwide economic depression that devastated the American economy. Businesses went bankrupt, banks collapsed, and unemployment rose to approximately 17 percent. The economy began to recover by 1897, and the beginning of World War I boosted the U.S. economy as European nations bought American goods.

In 1918, the United States emerged from World War I as a major economic power because it had helped finance the Allied war effort and produced large amounts of weapons and equipment. The American agricultural sector also prospered because European farms had been devastated by the war. This sent crop prices up, and farmers used the money to buy more land and equipment. Although the 1920s is usually depicted as an era of economic prosperity, agricultural prices fell after World War I, and farmers were unable to pay back their debts.

Stock market speculation increased during the 1920s, and investors borrowed money in order to purchase shares. This did not cause any concern as long as the stock market went up, but it led to disaster when stock prices fell sharply in October 1929 and investors were unable to repay their loans. The stock market crash may have triggered the Great Depression, but it did not cause it. The Great Depression spread around the globe as nations stopped trading with each other. In the United States, families lost their savings when banks failed because there was no federal insurance. The economy went into a downward spiral because as more people lost their jobs, they had little money to spend, which led to further layoffs and more economic contraction.

Unemployment peaked at 25 percent between 1932 and 1933.

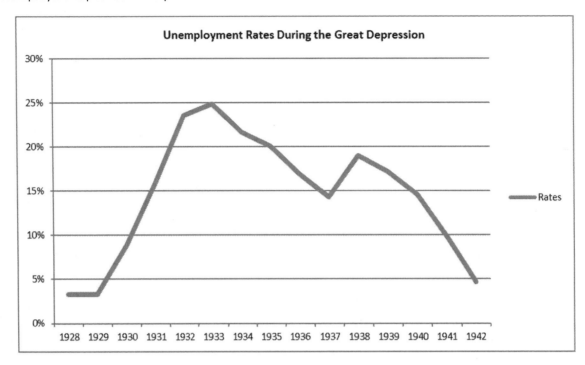

Unemployment Rates During the Great Depression

Democratic candidate Franklin D. Roosevelt was elected president in 1932 on his promise to help the economy recover by increasing government spending. After taking office in 1933, Roosevelt introduced a barrage of proposals, called the New Deal, that he hoped would boost employment, stimulate demand, and increase government regulation. Some elements of the New Deal were temporary, such as the Civilian Conservation Corps, which put young men to work improving parks between 1933 and 1942. Other New Deal programs endure to this day, such as the Social Security Administration, which has provided pensions to retirees, temporary payments to unemployed workers, and benefits to handicapped individuals since 1935. In addition, the Securities and Exchange Commission was created in 1934 and continues to regulate stock markets and investment companies. The Wagner Act of 1935 was also an important part of the New Deal because it guaranteed the right of workers to unionize and go on strike. The 21st Amendment was ratified in 1933 and repealed Prohibition, which had been hard to enforce and was unpopular. Roosevelt also hoped it would create jobs and stimulate spending. The New Deal helped reduce unemployment, but the economy did not completely recover until America entered World War II and production increased in order to support the war efforts.

Causes and Consequences of American Participation in World War I & II

World War I began in 1914 with the assassination of Franz Ferdinand, the apparent heir of the Austro-Hungarian Empire. A network of secret alliances meant that most European nations were quickly drawn into the conflict, although President Woodrow Wilson initially tried to keep the United States neutral. The war involved two major European alliances: the Triple Entente of Britain, France, and Russia, and the Central Powers, which included Germany and Austria-Hungary. The British implemented a naval blockade that was very successful, and the Germans retaliated by launching submarine attacks. German submarines attacked any ship carrying supplies to the Triple Entente, including the passenger ship RMS Lusitania in 1915. About 1,200 people died, including more than 100 Americans. The Germans temporarily halted their unrestricted submarine campaign, but eventually resumed the attacks in 1917. In addition, in 1917, Germany asked Mexico to attack the United States in a communiqué known as the

Zimmerman telegram. These events led the United States to join the Triple Entente in 1917, although significant numbers of American troops did not arrive in Europe until 1918. American reinforcement helped the British and French, who had been fighting continuously since 1914, launch a final offensive that defeated Germany in 1918. American forces suffered about 320,000 casualties. As previously noted, World War I also led to significant changes on the home front as women took on new responsibilities, and thousands of African Americans migrated north in search of work. World War I also led to a communist revolution that transformed Russia into the USSR in 1922.

After Germany was defeated in 1918, Wilson made a proposal known as the Fourteen Points and argued that the best way to resolve the conflict was by promoting free trade and democracy. For instance, Wilson wanted nations to respect the right to navigate in international waters and create a League of Nations that would resolve future disputes. Some of his suggestions, such as the League of Nations, were adopted, but many were not. In 1919, Germany was forced to sign the Treaty of Versailles, which imposed harsh economic penalties and restricted the German military. Ultimately, the Treaty of Versailles created resentment in Germany that lead to World War II. America emerged as an important player in world affairs after World War I because the American economy had supplied the Triple Entente with arms and equipment and American soldiers helped to achieve victory.

In the period between the world wars, fascism became popular in many European countries that were ravaged by the Great Depression. Fascism is a political ideology that advocates for a dictatorship in order to provide stability and unity. Adolf Hitler emerged as a prominent fascist leader in Germany and eventually brought the Nazi party to power in 1933. Germany, Italy, and Japan formed an alliance called the Axis and began to threaten other countries. The League of Nations could not diffuse the conflict. World War II broke out when Germany invaded Poland in 1939. Hitler quickly conquered most of Europe, except for Britain, and attacked the USSR in 1941. The United States sent military equipment and weapons to Britain and the USSR, but did not formally join the war until the Japanese attacked Pearl Harbor on December 7, 1941. Again, women played an important role on the home front by working in factories to build guns, tanks, planes, and ships. African Americans, Native Americans, and Japanese Americans also contributed by fighting on the front lines.

American forces first landed in North Africa where they, along with British and French troops, defeated German and Italian forces in 1942. In 1943, Allied forces invaded Italy, and Soviet troops began to push the German army back out of the USSR. Allied troops landed in France in 1944 and the Soviets began to advance on Germany as well. By May 1945, Hitler had committed suicide and Germany had been defeated.

This also brought about an end to the Holocaust. The Holocaust was a genocide committed by Hitler's Nazi Germany and collaborators that resulted in the deaths of more than 6 million Jews and 5 million Romans, gypsies, Afro-Europeans, disabled citizens, and homosexuals. A network of facilities in Germany and its territories were used to house victims for slave labor and mass murder, among other heinous crimes. The Nuremberg trials were part of the aftermath of the Holocaust, which served to prosecute important members of Nazi Germany leadership.

In the Pacific theater, American naval forces defeated the Japanese fleet in several key engagements, including the battle of Midway in 1942. American troops began recapturing territory in the Pacific as well and eventually pushed the Japanese back to their home islands in 1945. The Japanese refused to surrender until American planes dropped atomic bombs on the cities of Nagasaki and Hiroshima in August 1945.

Because World War II devastated most of Europe, the United States and the USSR emerged as the only superpowers when it ended. However, the erstwhile allies were suspicious of each other, which led to the Cold War.

Origins, Developments, and Consequences of the Cold War

Although the United States and the USSR worked together to defeat the Axis powers during World War II, the alliance quickly fell apart. As previously discussed, Americans had been afraid of communist influence since the Russian revolution in 1917. The USSR viewed the United States as a capitalist and imperialist power that threatened Soviet security. The USSR and United States divided Europe into spheres of influence, and this mutual hostility led to the Cold War. For example, the Soviets built a wall around the portion of Berlin, Germany that they occupied. The United States formed a military alliance, called the North Atlantic Treaty Organization, with its allies in Western Europe. The Soviets responded with their own defensive alliance in Eastern Europe, known as the Warsaw Pact. President Harry Truman announced that the United States would try to contain communist influence and would assist countries threatened by communist aggression. The domino theory predicted that once one country succumbed to communism, neighboring nations would also be at risk (thus following like a stack of dominoes). A resurgence of anti-communist sentiment occurred in the early 1950s when Senator Joseph McCarthy pledged to root out spies within the federal government. Known as the Second Red Scare in American history, McCarthy's communist "witch hunts" produced little evidence of his allegations and was censored in 1954 when he refused to reign in his attacks.

The resistance to communism led to a number of indirect conflicts around the globe between the United States and the USSR and China, which had become a communist regime in 1949. For example, Korea was divided into two portions after World War II (at the 38th parallel). When the communist regime in North Korea invaded South Korea in 1950, the United States sent troops to defend South Korea. The USSR and China sent troops, weapons, and equipment to support North Korea. The war ended in a stalemate in 1953, and Korea remains divided to this day. Today, it is divided at a unique demarcation line close to the original 38th parallel separation.

Vietnam was also partitioned into northern and southern regions after World War II. The United States supported South Vietnam and sent troops in ever-increasing numbers. The conflict intensified when North Vietnamese gunboats allegedly attacked a U.S. navy ship in 1964. However, U.S. forces were unable to defeat the Vietnamese communists, who preferred to use guerrilla troops and ambush tactics. The support for the war evaporated in United States as casualties mounted and the draft was unpopular as well. American troops also killed at least 300 civilians in the Vietnamese village of My Lai in 1968. National Guardsmen shot and killed four students and wounded nine others during an anti-war protest at Kent State University in 1970. These scandals made the war extremely unpopular. American troops withdrew in 1973, and South Vietnam was defeated in 1975.

The U.S. and USSR also vied for influence in South America and Africa as well. Some nations refused to pick sides and instead formed the Non-Aligned Movement.

The nuclear arms race and the space race were also important arenas in the Cold War. The Soviets took an early lead in the space race and successfully launched the first satellite into orbit in 1957. The Soviets also put the first man, cosmonaut Yuri Gagarin, into space in 1961. However, the United States surpassed the Soviet Union by landing the first man, Neil Armstrong, on the Moon in 1969.

The United States was the only nuclear power for a brief period after World War II, but the Soviets quickly caught up and detonated their own nuclear bomb in 1949. Both sides developed nuclear missiles during the 1950s. This became a very dramatic issue during the Cuban Missile Crisis. In 1962, President John F. Kennedy learned that the Soviets were installing nuclear missiles in Cuba, which had become a communist regime. The U.S. navy imposed a blockade, and tensions rose as the Soviets refused to back down. Eventually, negotiations ended the crisis and the Soviets agreed to withdraw the missiles in Cuba if the U.S. agreed to withdraw missiles from Turkey that threatened the USSR. Although tensions remained, the nuclear arms race slowed during the 1970s when the U.S. and USSR entered into negotiations. Both the U.S. and USSR promised to reduce nuclear weapons tests and limit their nuclear arsenals. Throughout the Cold War, a concept known as "Mutually Assured Destruction" (MAD) helped prevent nuclear war. Both the United States and the USSR each had thousands of warheads and MAD predicted that no matter who struck first, the other side would have enough surviving firepower to destroy the aggressor.

During the Cold War, a number of protests and demonstrations occurred in the Soviet satellites in Eastern Europe, including Hungary in 1956 and in Czechoslovakia in 1968. The uprisings were suppressed, but demands for reform continued and, in 1985, Mikhail Gorbachev became the leader of the USSR. He promised to make political and economic reforms, but protestors wanted change to occur more rapidly. Revolutions swept through Eastern Europe in 1989, and the communist regimes in Poland, Romania, and elsewhere crumbled. The Berlin Wall fell in 1989, and the Cold War ended when the USSR collapsed in 1991. This left the United States as the sole superpower, although other countries, such as India and China, have become more powerful. Recent scholars, however, are questioning whether the Cold War is once again beginning to heat up with the most recent tensions between Russia and the United States in the early 2000s.

Social, Economic, and Technological Changes Between 1950 and 2000

The post-World War II era led to a number of social, economic, and technological changes in the United States. The counter-culture phenomenon was one of the most powerful social movements in the latter half of the twentieth century in the U.S. The counter-culture movement challenged social norms and rejected traditional authority figures. The movement began in the 1950s with the beatniks, a group of non-conformist writers and artists who were dissatisfied with society. The beatniks sought inspiration in African and Asian cultures and many eschewed materialism.

The counter-culture movement became more popular during the 1960s as millions of children from the Baby Boomers generation entered into adulthood. Veterans came home after World War II and started families, and, by the 1960s, many of these young adults also felt disaffected and rebellious. Their parents criticized them because they began to wear colorful clothing and the boys let their hair grow out. Many members of the counter-culture movement, now called hippies, inherited the beatnik's interest in African and Asian cultures. Writer Ken Kesey traveled around the country on a bus encouraging people to experiment with psychedelic drugs, such as LSD. The counter-culture movement influenced musicians and avant-garde artists.

The counter-culture movement was also closely connected to other protest movements during the 1960s, including the Civil Rights movement, which will be discussed later. Many members of the counter-culture movement during the 1960s also opposed the war in Vietnam. The Baby Boomers could be conscripted to fight in Vietnam whether they wanted to or not. In 1965, young men began burning their draft cards, which was a criminal offense, in protest. Massive demonstrations against the war occurred around the country, especially on college campuses, but many other people also refused to support the war effort, including clergymen and even some veterans who had fought in Vietnam. The counter-culture movement disappeared during the 1970s but had a lasting impact on the social and cultural history of the United States.

Economic Changes

America emerged as one of the most powerful economies in the world after 1945. The US economy, especially manufacturing, was very prosperous during the 1950s and 1960s. The economy successfully switched from wartime production, and consumer demand was very high. During the Great Depression, few families had disposable income. Although most workers earned good wages during World War II, they had little to spend it on because most goods were rationed. Once production of consumer goods resumed, families used their savings to buy cars, household appliances, and televisions. This was good for the economy, and unemployment remained below 5 percent for most of the 1950s and 1960s. However, during the latter part of the 20th century, the manufacturing base in the North and Midwest began to crumble and the area became known as the Rust Belt. Manufacturing jobs began to move from the North and Midwest to states in the South and West, known as the Sun Belt, where land was cheap and wages were low.

The world economy also became increasingly interconnected during the post-World War II era. This accelerated the process of globalization, which is the integration of ideas and products from different cultures. This benefitted the United States economically because businesses, such as McDonald's and Coca-Cola, found many consumers around the world who were eager to consume American goods. However, the process works both ways, and many aspects of foreign culture, such as Japanese cartoons and animation, have become very popular in the United States. Many critics also point out that globalization has hurt the American economy in recent decades because manufacturing jobs have gone overseas to countries in South America and Asia where wages are low.

Technological Changes

Several technological changes have had a significant impact on the U.S. economy as well. The Cold War led to advances in nuclear power and aerospace engineering. The development of computers, in particular, has helped accelerate the transition to a post-industrial economy where information technology and other services have replaced traditional manufacturing jobs. The first computers were used to break coded messages during World War II and had very limited computing power. The invention of transistor technology in 1947 made computers cheaper, smaller, and more reliable. The invention of integrated circuits in the 1960s and 1970s increased computing power and gave birth to the first personal computers. The Internet was created in 1969, but widespread use in business and academia did not begin until the 1980s. These developments have made it much easier to share information and have increased economic opportunities. But, the increasing use of robots, especially in the manufacturing industry, have also made the economy more efficient while also causing layoffs.

Political Realignments from the New Deal and Great Society Through the Rise of Conservatism

President Franklin D. Roosevelt created the New Deal in order to stimulate the economy and improve government regulation. The New Deal also marked an important shift in American politics because the Democratic Party began to favor government intervention while Republicans opposed it. This was a reversal of the parties' previous platforms. The Democratic Party relied on a coalition of labor unions, Catholics, African Americans, and other minorities. The Republican Party included conservatives, evangelicals, and business leaders.

The Great Society was another major government program that the Democratic Party supported. President Lyndon B. Johnson sought to end poverty and improve education. For example, he raised the minimum wage and created programs to provide poor Americans with job training. The Great Society also implemented a number of Civil Rights laws that will be discussed in greater detail later.

The presidential election of 1980 was another watershed moment. Republican nominee Ronald Reagan carried forty-three states, and the Republicans won a majority in the U.S. Senate after twenty-eight years of Democratic control. Reagan presented an optimistic message and broadcasted a television advertisement that proclaimed "It's morning again in America." He promised to restore America's military power, cut government regulations, and reduce taxes. Reagan enjoyed the support of resurgent conservative Christian evangelicals, who wanted to restore morality to American society. They were particularly concerned about issues such as abortion. The Moral Majority, founded by Baptist minister Jerry Falwell in 1979, was one key group that helped Reagan win the election. This coalition helped realign party loyalties, as more liberal Republicans and conservative Democrats shifted their allegiance.

Impact of Race, Gender, and Ethnicity Throughout American History

Race, gender, and ethnicity have been important themes in American history from the colonial era to the present. Individuals from different races, ethnicities, and genders have had very different experiences throughout the same historical events or eras. It is important to distinguish between race and ethnicity: race refers to a group of people with common ancestry, while ethnicity refers to cultural background, such as language and tradition.

Race played an important part in colonial America because both Caucasians and Africans occupied positions of servitude. White immigrants who could not purchase passage to the New World sometimes agreed to become indentured servants. Their employers paid for their passage across the Atlantic, and in exchange, the indentured servant agreed to work without wages for at least five years. However, African slaves were rarely able to free themselves. The strong connection between slavery and race meant that all blacks, whether free or enslaved, were viewed as inferior. After the American Revolution, most free blacks, even those living in northern states, were denied the right to vote. Although the Civil Rights Movement in the 1960s made great gains, many activists claim more must be done in order to overcome the legacy of racial inequality in America.

Chinese and Japanese have also been the victims of discrimination throughout American history as well. For example, in 1882 Congress prohibited Chinese immigration in an act known as the Chinese Exclusion Act. This was the first law to ever prevent an entire ethnic group from immigrating to the United States. Japanese Americans also experienced discrimination during and after World War II, specifically with the implementation of Japanese internment camps in America. This forced 110,000 to 120,000 Japanese Americans into camps, 62 percent of which were United States citizens.

Discrimination against certain ethnicities is also prominent throughout American history as well. For example, many Americans resented the arrival of German and Irish immigrants during the 1800s because they spoke a different language or practiced different religions. Hispanics were also subject to discrimination, and in 1943, a number of Hispanic youths were attacked during the Zoot Suit Riots.

Gender differences in the United States have also been impossible to ignore. For example, until the 1840s, most married women in the United States were unable to enter into contracts, own property, or retain their own wages. As previously discussed, women were unable to vote until the 19th Amendment was ratified in 1920. The Women's Rights Movement in the U.S. ranged from 1848 to 1920. This movement called for a woman's right to vote, the right to bodily autonomy, freedom from sexual violence, the right to hold public office, the right to work, the right to fair wages and equal pay, and the right to own property and obtain an education. Women continue to demand change during the 21st

century for reasons such as the gender wage gap, better resources for women's health, female reproductive rights, and for protection of basic human rights, such as bringing greater awareness to rape culture, violence against women, and protection against female sex trafficking.

How Participants in the Political Process Engage in Politics and Shape Policy

The Constitution provides for a series of checks and balances between the legislative, executive, and judicial branches of the federal government. Members of Congress debate and vote on legislation, although the president may request that legislators consider a certain proposal. The president may veto legislation that he or she disagrees with, but Congress can override the veto with a two-thirds majority in both chambers. The Supreme Court may review legislation and declare it unconstitutional. The president selects nominees to the Supreme Court but the Senate must confirm them.

Branch	Role	Checks & Balances on Other Branches	
Executive	Carries out the laws	**Legislative Branch** • Proposes laws • Vetoes laws • Calls special sessions of Congress • Makes appointments • Negotiates foreign treaties	**Judicial Branch** • Appoints federal judges • Grants pardons to federal offenders
Legislative	Makes the laws	**Executive Branch** • Has the ability to override a President's veto • Confirms executive appointments • Ratifies treaties • Has the ability to declare war • Appropriates money • Has the ability to impeach and remove President	**Judicial Branch** • Creates lower federal courts • Has the ability to impeach and remove judges • Has the ability to propose amendments to overrule judicial decisions • Approves appointments of federal judges
Judicial	Interprets the laws	**Executive Branch** • Has the ability to declare executive actions unconstitutional	**Legislative Branch** • Has the ability to declare acts of Congress unconstitutional

Constituents, businesses, professional associations, civic organizations, and other interest groups may lobby members of Congress and ask them to propose legislation or support a certain proposal. Interest groups may also lobby the president and other executive branch officials in order to try and influence policies. The president appoints fifteen men and women to head a variety of executive departments, including defense, transportation, education, and many others. These officials are known as the president's cabinet, and they advise the president on various matters. These discussions are used to help formulate policies, and the cabinet members are responsible for putting the decisions into action. The president may also issue executive orders that instruct federal employees how to enforce certain policies. For example, in 1948, President Harry S. Truman issued an executive order that established racial integration within the armed forces.

Elections are an essential part of our democracy. Although members of Congress are prohibited from accepting gifts, individuals and interest groups can make campaign contributions during elections, which occur every two years in the House, four years for the White House, and six years in the Senate. Individuals can give a maximum of $2,700 per year to individual candidates. Since 2010, individuals, corporations, labor unions, and other contributors can give an unlimited amount to organizations known as super PACs (Political Action Committees). Super PACs may not give money to candidates or parties but can air commercials that support a specific issue.

Although President George Washington warned against creating political parties in his farewell address in 1796, they have been a part of American politics since the founding of our country. The Republicans and Democrats hold conventions to nominate candidates for state and national elections. The parties also create a platform, which is a set of goals and principles, at each convention in order to set priorities and inform members about issues. During elections, parties also organize rallies and urge voters to support their candidates and issues. Some Americans belong to either the Republican or Democratic Party, but voters who belong to neither party are known as independents.

Emergence of the United States as a World Power and the Evolving Role of United States in the World

The United States gained prestige and international status after the Spanish-American War of 1898, because the United States defeated Spain and acquired several colonies. American participation in World War I made the United States an economic and financial leader as well. The United States loaned money to Britain and France and supplied weapons and equipment that helped the Triple Entente achieve victory. The United States and USSR emerged from World War II as the only surviving superpowers because so much of the rest of the world had been devastated. This system was described as bipolar because there were two centers of power.

The United States was the leader of the free world during the Cold War and formed military and economic alliances with other nations. With the collapse of the USSR in 1991, the United States was the only surviving world power. This era was a unipolar system because there were no other major powers that could rival the United States.

Although the U.S. was still considered a world power, September 11, 2001 demonstrated that America was nevertheless vulnerable to attacks. The attacks on 9/11 killed more than 3,000 civilians and first-responders. Although American troops have been stationed in Iraq and Afghanistan for more than a decade, both nations are still unstable, and the lack of progress has damaged American prestige. Furthermore, new economic and military powers have risen to challenge American dominance in world affairs. The Chinese economy has grown significantly, and the Chinese government has expanded and improved its armed forces. India has also boosted its manufacturing industry and has purchased new fighter jets and an aircraft carrier. The European Union, Russia, and Brazil have also emerged as potential rivals that might create a multipolar environment. However, the United States is still the world's largest economy and remains a cultural leader.

The Influence of Religion Throughout American History

Religion has also been an important, albeit divisive, theme in American history since the colonial period. The British colonies in North America attracted settlers from many different religions, including Catholics in Maryland, Quakers in Pennsylvania, Puritans in New England, and Anglicans in Virginia. This led to conflict and tension. For example, Puritans in New England expelled dissenters and even executed four Quakers between 1659 and 1661.

In the 1730s and 1740s, a religious revival known as the First Great Awakening swept through the British colonies in North America. This movement emphasized a more personal connection to Christ, and some Protestant preachers, such as Jonathan Edwards, began to present their sermons in a more passionate and emotional style. This "fire and brimstone" form of religious dissemination became the cornerstone of the First Great Awakening. These passionate sermons—and the emotions that they stirred—caused divisions within Protestant congregations. Those who supported the Great Awakening were known as New Lights while those who opposed it were called Old Lights. The Baptists and Methodists became more popular during the revival because they embraced this new style of preaching.

The Second Great Awakening occurred in the early 1800s and urged Protestants to work not only for their own salvation but for the salvation of others as well. This helped fuel a social reform movement that promoted the abolition of slavery, temperance, and prison reform. The question of slavery caused schisms in the Baptist and Methodist churches during the 1840s. The Second Great Awakening, much like the First Great Awakening, inaugurated the creation of several New Religious Movements (NRMs) in the United States, especially in the southern states.

A third revival occurred in the late 1800s that emphasized temperance. As previously discussed, the religious right emerged after World War II and began to play an important part in American politics, especially during the election of President Ronald Reagan in 1980.

Although Catholics were a minority during the colonial period of American history, Catholicism has become the largest religious denomination in the United States. Many colonial governments actually banned Catholicism, but the American Revolution brought more toleration. However, anti-Catholic sentiment renewed in the 1800s as immigrants from Ireland and Germany, many of whom were Catholic, arrived in ever-increasing numbers. The arrival of Italian immigrants in the late 1800s and early 1900s also increased Protestant-Catholic tension in America. Many Americans feared that Catholic immigrants would be more loyal to Pope than they would be to the Constitution. This led to the creation of the Know-Nothings who sought to limit immigration and physically attacked Catholics. Anti-Catholic sentiment remained an issue even until the presidential election of 1960 when John F. Kennedy, a Catholic, won the Democratic nomination. Kennedy helped allay fears by promising to respect the separation of church and state. Since then, anti-Catholicism has largely disappeared.

Small numbers of Jews immigrated to the U.S. during the colonial period, but large numbers of Jews from Eastern Europe began to arrive in the late 19th and early 20th centuries. Jews contributed to the American economy in many different ways but drew criticism from anti-Semites because of their prominence in the financial industry. The Anti-Defamation League was founded in 1913 to combat anti-Semitic sentiments. In the 1920s, the resurgent Ku Klux Klan revived anti-Semitism. The Anti-Defamation League sponsored events after World War II to commemorate the Holocaust and repudiate Holocaust deniers. Anti-Semitism has declined, but the Anti-Defamation League reported that more than 900 anti-Semitic incidents occurred across the country in 2014.

Muslim immigration in the 1800s remained modest. The first mosque was not constructed in the United States until the 20th century. In the latter part of the 20th century, more Muslims, especially from Pakistan, began arriving in the United States. In the wake of the 9/11 attacks, Islamophobic incidents increased, and Muslims were victims of harassment, intimidation, and assaults. The United States' current battle with ISIS in the Middle East, North Africa, and Europe has also increased Islamophobia, paving the way to an anti-refugee right-wing faction in the current Republican Party. The religious morality of the nation has once again become a hot-button topic in the wake of the recent Clinton-Trump debates for the U.S. Presidency.

Major Economic Transformations in the United States

The American economy has changed dramatically since the 1700s, a century where agriculture was the main economic activity. The First Industrial Revolution began in the early 1800s when steam-powered machines were used to increase productivity, especially in the textile industry. The invention of steamboats and railroads made it much cheaper and faster to ship goods across the country in the mid-1800s as well. After the Civil War, the Second Industrial Revolution led to increased productivity and efficiency in the many industries, including metallurgy, chemicals, telecommunications, and energy. This led to significant social changes as immigration and urbanization increased. Workers began to form labor unions in order to demand better wages and working conditions, which led to strikes and conflict with law enforcement officials.

In the early 20th century, Henry Ford introduced the moving assembly line to the automobile manufacturing industry, which made it easier for middle- and working-class families to buy cars. Other industries adopted Ford's methods, which led to lower prices for many consumer goods. The stock market crash in 1929 helped trigger the Great Depression, which resulted in a vicious downward economic spiral. Franklin D. Roosevelt introduced the New Deal to try and boost the economy, but only the outbreak of World War II led to full employment. The United States emerged from World War II as the world's largest economy and pent-up consumer demand fueled prosperity during the post-war era.

The development of computers in the latter part of the 20th century improved communications and led to greater economic efficiency. However, it also marked the beginning of the post-industrial economy in the United States. Traditional manufacturing jobs began to disappear as robots replaced unskilled workers. On the other hand, careers in the information technology sector grew and became a key component of the new high-tech economy. Many unskilled manufacturing jobs also went overseas to countries in Asia and South America as the global economy became more interconnected.

The Causes and Consequences of Changing Immigration Patterns to the United States

Immigration has always played an important role in American history, although patterns have changed over time. Most immigrants came to the United States in search of better economic opportunities, although some have sought religious and political freedom as well. During the colonial period, most immigrants came from Britain, but during the mid-1800s that began to change. In the 1840s, a fungus destroyed the potato crop in Ireland, which led to widespread famine. Many Irish starved, but millions also emigrated, with many heading to the United States. A wave of revolutions also swept across Europe in 1848 and many participants, especially Germans, fled to the United States when the movements failed. This shift led to tension and conflict between immigrants and those born in America. Native-born Americans resented the immigrants' cultural differences and the increased competition for jobs. In the late 1800s, immigration patterns changed again and arrivals from Southern and Eastern Europe began to increase. In 1924, Congress passed an act that limited immigration from these areas.

In 1965, immigration patterns changed again when Congress passed the Immigration and Nationality Act of 1965 act that changed the way immigration quotas were calculated. Immigrants from Central and South America, as well as Asia, became very numerous. Like their predecessors, most came in search of jobs. Recently, many refugees are fleeing violence that erupted from the U.S. invasion of Iraq in 2003 and the revolutions that swept through the Middle East between 2010 and 2012. Cultural differences and economic competition between immigrants and native-born American citizens continue, especially against Mexicans. Vigilante groups have formed in order to prevent illegal immigrants from crossing the U.S.-Mexico border.

Internal Migration

Migration within the United States has also been an important theme since the colonial period. During the 18th and 19th centuries, the focus was on westward expansion because settlers sought cheap land. This often led to violence between settlers and Native Americans who refused to relinquish their territory.

The 19th century also saw an increase in migration from rural areas to cities as individuals sought employment in factories. This trend continued until the late 20th century and more than 80 percent of Americans now live in cities. World War I led to the Great Migration of African Americans from the South to the North. This influx also created more competition for jobs and housing and resulted in a wave of race riots in 1919.

The Struggles and Achievements of Individuals and Groups for Greater Political and Civil Rights Throughout American History

Although the Declaration of Independence declared "all men are created equal," blacks, women, and other minorities struggled for more than a century to make this dream a reality. The U.S. Constitution legalized slavery, and it was not abolished until the 13th Amendment was ratified in 1865. The 14th Amendment, ratified in 1868, granted African Americans citizenship, and the 15th Amendment, ratified in 1870, explicitly granted them the right to vote. However, white Southerners passed laws, known as the Jim Crow system, that prevented blacks from exercising their rights and, when that failed, they relied on violence and intimidation to oppress African Americans. For example, many Southern states required voters to pass literacy tests and used them to prevent blacks from casting a ballot. Whites were either exempt from the test or were held to much lower standards. Blacks who protested their oppression could be assaulted and even killed with impunity. In the 1896 decision *Plessy vs. Ferguson*, the U.S. Supreme Court ruled that "separate but equal" schools for white and black students were permissible. In reality, black schools were almost always inferior to white schools.

The emergence of the Civil Rights Movement after World War II finally destroyed the Jim Crow system. In the 1954 decision *Brown vs. Board of Education*, the Supreme Court reversed the "separate but equal" doctrine and declared that separate schools were inherently unequal because they stigmatized African American students. In 1957, President Dwight D. Eisenhower used federal troops to force the high school in Little Rock, Arkansas, to integrate and accept nine black students. This encouraged civil rights activists to demand additional reforms. In 1955, Rosa Parks refused to give up her seat on a bus in Montgomery, Alabama, which led to a boycott. Martin Luther King Jr. led the bus boycott and became a national leader in the Civil Rights Movement. In 1960, four students in Greensboro, North Carolina, launched a peaceful sit-in at a segregated lunch counter, which sparked similar protests around the country. White activists from the North went south to help blacks register to vote, and in 1964 three activists were murdered in Mississippi. That same year, King led 250,000 protesters in a march on Washington D.C. where he delivered his famous "I Have a Dream Speech."

Although King advocated for peaceful protests, many other civil rights activists disagreed with him. For example, Malcolm X believed that blacks should use violence to defend themselves. Furthermore, King worked with white activists while Malcom X rejected any cooperation. Malcolm X was assassinated in 1965, and, despite his reputation as a non-violent leader, King was also gunned down in 1968.

Under mounting pressure, Congress passed several important pieces of legislation. The 1964 Civil Rights Act banned discrimination based on race, color, religion, sex, or national origin. The Voting Rights Act of 1965 prohibited the use of poll taxes or literacy tests to prohibit voting. The Civil Rights Act of 1968 banned housing discrimination. In 1967, Carl Stokes became the first black mayor of a major American city, Cleveland. That same year, Thurgood Marshall became the first African American to serve on the Supreme Court. President Gerald Ford declared February to be black history month. In 1989, Colin Powell became the first black chairman of the Joint Chiefs of Staff. Despite these reforms, activists claim institutional racism is still a problem in the 21st century. The Civil Rights movement inspired women, Latinos, and other groups to make similar demands for equal rights.

Women

In 1776, Abigail Adams urged her husband, founding father John Adams, to advocate for women's rights, but it would take more than a century before women could vote. In 1848, activists organized a convention in Seneca Falls, New York, to organize the women's suffrage movement, and their efforts slowly gained momentum. The ratification of the 19th Amendment in 1920 finally gave women the right to vote.

Although women had achieved political equality, they continued to demand reform throughout the 20th century. In the early 1900s, Margaret Sanger provided women with information about birth control, which was illegal at the time. Women entered the industrial workforce in large numbers during World War II, but when the war ended, they were fired so that veterans would have jobs when they came home. Many women were frustrated when told they had to return to their domestic lives. Simone de Beauvoir, a French writer, published her book "The Second Sex" after World War II, and an English translation was published in 1953. It highlighted the unequal treatment of women throughout history and sparked a feminist movement in the United States. In 1963, Betty Friedan published a book, called "The Feminine Mystique," that revealed how frustrated many suburban wives were with the social norms that kept them at home. During the 1960s, women participated in the sexual revolution and exerted more control over their own sexuality. In 1972, Congress passed Title IX, which prohibited sexual discrimination in education and expanded women's sports programs. In the 1970s, women's rights activists also pushed for greater access to birth control, and in 1973 the Supreme Court issued the landmark decision *Roe vs. Wade* which removed many barriers to abortion services. Women also demanded greater protection from domestic abuse and greater access to divorce.

During the 20th century, many American women made notable achievements, including Amelia Earhart, who was the first woman to cross the Atlantic in an airplane in 1928. In 1981, Sandra Day O'Connor became the first woman to serve on the Supreme Court. In 1983, Sally Ride became the first female astronaut. In 1984, Geraldine Ferraro became the first woman to run for vice-president, although she was unsuccessful. However, many activists continue to demand reform in the 21st century. For example, women only account for 20 percent of the U.S. Senate and House of Representatives. Furthermore, women only earn 79 percent of what men in similar jobs are paid. In 1980, President Jimmy Carter declared March to be women's history month.

Hispanics

After World War II, many Hispanics also began to demand greater equality. In 1949, veterans protested a refusal by a Texas town to bury a Mexican American soldier, who died during World War II, in the local cemetery, because only whites could be buried there. Activists called themselves Chicanos, a term that previously was used as a pejorative to describe Mexican Americans. Cesar Chavez was a labor union activist who organized transient Hispanic agricultural workers in an effort to obtain better working conditions in the 1960s and 1970s. Activists encouraged a sense of pride in Chicano identity, especially in arts and literature. In 1968, President Lyndon B. Johnson declared National Hispanic Heritage Month would run from mid-September to mid-October.

In 1959, biochemist Severo Ochoa became the first Hispanic to win a Nobel Prize. Franklin Chang-Diaz became the first Hispanic astronaut in 1986, and he flew a total of seven space shuttle missions. In 1990, Oscar Hijuelos became the first Hispanic American to win the Pulitzer Prize. Sonja Sotomayor became the first Hispanic to serve on the Supreme Court in 2009.

Native Americans

Native Americans suffered centuries of oppression at the hands of European colonists, and later American settlers as they pushed further west. Native Americans resisted attempts to encroach on their lands but were pushed onto smaller and smaller reservations. The Massacre at Wounded Knee in 1890 was the last major conflict between Native Americans and U.S. forces. However, American officials continued to try and force Native Americans to assimilate into white culture.

In 1968, a group of Native Americans formed the American Indian Movement in order to combat racism and demand greater independence. Between 1969 and 1971, a group of Native American activists occupied the federal prison on Alcatraz Island near San Francisco, although it had been closed since 1963. The activists offered to buy back the island for $9.40 in order to draw attention to how the federal government had forced tribes to sell their lands at low prices. Other activists disrupted Thanksgiving Day ceremonies aboard a replica of the Mayflower in Boston in 1970. In 1971, Native American activists also occupied Mount Rushmore, which is located on ground the Native Americans consider sacred. Violence broke out between activists and law enforcement officials in 1973 when Native Americans occupied the town of Wounded Knee, sight of the famous massacre.

In 1970, President Richard Nixon granted Native American tribes more autonomy. In 1978, Congress passed the American Indian Religious Freedom Act, which guaranteed Native Americans' rights to practice their religious ceremonies and visit sacred sites. In 1990, President George H.W. Bush declared November Native American History Month. In 1969, Navarre Scott Momaday became the first Native American to win a Pulitzer Prize for his book "House Made of Dawn." In 2014, Diane Humetewa, a member of the Hopi tribe, became the first Native American woman to serve as a federal judge. However, many Native American communities still suffer from high rates of unemployment, alcoholism, and domestic abuse.

Asian Americans

Asian Americans also faced discrimination throughout American history and in 1882, Congress passed a law banning all Chinese immigrants. During World War II, more than 100,000 Japanese Americans were interned in concentration camps. In 1982, two American autoworkers beat Vincent Chin to death with a baseball bat because his assailants blamed him for the loss of jobs in the automotive manufacturing industry.

In the 1960s, activists demanded that the term "Asian American" replace the word "oriental," because it carried a stigma. Asian Americans also promoted a sense of pride in their cultural identity and successfully pushed for the creation of ethnic studies programs. Ellison Onizuka became the first Asian American astronaut in 1985, although he perished in the space shuttle Challenger disaster. In 1990, President George H.W. Bush declared May Asian Pacific American Heritage Month and Sheryl WuDunn became the first Asian American to win a Pulitzer Prize that same year.

Practice Questions

1. Which of the following documents outlawed slavery throughout the United States?
    a. U.S. Constitution
    b. Compromise of 1850
    c. Emancipation Proclamation
    d. 13th Amendment

2. What were the consequences of the Spanish-American War?
    a. The U.S. acquired colonies in the Caribbean and Pacific oceans.
    b. The U.S. acquired large swaths of territory in the Southwestern United States.
    c. It led to the formation of the League of Nations.
    d. It ended the Great Depression.

3. Which constitutional amendment gave women the right to vote in the United States?
    a. 15th
    b. 18th
    c. 19th
    d. 20th

4. What consequences did the Great Migration have?
    a. It led to conflict with Native Americans in the West in the 1800s.
    b. It led to increased racial tension in the North in the early 1900s.
    c. It led to increased conflict with Mexican immigrants in the 1900s.
    d. It led to increased conflict with Irish and German immigrants in the 1800s.

5. Which Supreme Court decision struck down the "separate but equal" doctrine?
    a. *Roe vs. Wade*
    b. *Brown vs. Board of Education*
    c. *Plessy vs. Ferguson*
    d. *Marbury vs. Madison*

6. Which of the following led to the American Revolution?
    a. The Stamp Act
    b. The Boston Massacre
    c. The Boston Tea Party
    d. All of the above

7. Which event(s) contributed to increasing sectional tension before the Civil War?
    a. Malcom X's death
    b. The "Bleeding Kansas" conflict
    c. The 13th Amendment
    d. Shay's Rebellion

8. Which of the following caused America to join World War I in 1917?
    a. Germany's unrestricted submarine warfare
    b. The destruction of the USS Maine
    c. The Japanese attack on Pearl Harbor
    d. Franz Ferdinand's death in 1914

9. What consequences did World War II have?
    a. It led to the creation of the League of Nations.
    b. It led to a communist revolution in Russia.
    c. It made the U.S. the only superpower in the world.
    d. None of the above.

10. Which event was the last major armed conflict between U.S. forces and Native Americans?
    a. Trail of Tears
    b. Tecumseh's War
    c. Massacre at Wounded Knee
    d. Battle of the Little Big Horn

11. What consequences did the Neolithic Revolution have?
    a. Native Americans domesticated cattle and horses.
    b. Native Americans began to grow crops.
    c. Native Americans developed steel weapons and tools.
    d. Native Americans began to emigrate to Canada.

12. Which document established the first system of government in the United States?
    a. Declaration of Independence
    b. Constitution
    c. Articles of Confederation
    d. Bill of Rights

13. What consequences did the New Deal have?
    a. It established a number of federal agencies and programs that continue to function in the 21st century.
    b. It led to a third political party.
    c. It established a two-term limit in the White House.
    d. It led to the Great Depression.

14. What advantage(s) did the North have over the South during the Civil War?
    a. The North was defending their homes from damage.
    b. The North had free labor at home.
    c. The North had a larger navy.
    d. The North had more experienced military leaders.

15. In which of the following areas did the United State achieve victory during the Cold War?
    a. The Korean War
    b. The Space Race
    c. The Vietnam War
    d. The Battle of Gettysburg

16. The presidential cabinet has which of the following duties?
    a. Advise the president.
    b. Act as spokesperson for the U.S. government administration.
    c. Solicit donations for the president's re-election campaign.
    d. Preside over the Senate.

17. What organization helped Ronald Reagan win the White House in 1980?
    a. Great Awakening
    b. Moral Majority
    c. Know-Nothings
    d. Anti-Defamation League

18. Since 1965, most immigrants to the United States have come from what region(s)?
    a. Central and South America and Asia
    b. Australia
    c. Europe
    d. Antarctica

19. Which event helped sparked the gay and lesbian rights movement in 1969?
    a. The Stonewall Inn Riot
    b. The murder of Matthew Shepard
    c. The murder of Vincent Chin
    d. The emergence of AIDS

20. Which of the following were characteristics of the Gilded Age?
    a. Social inequality
    b. Increasing urbanization
    c. Expanding industrialization
    d. All of the above.

21. Which of the following were characteristics of the American political environment in the early 1900s?
    a. The Federalists and the Democratic Republicans
    b. The Populist Party and Progressive Reformers
    c. The Whig Party and the Democrat Party
    d. National Union Party and the Democrat Party

22. Which of the following motivated Christopher Columbus to sail across the Atlantic Ocean?
    a. A desire to establish a direct trade route to Asia.
    b. A desire to confirm the existence of America.
    c. A desire to prove the world was round.
    d. A desire to spread Judaism.

23. Which battle of the Revolutionary War was a key turning point in 1777 because it brought France into the war?
    a. The Battle of Lexington and Concord
    b. The Battle of Saratoga
    c. The Battle of Trenton
    d. The Battle of Bunker Hill

24. What did Radical Republicans hope to accomplish during Reconstruction?
    a. Equal rights for freed slaves.
    b. Leniency for former Confederates.
    c. Acquittal of President Johnson during impeachment.
    d. Effective segregation laws.

25. Which of the following were characteristics of the American economy after World War II?
    a. A return to the Great Depression.
    b. Increased use of computers.
    c. The decline of the Sun Belt.
    d. The fall of the stock market.

26. Which of the following agreements allowed territories to vote on whether or not they would become free or slave states?
    a. The Connecticut Compromise
    b. The Missouri Compromise
    c. The Compromise of 1850
    d. The Three-Fifths Compromise

Answer Explanations

1. D: 13th Amendment. The U.S. Constitution, Choice A, actually legalized slavery by counting slaves as three-fifths of a person. The Compromise of 1850, Choice B, banned the slave trade in Washington D.C. but also created a stronger fugitive slave law. The Emancipation Proclamation, Choice C, only banned slavery in the Confederacy. The 13th Amendment finally banned slavery throughout the country.

2. A: The Spanish-American War of 1898 made the U.S. a colonial power because it acquired many former Spanish colonies. The Mexican-American War of 1846-48 led to the acquisition of California, Nevada, Utah, Arizona, and New Mexico, Choice B. World War I led to the formation of the League of Nations in 1919, Choice C. The Great Depression ended when Americans joined World War II in 1941, Choice D.

3. C: The 19th amendment gave women the right to vote. The 15th Amendment, Choice A, gave blacks the right to vote. The 18th Amendment, Choice B, introduced alcohol prohibition. The 20th amendment, Choice D, repealed prohibition.

4. B: More than one million African Americans in the South went north in search of jobs during and after World War I. The Great Migration led to increased racial tension as blacks and whites competed for housing and jobs in northern cities. The Great Migration also led to the Harlem Renaissance.

5. B: *Brown vs. Board of Education* ruled that separate schools for blacks and whites were inherently unequal and sparked demands for more civil rights. *Roe v. Wade* in 1973, Choice A, increased access to abortion. *Plessy vs. Ferguson*, Choice C, established the "separate but equal" doctrine. *Marbury vs. Madison* in 1803, Choice D, established the doctrine of judicial review.

6. D: All three events led to increasing tension and conflict between the colonists and the British government, which finally exploded at the Battle of Lexington and Concord in 1775. The Stamp Act of 1765 imposed a tax on documents. It was repealed after colonists organized protests. The Boston Massacre resulted in the death of five colonists in 1770. The Boston Tea Party was a protest in 1773 against a law that hurt colonial tea merchants. The British responded to the tea party by punishing the colony of Massachusetts, which created fear among the other colonies and united them against the British government.

7. B: The "Bleeding Kansas" conflict contributed to sectional tension before the Civil War. The application of popular sovereignty in Kansas led to conflict as free-soil and pro-slavery forces rushed into the territory. Malcolm X's death, Choice A, was in 1965, almost 100 years after the Civil War ended. The 13th Amendment, Choice C, was ratified in 1865 and was approved at the very end of the Civil War. Shay's Rebellion, Choice D, was an uprising during 1786 and 1787 in Massachusetts.

8. A: Because the British naval blockade during World War I was so effective, Germany retaliated by using submarines to attack any ship bound for Britain or France. This led to the sinking of the RMS Lusitania in 1915, which killed more than 100 Americans. The destruction of the USS Maine, Choice B, sparked the Spanish-American War in 1898. The Japanese attack on Pearl Harbor in 1941, Choice C, brought America into World War II, not World War I. Franz Ferdinand's death in 1914, Choice D, sparked the outbreak of World War I, but America did not join the war until 1917.

9. D: World War I led to the League of Nations and the communist revolution in Russia, Choices A and B. The USSR and U.S. both emerged as two rival superpowers after World War II. It was thus a bipolar, rather than unipolar, world. The tension and mistrust between the U.S. and USSR eventually led to the Cold War, which ended in 1991.

10. C: Massacre at Wounded Knee. The Massacre at Wounded Knee in 1890 left at least 150 Native Americans dead, including many women and children, and was the last major engagement between Indians and American soldiers. The Trail of Tears, Choice *A*, involved the forced relocation of tribes from the American Southeast in the 1830s. Although thousands of Native Americans died along the way, it was not a battle. Tecumseh launched his uprising in 1811, Choice *B*, and conflict between Native Americans and U.S. soldiers would continue for decades as the country expanded further west. The Battle of Little Big Horn in 1876, Choice *D*, was a great Native American victory that led to the death of General Custer and more than 200 men.

11. B: Native Americans began to grow crops. During the Neolithic Revolution, Native Americans began to cultivate beans, squash, chilies, and other vegetables. However, they did not domesticate many large animals, Choice *A*—only the dog in North America and the llama in Central America. Horses and cattle only arrived in North America as a result of European exploration. Native Americans also did not develop steel or iron, Choice *C*—Native Americans only obtained these items by trading with Europeans. Despite these limits, Native Americans did develop a semi-sedentary lifestyle, formed social hierarchies, and created new religious beliefs.

12. C: Articles of Confederation. Issued in 1776, the Declaration of Independence, Choice *A*, explained why the colonists decided to break away from England but did not establish a government. That was left to the Articles of Confederation, which were adopted in 1781. The Articles of Confederation established a very weak central government that was replaced by the Constitution, Choice *B*, in 1789. It established a stronger executive branch. In 1791, the Bill of Rights, Choice *D*, amended the Constitution by guaranteeing individual rights.

13. A: The New Deal introduced a number of programs designed to increase regulation and boost the economy. Many of them remain in effect today, such as the Social Security Administration and the Securities and Exchange Commission. The New Deal also led to the Republican and Democratic parties to reverse their ideological positions on government intervention. It did not lead to a third party, Choice *B*. President Franklin D. Roosevelt was actually elected to four terms in office and the official two-term limit was not established until the 22nd Amendment was ratified in 1951. Until then, the two-term limit had been an informal custom established by President George Washington when he left office in 1797. Thus, Choice *C* is incorrect. Choice *D* is also incorrect. The Great Depression led to the New Deal, and not the other way around.

14. C: The North had a population of about 18.5 million while the South had only 5.5 million citizens and 3.5 million slaves. This meant the Union could more easily replace men while the Confederacy could not. The South was defending their homes from damage, since most of the war happened in the South, so Choice *A* is incorrect. Choice *B* is incorrect—the South had free labor at home, so they didn't have to worry about leaving their farms to go to war. Finally, Choice *D* is incorrect; the South had more experienced military leaders due to their participation in the Mexican-American War.

15. B: Although the United States initially lagged behind the Soviets, the U.S. successfully landed the first man on the Moon in 1969. However, the Korean War resulted in a stalemate in 1953, leaving Choice *A* incorrect. The Vietnam War, Choice *C*, was a defeat for U.S. forces. Despite sending more than 500,000 troops to Vietnam, the Vietnam War became increasingly unpopular and the United States eventually withdrew in 1973. The communist North Vietnamese eventually captured the southern capital of Saigon in 1975. Choice *D*, Battle of Gettysburg, is part of the Civil War.

16. A: Although the Constitution makes no provisions for a presidential cabinet, President George Washington created one when he took office. Members of the cabinet advise the president on a wide variety of issues including, but not limited to, defense, transportation, and education. The White House Press Secretary acts as spokesperson for the U.S. government administration, Choice *B*. The cabinet members are not required to raise money for the president's re-election effort, Choice *C*. The Vice President, not the cabinet, is who presides over the Senate, Choice *D*.

17. B: Conservative evangelicals formed the Moral Majority in 1979 in an effort to address issues like abortion. Their enthusiasm helped carry Reagan into the White House and bring the U.S. Senate under Republican control for the first time in twenty-eight years. The First Great Awakening, Choice *A*, occurred in the 1700s and the Second Great Awakening began in the 1800s. These movements encouraged Protestants to have a more personal connection to Christ. The Know-Nothings, Choice *C*, opposed Catholic immigration during the 1800s. The Anti-Defamation League, Choice *D*, focused on combating anti-Semitism and Holocaust deniers.

18. A: Congress passed immigration reform in 1965 that made it much easier for immigrants from Central and South America, as well as Asia, to enter the United States. During the colonial period, most immigrants came from Britain. During the mid-1800s, Irish and German immigrants became more numerous. That changed again around 1900 when an influx of immigrants from Southern and Eastern Europe began.

19. A: The Stonewall Inn Riot in 1969 helped ignite the gay and lesbian rights movement when patrons fought back against a police raid. The site became a national monument in 2016. Although he became an icon of the gay and lesbian rights movement, Matthew Shepard was murdered in 1998. Thus, Choice *B* is incorrect. The murder of Vincent Chin, Choice *C*, in 1982, became a rallying cry for Asian American activists. The gay and lesbian rights movement was well established when activists campaigned to raise awareness of AIDS during the 1980s and 1990s, making Choice *D* incorrect.

20. D: Mark Twain called the late 1800s the Gilded Age because the appearance of extreme wealth covered up massive social inequality. While many wealthy industrialists became very rich, many workers worked in poor conditions for low wages. The onset of the Second Industrial Revolution led to an expansion of the chemical, telecommunications, and metallurgical industries. Urbanization also increased during this period as workers crowded into cities in search of work.

21. B: Progressive reformers sought to remedy some of the abuses that emerged during the Gilded Age. They wanted to break up monopolies that interfered with economic competition. Muckraking journalists, including Upton Sinclair and Jacob Riis, also exposed political corruption and social inequality. The Populist Party sought political reforms that would alleviate the plight of farmers and the working class, such as the abolition of national banks and government regulation of railroads.

22. A: King Ferdinand and Queen Isabella agreed to support his mission because he promised to establish a direct trade route to Asia that would allow European merchants to bypass Middle Eastern middlemen. Columbus had no idea that America existed, Choice *B*, and he believed he had landed in India when he arrived in the Caribbean. That's why he mistakenly called the natives *Indians*. It is a common myth that Columbus sought to prove experts wrong by showing them the world was round, not flat. Most European thinkers already knew the world was round, making Choice *C* incorrect. Choice *D* is also incorrect; Christopher Columbus practiced the Christian faith, not Judaism.

23. B: Battle of Saratoga. The Battles of Lexington and Concord marked the start of the American Revolution in 1775. The Battle of Bunker Hill in 1775 was a defeat for the Patriot cause but showed they could stand up to the British army. The Battle of Trenton in 1776 bolstered morale in the Continental army but was not as significant as the Battle of Saratoga in 1777. In this engagement, the Continental army captured thousands of British troops. This victory convinced the French king to support the Patriot cause and his military aid was an important factor in the success of the American Revolution.

24. A: Radical Republicans wanted to ensure that recently freed slaves had the economic and political rights that would enable them to achieve self-sufficiency in the post-Civil War era. Democrats, such as Andrew Johnson, preferred leniency towards the South while Radical Republicans wanted a harsher punishment, making Choice *B* incorrect. This led to conflict between Johnson and Radical Republicans who almost succeeded in having him impeached in 1868.

25. B: World War II brought about an end to the Great Depression by switching over to wartime production. After the end of World War II, consumer demand remained high and unemployment was usually low. Computers began to become more powerful, efficient, and inexpensive in the latter part of the 20th century, and they became more common in business. The Sun Belt actually expanded after World War II as the traditional manufacturing base in the North and Midwest fell into decline. Land was cheaper in the South and West and wages were also lower too, so these regions were very attractive to businesses.

26. C: The Compromise of 1850. The Connecticut Compromise, Choice *A*, formed the basis for the Constitution by proposing a bicameral Congress. The Missouri Compromise, Choice *B*, banned slavery north of the 36°30' parallel in the Louisiana Territory. The Compromise of 1850 essentially undid the Missouri Compromise by introducing popular sovereignty, which allowed voters in territories to decide whether or not the state constitution would ban slavery. The Three-Fifths Compromise, Choice *D*, counted slaves as three-fifths of a human being when allocating representatives.

World History

Formation, Organization, and Interactions of the Classical Civilizations of Greece, Rome, Persia, India, and China in the period 1000 BCE to 500 CE

Age of Antiquity

The study of history from a global perspective is called *world history, global history,* or *transnational history*. Unlike comparative history, world history examines common patterns across nations and cultures on a global scale. A world historian studies how cultures and nations are drawn together and how they are distinct.

The classical civilizations of the world emerged out of the Iron Age, 1200-1000 BCE, with advanced metal tools, written languages, and specialized farming. The characteristics of a civilization include a written language, a geographic state, metal weapons and tools, and the use of a calendar. The prehistoric world developed near fertile river valleys near the Nile River in Egypt, Mesopotamia near ancient Greece, the Indus River in South Asia, and around the Hwang Ho in China. The classical civilizations that emerged out of the ancient world were Greece, Rome, Persia, India, and China.

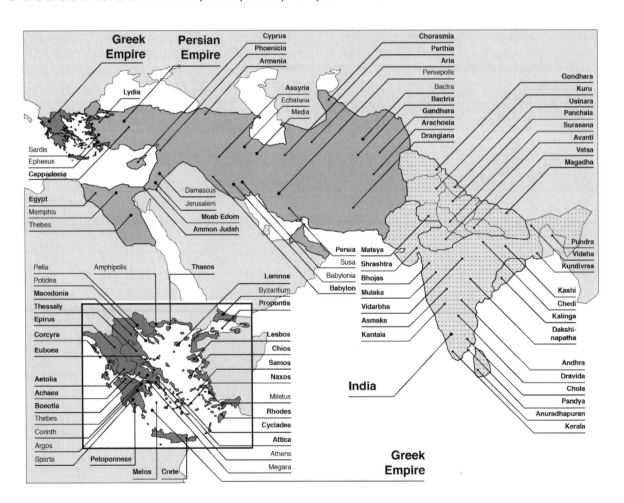

Ancient Greece

Ancient Greece formed from scattered farming communities between 800 BCE and 500 BCE. In this early era of Greece, the polis, or city-state, held all of the political power locally. City-states were self-ruling and self-sufficient. The idea of a self-governing state had an enduring effect on the government of Greece and would result in the demokratia (rule by the people), which would spread and influence the world. As farming villages grew and marketplaces were built, a government with laws, an organized army, and tax collection took shape.

Each city-state was different from one another, but some unifying traits included a common language, a shared belief system, an agriculturally based economy, and rule by several wealthy citizens instead of rule by a king or queen. However, these few aristocratic rulers, known as *oligarchs,* often owned the best and most land, which created tension as the population grew. As a result, many citizens moved to less populated or newly conquered areas. By 800 BCE, there were over 1500 city-states, each with its own rulers and rules. Greek city-states were concentrated on the coast, resulting in greater contact with other civilizations through trade. City-states' governments and culture continued to diverge as time progressed. For example, in the fifth century BCE, Athens became the first direct democracy in the world, and Athenian citizens would vote directly on legislation. Only adult, male, landowning citizens could vote, but it was a remarkable departure from all contemporary forms of government to provide for direct democracy, especially relative to other city-states' oligarchies. Another world-renowned example is Sparta, which based its entire social system and constitution on military training and ability.

The Greek religion was polytheistic. Every city-state had a temple dedicated to a particular god or goddess; however, the whole of ancient Greece believed that Zeus, residing in Mount Olympus, was the most powerful of the gods. The physical presence of the temple, the rituals and festivals that dotted the Greek year, and the widespread belief in the gods controlling every aspect of human life heavily influenced their agricultural economy, government, and interactions with other ancient civilizations.

The ancient Greeks were known for their citizen-soldiers, known as *hoplites.* No ancient civilization could field a professional military due to economic restraints, such as a lack of a banking system and the need for agricultural laborers, but the hoplites were famous in ancient times for their tactics and skill. Hoplites were armed with spears and large shields, and they would fight in a phalanx formation. The Romans would later adopt many of the Greek military principles. Greek city-states fought numerous wars among each other, the largest being the Peloponnesian War, as well as wars against Persia. Fought between 499 BCE and 449 BCE, the Greco-Persian Wars pitted the Greek city-states against the mighty Persian Empire after the latter invaded. Although ancient sources are difficult to authenticate, it is certain that the Persian forces vastly outnumbered the Greeks who historically struggled to unite, even against a common enemy. This conflict included the legendary Battle of Thermopylae where three hundred Spartans, led by the Spartan king Leonidas, held off the elite contingent of the Persian army, the Immortals, for two days. After several setbacks and disastrous turns, the Greeks eventually defeated the Persian fleet at the naval Battle of Mycale and forced the Persians out of Europe. Greek unification did not last beyond this victory, and by 404 BCE, Sparta crushed Athens in the Peloponnesian War. Athens would never again attain its status as the leading city-state.

Alexander's father, King Phillip II of Macedon, conquered the Greek city-states, ultimately achieved at the Battle of Chaeronea in 338 BCE, and established the first centralized Greek state in ancient history. Phillip II then set his sights on the Persian Empire and began preparing for an invasion; however, he was assassinated by sources disputed by contemporary historians. Some speculate they were Persian assassins; others claimed that unhappy leaders of the recently conquered city-states executed the assassination. In any event, Alexander the Great succeeded his father and seized control over their new empire at twenty years old.

In the thirteen years between Alexander's accession to the throne and his own death, he conquered the Persian Empire, which stretched from the Mediterranean to India, fulfilling his father's plans. During this period, education and literacy spread, and new genres of writing were created. The rich cultural interactions between the great ancient civilizations ushered in the Hellenistic period. Architecture was more lavish, and the scientific advancements that began with Aristotle continued throughout the empire. The spread of Greek culture, as well as its interaction with foreign civilizations, had a lasting effect on religion, language, and innovation that endured until Rome conquered Greece and adopted much of the Hellenic culture.

Persian Empire

Cyrus the Great established the First Persian Empire in 550 BC after stifling the great rebellion of the Medes and subsequently defeating the kingdom of Lydia and the Neo-Babylonian Empire. Initially nomadic shepherds, the Persians steadily consolidated power and created a strong infrastructure and military. At its height, the Persian Empire was the largest in the ancient world and stretched from Eastern Europe to Central and South Asia. His successors, including Darius I, continued to expand the empire until Alexander the Great conquered much of Persia, creating the largest empire until the founding of Rome.

The Persian Empire consisted of multiple countries, religions, languages, and races governed by a central government. Cyrus the Great was known for his social and political acumen. He was able to navigate the empire's diversity with his "carrot or stick" approach. Cyrus the Great would offer foreign civilizations some degree of home rule, as long as they paid tribute to Persia and adopted some of its norms, or else the might of the legendary Persian military would crush them. As long as the citizens of Persia paid taxes and were peaceful, they were allowed to keep their own religious customs, local culture, and local economies. It was not until his successors that this political policy began to wan with the onset of multiple rebellions that weakened the centralized government.

The government of Persia delegated power among four governing capitals. Each state had a satrap, or governor. The satrapy government allowed for regional self-governance with a military leader and an official record-keeper that reported to the central government. The empire was also innovative in its road construction and postal systems. By allowing some degree of regional autonomy, Persia was able to rule over an unprecedented territory in ancient history. For example, Babylon even requested to be part of Persia because of its unique policies. The empire's enormity and vast scope influenced world history for centuries. Persian scholars and political philosophers would later influence rulers in the Renaissance and Enlightenment eras.

Maurya Empire

The Maurya Empire was the most powerful and influential kingdom in the history of ancient India, ruling from 322 BCE to 185 BCE, and it was one of the largest empires in the word for its time period. The first emperor of Maurya was Chandragupta Maurya, who overthrew the Nanda Dynasty, unified India, and expanded the empire. His success occurred after Alexander the Great's armies withdrew from India, and Chandragupta's armies defeated the satraps and Greek armies that were left behind.

The Maurya Empire established a centralized government to govern its vast territories, and it specialized in tax collection, administration, and the military. It was modeled after the Greek and Persian governments, who, through trade and invasion, had influenced Chandragupta's government layout. Previously, regional chieftains and small armies governed India, which led to continuous skirmishes and wars. Chandragupta cleared out the chieftains and imposed regulated laws and tax reforms. The centralized form of government allowed for a period of peace, scientific advancement, and religious growth.

The centralized government was made up of four provinces organized under one capital. Each emperor had a cabinet of ministers known as a *Mantriparishad,* or Council of Ministers, to help guide him—an idea that is still used in governments across the world. Princes, or Kumaras, likewise oversaw each province, with a council of ministers called the *Mahamatyas.* A civil service was developed to govern many aspects of life and infrastructure, including waterworks, roads, and international trade. The army was expanded into one of the largest in the world at the time. Trade became a major source of revenue as other empires sought spices, food, and cloth from India.

India's three main religions flourished in this period. Hinduism, a blend of multiple beliefs, appeared in the Epic Age and became a central religion. Buddhism appeared as a consequence of the harsh social structure that had left a wide gap in the social and economic freedoms of the people. Chandragupta later accepted Jainism, a religion of total peace and unity with the world. Overall, the Maurya Empire featured a balance of religions that promoted peace as foundational and sought social harmony. The centralized government discouraged the infamous Indian caste system, which organized society by social status and led to discrimination against the lower castes.

Chinese Empire

Between 1000 BCE and 500 CE, ancient China was unified under three successive dynasties: the Zhou Dynasty, the Qin Dynasty, and the Han Dynasty, in respective chronological order. The Zhou Dynasty was the longest dynasty in Chinese history and began after the fall of the Shang Dynasty. Originally, the Zhou Dynasty had moved away from the Shang Empire, created their own government, and formed alliances with enemies of the Shang. When war eventually broke, the people of Shang, so angered by their own government's foolishness, put up little resistance against the rebellion.

Under the Zhou Dynasty, the kingdom's ruler legitimized their power through the Mandate of Heaven, meaning they believed the rulers of the land were put in place by a higher being that could not be disposed. The Zhou claimed that the Shang Dynasty had forfeited their claim due to their mismanagement of the kingdom. This would be a common theme for dynasty takeovers. A centralized government was established, but the Zhou Dynasty never achieved complete centralized control across the kingdom. The economy was heavily agricultural and organized based on feudalism, an economical system in which a wealthy, landowning class rules the peasant class. These aristocratic rulers retained considerable power and regularly rebelled against the central government.

The Qin Dynasty was the first imperial dynasty, originally organized under Emperor Qin Shi Huangdi. The imperial state had a more centralized government, which limited the aristocratic landowners' power, stabilized the economy, and boosted the army. The Qin Dynasty formed a political structure that allowed China to start seriously building projects like the Great Wall of China. Its form of government would be adopted by many dynasties in China's history. The Qin Dynasty was short-lived and ended when Emperor Qin Shi Huangdi died prematurely, and rebel leaders fought for control of the kingdom. Liu Bang of Han defeated Xiang Yu of Chu at the Battle of Gaixia in 202 BCE, establishing the Han Dynasty.

Like the previous imperial dynasty, power was consolidated under a single emperor who dominated the Han Dynasty's centralized government. Under the emperor, a cabinet of ministers and chosen nobility acted as advisors who retained limited power. The Han dynasty was a golden era of Chinese innovation and technology, all driven by the tremendous growth in commerce and trade. To facilitate commerce, the Han Dynasty issued one of the world's earliest currencies under a money economy. Han coinage would remain the dominant currency from its introduction in 119 BCE until the Tang Dynasty in 618 CE. A uniform currency was an essential part of the legendary Silk Road, which began under the Han Dynasty.

The vast deserts and mountains that sit between China and the rest of the world left China untouched by outside influences for many years. It was not until the Silk Road that opened up trade routes between China and the rest of the world that some technology, culture, and ideas began to influence the West.

Roman Empire

The formation of Rome is steeped in legend and lore befitting its status as the greatest successor to all previous empires. According to legend, twin brothers Romulus and Remus set out to found a new city but disagreed as to its location. Tensions led to Romulus killing his twin brother and founding a city on the Palatine Hill called Rome. Conquering land from Britain to northern Africa and the Middle East, Rome solidified itself as the greatest empire of the ancient world. At its height, Rome's military conquered and held an unprecedented amount of territory.

Throughout its history, Rome transitioned from a monarchy to a republic and then to an autocratic empire. Historians dispute when Rome was founded, but most agree that it was established somewhere between the tenth and eighth centuries BCE by the Latin tribe of Italy. The Etruscans established control over the region by the late seventh century BCE and were ruled by an aristocratic elite and monarch. Sometime during the latter half of the sixth century BCE, the Latin tribe regained power and established the Roman Republic. Around 509 BCE, a constitution and system of government based on checks and balances and separation of powers was established. The senate functioned as the elected legislative branch, and nobility known as *patricians* controlled it. Consuls functioned as the executive branch, and the senate appointed the consuls for limited terms. The Roman Republic would rise to greatness after first defeating Carthage in the Punic Wars and then the Macedonian and Seleucid empires in the second century BCE. Although still a republic, Rome constituted the premier empire in the Mediterranean, well positioned for expansion.

Although already one of the world's most powerful civilizations, Rome began to strain under political pressure and domestic unrest in the mid-first century BCE. In 48 BCE, Gaius Julius Caesar seized power over the republic, but his assassination in 44 BCE on the Ides of March threw the republic back into turmoil. Caesar's great-nephew turned son adopted by will, Octavian, eventually emerged as the sole leader of Rome, and historians define this point as the beginning of the Roman Empire. Octavian would serve as the first emperor under the name Augustus. His rule would be one of the most peaceful and prosperous in Roman history, often referred to as the *Pax Romana* or *Pax Augusta*. Although the Roman Empire did not adhere to the republic's democratic principles and separations of powers, the Roman Empire would be the vehicle that enabled Rome to conquer and administer enormous territory.

As Rome became an empire, its influence both in the ancient world and in the modern world began to take shape. Rome's ability to absorb and adapt the cultural achievements of Greece and push them on conquered cultures was a key to their success. Rome was highly influenced by Greek culture, religions, ideas, literature, and politics but kept at its roots the Roman ideals of simplicity, honesty, and loyalty. Rome was able to hold together a government that included multiple races, languages, and cultures in peace through the successful use of these ideas. In addition, Rome applied concepts developed by the Persians in the administration and political organization of its territories. By the time Rome became an empire, the government was highly structured with a complex civil service that addressed and administrated localized affairs.

Rome's decline began well before its eventual fall. There are many aspects to Rome's demise, including social, political, moral, religious, and economic. Each took their toll on the strength of the empire, and by 400 CE, Rome collapsed under public unrest and religious discord, along with the invasion of the Huns of Mongolia and Germanic tribes. Although ultimately defeated, Rome's legacy extends all the way through to the present day. The Roman Republic's democratic elements and robust civil service would be the model for much of the West, especially the United States. That is to say nothing of the advancements in literature, technology, architecture, urban planning, and hygiene across the empire that influenced every future Western civilization.

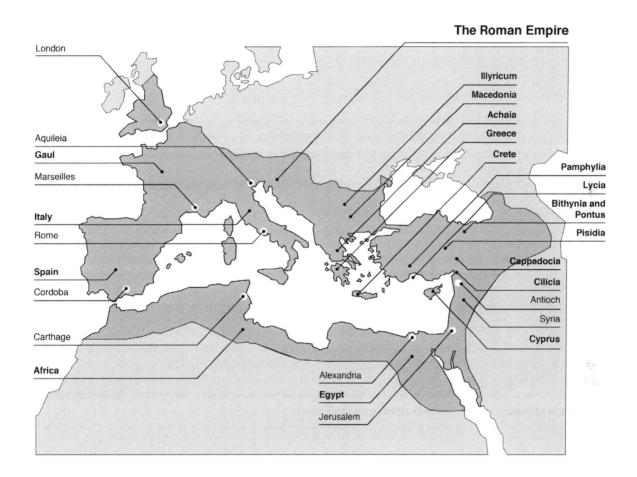

The Roman Empire

The Transformation of Classical Civilizations as a Result of Invasions, Trade, and the Spread of Religions in the Period 300 CE to 1400 CE

Early Middle Ages
The Middle Ages refers to the period from the fifth century to the fifteenth century, beginning with the fall of the Roman Empire and ending with the Renaissance and Age of Exploration. Sharp population decline, intensely localized governance, frequent invasions, famine, and disease defined the early Middle Ages and explain why it is sometimes referred to as the *Dark Ages*. Manorialism and feudalism were the dominant economic systems of the period. Peasants would rent patches of land to farm on enormous manors of aristocrats, while knights and lower nobles would exchange military service with the aristocracy in exchange for control over a manor. In addition, much of the knowledge gained during the Age of Antiquity was lost during this period.

Following the collapse of the Roman Empire into fragmented territories in 476 CE, the former eastern territory retained its power and regained control over some of Rome's other territories, establishing the Byzantine Empire. Although originally part of the Roman Empire, the Byzantine Empire adopted significantly different policies and cultural practices during and after Rome fell. Under Theodosius I, the Byzantine Empire adopted Christianity as the official religion during the third century. During the sixth century, under the reign of Heraclius, the empire adopted Greek as the official language in its administration and military. The Byzantine Empire protected and advanced the rich culture of art, literature, and philosophy developed by the Romans. The emperor Justinian is by far the most heralded and influential Byzantine ruler. He successfully invaded to reorganize governments and spread law. The Code of Justinian, also known as the *Corpus Juris Civilis*, issued from 529 CE to 534 CE, is a fundamental collection of jurisprudence, and it was intended to be the complete collection of laws governing the Byzantine Empire. The Code of Justinian is one of the most influential pieces of legislation in world history, serving as the basis for future civil law jurisdictions and canon law of the Roman Catholic Church.

Christianity played a special role in the Byzantine Empire, as it was able to take over much of the authority lost by civil and military rulers. Christianity was also able to keep literacy, culture, and philosophy of the ancient world alive. In addition, the Byzantine Empire's Christian faith would pit it against Muslims in numerous bloody conflicts. By Justinian's time, the church of the east and the west had grown apart. Concerned with growing differences between the two, Justinian sent out missionaries and suppressed heresy and paganism. His attempts failed in the long term and, as a result, the east and west churches split irrevocably into Roman Catholicism and Eastern Orthodox Christianity with the Schism of 1054 CE.

In 768 CE, Charlemagne, or Charles the Great, took power and worked to unify an empire under the Roman Catholic Church. By 800 CE, he was crowned emperor of the Holy Roman Empire. The Holy Roman Empire controlled a complex set of territories in central Europe from the early Middle Ages until it dissolved in 1806. The predominance of Christian thought in Charlemagne's government covered all aspects of government and allowed for a revival in literature and the arts. It also included copying Latin text to preserve knowledge for future generations. This contrasted sharply with the rest of the West, where much of the former Roman territories lived in localized and unorganized communities. The Holy Roman emperors claimed to be the heir to the Roman Empire and clung to the prestige of that claim. Even in the Holy Roman Empire, the West failed to develop the technology and advance the knowledge gained under the Roman Empire. Although the Holy Roman Empire retained the name and wielded substantial power, the actual government was extremely decentralized, like that of other feudal territories with lesser names.

High Middle Ages

During the High Middle Ages, signs of revival began to emerge. Christians began to see the need to live out the fundamental convictions of Christianity and also saw the need for the clergy to exemplify Christ. After several reforms, religious orders developed, such as the Franciscans and Dominicans. The orders protected the knowledge and texts of the church, becoming a strong intellectual body. As a consequence, there was a revival in learning in the monasteries that trickled out to the cathedrals and then to schools.

Around 570 CE, the Islamic prophet Muhammad was born in Mecca. Muhammad was a trade merchant who, coming into contact with Christian and Jewish traders, blended their religions with his own religious experience in which he believed that Allah was the one true god. He believed that Allah had called him to preach the Islamic religion. At first, he met with little success, as most Arabs believed in many and differing gods. However, in a few years, he was able to unite the nomadic tribes under Islam.

After Muhammad's death, his successors, known as *caliphs,* developed the religion of Islam into a system of government and spread the faith and government control into the Middle East, North Africa, Spain, and southern France. At one point, the Islamic Empire was larger than the Roman Empire. With invasion, Islam spread the Arabic language and embraced Greek science and Indian mathematics. From 900 CE to 1100 CE, Islam experienced a golden age.

In 1095, European Christians launched military strikes against Muslims in the Holy Land, and the entire series of armed religious conflicts is known as the *Crusades.* During the Crusades, Italy's trade flourished because the movement of people facilitated commerce and communication with the Middle East and Africa. In the High Middle Ages, Italy expanded trade into Europe, and merchants across Europe began to settle in areas with good trade routes. Others who had a trade to sell settled in these areas, forming towns and local governments. The development of commerce would be the impetus for the Renaissance.

India
The classical age of India came to a sudden end in 535 CE when the Huns invaded. Under Hun rule, India held on to its religious and cultural traditions. By the 600s, a Hindu confederation pushed back the Huns, and Harsha, the Hindu king, united the empire once again. At first, his rule was peaceful and humane, but in his later years, oppressive acts caused another overthrow of the empire. This time, it was from the Rajput Indians, descendants of central Asians who had intermarried with Hindus after invading some centuries before.

The Rajput kingdoms were small, regionally ruled areas weakened by disunity. After the spread of Islam in the Middle East, Muslim Turks began to invade India. Beginning in the north, Muslims streamed in and began to convert Hindus to Islam. It took from 712 CE to 1236 CE for Muslims to control the northern part of India and another hundred years to gain the southern part.

After setting up a new capital in Delhi, the Muslim invaders used sultans, or Muslim authorities, to rule over India. Their government was called the *Delhi Sultanate,* and it was cruel toward those who had not converted to Islam. The sultans remained in power until 1526 CE. The laws established higher taxes for non-Muslims, which caused many to convert. The strict caste system of Hindu also caused many to convert to the socially equal Muslims. As a result of the invasion and religious conversion, India was divided into Hindus and Muslims, and it remains a dividing point today.

China
The harsh terrain between China and the rest of the world kept it in relative peace and stability for most of Europe's Middle Ages. However, after the Han Dynasty fell, China was in turmoil for nearly four hundred years until a Chinese general, Yang Chien, founded the Sui Dynasty in 581 CE. It was the Sui Dynasty that rebuilt the foundations of the government and allowed the next two dynasties to flourish with two more golden ages.

Following the collapse of the Sui Dynasty in 618 CE, the Li family took control of the empire and established the T'ang Dynasty, which lasted for almost two hundred years. Under T'ang, the government moved to a highly centralized, highly regulated form of government run by the empire's scholars. The economy grew with building projects that opened new avenues of trade. Canals and ports allowed thousands of foreign merchants to trade in China. The dissemination of ideas and culture, combined with long peaceful stability, allowed the Chinese time to create world-changing inventions, such as gunpowder and block printing. The decline of the T'ang Dynasty began after a series of weak emperors, overtaxation, and persecution led to the deposition of the last T'ang emperor by Chao K'uang-yin.

In 960 CE, Chao K'uang-yin established the Song Dynasty. Though it would last until 1279 CE, the Song Dynasty was often fighting off Mongol invaders. The early Khitan invaders were paid off with silver and silk, but the Tungusic people, known as the *Jurchen,* from Manchuria, divided the empire into two—Jurchen's Jin Empire to the north and the Song Empire to the south. Under Song rule, the southern empire flourished, despite the split. Trade increased with the opening of new commercial colonies and ports. As the Chinese began to travel to trade their wares, they introduced new ideas and technology to the world. They also improved sea travel and invented important navigational equipment.

With the empire split, the Jin Dynasty came under attack by Mongols, and after many years of tribute or fighting off, the dynasty gave way under the attacks of Genghis Khan, a brutal but highly effective military commander. In 1215 CE, Genghis Khan conquered the Jin Dynasty and moved to the West, occupying parts of Russia, Persia, Iraq, and northern India. Genghis Khan's grandson, Kublai Khan, united the empires once again by overthrowing the Song Dynasty in 1279 CE and adding the Asian states of Burma, Annam, and Cambodia. He then established the Yuan Dynasty, making Kublai the first foreign ruler in Chinese history.

The Major Political, Social, and Economic Developments in Europe from the Renaissance Through the Enlightenment

While Europe was experiencing a low point in the Middle Ages, with little progress in the arts, technology, or culture, India and China were experiencing multiple golden ages. However, by the 1300s, the tide had shifted. Europe was coming out of its dark age and moving toward a period that would surpass the cultural achievements, wealth, and power that India and China had gained during the Middle Ages. In this emerging Western dominance, the East declined, but it did not remain isolated due to European exploration and colonization.

For Europe, the Middle Ages were a time of feudalism and religious orthodoxy. As the period ended, people began to shift toward the idea of individualism, as they began to seek out political and economic freedom, independence of thought in religious matters, and a desire for greater knowledge. The idea of a "Renaissance man" developed, with Leonardo da Vinci representing the ideal: a person who achieved mastery in many forms or subjects.

The Italian Renaissance
The Renaissance, meaning *rebirth*, began in the fourteenth century in Italy and spread throughout Europe during the fifteenth century. Its philosophy was humanism, or the study of man and his relationship with the world. It was a time when reason and knowledge were highly valued. The Roman Catholic Church kept pace with Europe's focus on mankind and nature, instead of heaven and heavenly beings. Popes sponsored educational enhancements and were, in some instances, as is the case with Pope Pius II, trained as classical scholars. In the early 1500s, Julius II had masters such as Michelangelo create artistic masterpieces that celebrated humans. Indeed, the arts moved toward a more realistic and proportional style with Italian painters such as Leonardo da Vinci, Raphael, and Titian leading the way.

The literary greats of the age were writing in their own vernacular, or language, instead of Latin. This was one of the greatest leaps forward; it not only built their native language, but it also allowed the Italian people to learn and grow in literacy. This and the advances in printing made the written word more accessible and widely dispersed than ever before. The dissemination of knowledge to larger groups of people would change the world, especially as the Renaissance spread to other European nations.

Renaissance in Northern Europe

The ideas in Italy began to spread northward, allowing the arts to flourish in Germany, such as Albrecht Dürer, and in the Netherlands, like Johannes Vermeer and Rembrandt. England began a long history of great literature with Geoffrey Chaucer's *The Canterbury Tales* and Edmund Spenser's *The Faerie Queene*. The highest literary achievements of the Renaissance came from two English playwrights, Christopher Marlowe and his better-known contemporary, William Shakespeare. But the Renaissance did not stray far from religious themes; instead, they humanized them, as is the case of Italian works of art. It was also an early changing point in Christianity, as theologians like Meister Eckhart, Thomas à Kempis, and Sir Thomas More began to use humanism to question the need for priestly intervention, favoring instead direct worship of God.

The invention of movable type by Johannes Gutenberg in 1439 started a revolution in printing that saw the expansion of books go from approximately 100,000 laboriously hand-copied books in Europe to over 9 million by 1500. The literacy rate in Europe improved vastly, as did the printing of religious writings. News could now travel to distant places, allowing for unprecedented communication both locally and globally. Movable type would be one of the major inventions of the Renaissance, heavily influencing the Reformation and Enlightenment.

The Reformation

In 1517, Martin Luther, a German monk and professor of theology, nailed his famous *Ninety-Five Theses,* or *Disputation on the Power of Indulgences,* to the door of the cathedral in Wittenberg, Germany. Pope Leo X demanded Luther to rescind, but Luther stood his ground, which launched the Protestant Reformation. There were serious problems in the Catholic Church, including clergy accepting simony, or the sale of church offices; pluralism, or having multiple offices; and the violation of vows. In addition, the worldly behavior of the church leaders and the biblical ignorance of the lower clergy prompted Luther to ignite a fire that could not be swept away or cleared up. The Roman Catholic Church could not weather this call for reform like it had done before. This was instead a call to cast off the Catholic faith for Protestantism. Many church denominations were formed under Protestantism, the first being Lutheranism, which gained strength in Germany and Switzerland.

Shortly after, the Roman Catholic Church issued a Counter Reformation in an attempt to quell the spread of Protestantism by addressing some of the complaints. In its initial stages, the Counter Reformation had little effect, and many Germans adopted Lutheranism as its officially recognized religion. By 1555, the Catholic Church recognized Lutheranism under the Peace of Augsburg, which allowed rulers to decide on which religion their kingdom would follow. In Germany there was peace, but civil wars broke out in France and the Netherlands. The Spanish-ruled Netherlands' struggle was as political as it was social, with other countries joining the fight against Catholic Spain.

In the 1600s, the peace in Germany faded as the country allied itself with either the Protestant Union or the Catholic League. The Thirty Years' War broke out in 1618 and became one of the most destructive wars in European history. It was a war of political and religious hostility that would involve Germany, Denmark, France, Austria, Spain, and Sweden, to some degree. Though it ended in 1648 with the Peace of Westphalia, France and Spain would wage war until 1659. The Treaty of Westphalia emphasized national self-determination, which directly led to the development of the nation-state. For the first time in human history, local people controlled the right to build a nation-state with the accompanying legitimacy to control their region. The new states, most of which were carved out of the Holy Roman Empire, were allowed to determine their religion, including Catholicism, Lutheranism, and Calvinism.

The Enlightenment

In the Enlightenment, also known as the *Age of Reason,* that followed the Renaissance, Europe began to move toward a view that men were capable of improving the world, including themselves, through rational thinking. The Enlightenment placed a heavy emphasis on individualism and rationalism. During the Renaissance, scholars looked at the Middle Ages as a lost period and considered their own time as modern and new. The Enlightenment, building on the foundations of humanism, began a prolific era of literature, philosophy, and invention.

By the 1700s, Europe had entered the High Enlightenment Age, where events started to take place as a result of the rational thought promoted by the first half of the age. The idea that everything in the universe could be reasoned and cataloged became a theme that set Diderot to work at the first encyclopedia and inspired Thomas Paine and Thomas Jefferson during the initial political unrest in the American colonies.

In the later years of the Enlightenment, the ideal vision that society could be reborn through reason was tested in the French Revolution of 1789. Instead of becoming a leader in rational thinking and orderly government, the revolution turned into the Reign of Terror that saw the mass execution of French citizens and opened the way for the rise of Napoleon.

The Major Political, Social, Economic, and Biological Causes and Effects of Growing Global Interactions

Economic Revolution

During the Renaissance, commercial trade was revived and caused a revolution in the European marketplace and economy. The division of labor, urbanization, and population growth led to a more advanced market economy. Europeans were buying what they had historically made for themselves and were working in a particular trade, which transformed the economy and increased commercial productivity. By 1760, the Industrial Revolution began in England and revolutionized commerce when mechanized textile manufacturing, steam power, and iron making became the norm.

Europe mainly traded among itself, as India and China were not interested in Europe's exports, seeing them as primitive. Europe, however, desired the spices, silk, and tea only available from the East. China especially demanded coin money for exchanges, which at first made it difficult and expensive to purchase such items. The need for a monetary system was evident. During the sixteenth century, European countries would adopt mercantilism as their economic policy, which promoted governmental regulation of the country's economy for the purposes of increasing national wealth. Mercantilist policies developed national currencies, monetary reserves, and positive trade balances to ensure that imports exceeded exports. The Commercial Revolution transformed Europe from a humble trading system into a sophisticated market economy with banking, stocks, and government protection to promote trade. The revolution of trade coincided with exploration and colonization, which brought slave labor into the market, further increasing productivity.

Age of Exploration

The traveling merchants, the Crusades, the conquests of foreign lands, and the writings of ancient Greece expanded the known world of Europeans to include Europe, northern Africa, the Middle East, and Asia. Early explorers such as Marco Polo brought back amazing stories and exotic goods from Asia, while ports in the Middle East and around the Mediterranean spread cultures through trade. However, the very existence of America and Australia was unknown to the ancient and medieval world. Likewise, there was very little knowledge of sub-Saharan Africa until the late Renaissance era.

In an effort to find better trade routes to China, explorers discovered unknown lands that would change the world in dramatic fashion. Over a two hundred year period from 1450 to 1650, the great explorers of the age would discover new lands, unknown people, and better trade routes to the silks, spices, precious metals, and other sought-after goods Europe was eager to own.

Portugal and Spain funded the first explorations and, along with Italy, dominated the discovery of new lands and trade routes for the first one hundred years of exploration. In 1488, Portuguese explorer Bartolomeu Dias became the first European to sail around the Cape of Good Hope in South Africa and the first European to sail from the Atlantic Ocean to the Indian Ocean. On a voyage lasting from 1497 to 1499, Vasco da Gama, another Portuguese explorer, followed the route of Dias and became the first European to reach India by sea.

Portuguese explorers' success led to Portugal's dominance over trade with Africa and Asia. In West Africa, the Portuguese traded for slaves, and in east Africa, they captured city-states and opened trading posts. The coastal trading posts were utilized to launch further exploration and trade farther east with China and Japan. During a voyage launched in 1500, Dias went on to reach Brazil after his ship was blown off course to Africa. Brazil would later become Portugal's most lucrative colony due to the sugar plantations farmed by African slaves and indigenous people.

Hernàn Cortés was the first great Spanish explorer and conquistador, and he conquered present-day Mexico, defeating the mighty Aztec Empire. Within two years of his landing in 1519, most of the vast Aztec Empire fell under Spanish rule. Gold and silver were the prizes for the Spanish in Mexico, as they robbed the Aztecs of much of their precious metals. Francisco Pizarro explored modern-day Peru and conquered the Incan Empire in 1533, making it the second of the two most powerful ancient civilizations in the history of the Americas to fall under Spanish rule. Spain sent thousands of new settlers to America to mine precious metals and start plantations and ranches.

By the 1530s, France, England, the Netherlands, and Scotland were beginning to send explorers on their own expeditions. In 1534, the king of France sent Jacques Cartier to discover a western passage to the Asian markets, and during his voyage in 1534, Cartier became the first European to travel down the Saint Lawrence River and explore Canada, which Cartier named after Iroquois settlements that he encountered. Englishman Francis Drake was the first European to successfully circumnavigate the world, completing the three-year voyage in 1580. Another Englishman, Henry Hudson, was hired by the Dutch East India Company to find a northwest passage to India, and he explored the modern New York metropolitan area in the early seventeenth century. The Dutch would use this knowledge to colonize the area around the Hudson River, including New Amsterdam.

Even more devastating than the loss of their land, contact by Europeans exposed the indigenous people of America to devastating new diseases. Without any type of immunization, mild European diseases decimated the populations of the natives. Often the illness and death of natives made conquering the areas swift, and with it the loss of the culture, traditions, and languages of the native people. However, diseases such as syphilis and cholera were brought back from expeditions, ravaging European countries. The high death toll from disease, coupled with the deaths from native-born slave labor, caused a labor shortage that the Spanish replenished with slaves from their trade deals in West Africa. These slaves were mainly brought to the Caribbean Islands, though they were shipped to other Spanish colonies. The

British colonies would later import millions of slaves to the modern-day American South to harvest cotton.

Colonialism

Although the European explorers never did discover an effective northwest passage to Asia, Europe quickly realized the economic value of their discovery. Mercantilist economic policies viewed the exploitation of colonies and slaves as a positive because it increased the wealth of the home country. Often European nations sought wealth, first through the possibility of finding areas rich in gold, then through agricultural endeavors. The colonies were a way for a country to import goods from their own colonies, becoming more self-sufficient and reducing their reliance on trade with rival powers. As the trade routes became more efficient and the colonies more stable, the transfer of slaves for plantation work in sugar cane and tobacco fields became an ever-increasing source of revenue. To incentivize the creation of permanent colonies, colonists were often given more freedoms than in their home country. Colonial populations also increased as a result of religious persecution throughout Europe.

Spain set up the first colonies in the Caribbean Islands, Florida, California, Mexico, and South America. New Spain, as they called their colonies, was established in the mid-1500s. In 1565, the fort, St. Augustine, was established in modern-day Florida, making it the oldest European settlement in the modern-day United States. Colonies founded by the French, Dutch, and English in the Americas began in the 1600s, including settlements along the eastern coast of North America, eastern Canada, Newfoundland, Great Lakes area, and later along the Mississippi River. In 1624, the Dutch, seeking arable ground, established the New Amsterdam settlement near modern-day Manhattan, which would become an important trading center. The English would capture the New Amsterdam settlement in 1664 and rename it New York City, after the Duke of York.

Sir Walter Raleigh sent an expedition to settle land in the Americas in 1585. The initial attempt to settle Roanoke Island, North Carolina, failed, and the colonists sailed back to England with Sir Francis Drake, who arrived after successfully raiding and pillaging the Spanish colonies in the Caribbean. A second attempt in 1587 also failed. The fate of the "Lost Colony" remains disputed as a relief ship, returning to the area in 1591, found no trace of the settlement. England's first permanent settlement was founded in Jamestown, Virginia, in 1607, and subsequently the Virginia Colony was established.

In 1620, the Pilgrims, an English religious group of Anglicans and Separatists, settled in the Cape Cod Bay area of Massachusetts and drew up their own plans for governing their colony. After enduring religious persecution in England, the Mayflower Compact detailed the plan for a colony founded in fair and just laws, offering citizenship to all adult males. Unlike most other colonies, the Plymouth colony did not have a royal charter, so the Mayflower Compact is unique in that it provided one of the first forms of self-government in the colonies. By their eighth year, the Pilgrims had successfully established the Massachusetts Bay Colony, the second of the eventual thirteen British colonies in North America.

The rest of the thirteen colonies formed when royal charters were granted, either to individuals or corporations. The thirteen colonies were allowed limited self-rule. A governor for the colonies was appointed by England, but each colony could rule by its own laws enacted by colonial assemblies. The method in which these men were appointed, and the laws of each colony, differed based on the type of charter each had, if any. In royal colonies, those of Virginia, Massachusetts, New Hampshire, New York, New Jersey, North Carolina, South Carolina, and Georgia, the king of England was the direct authority of the colony and chose the governor, among other things. Proprietary colonies, which included Pennsylvania, Delaware, and Maryland, were under the authority of the owner of the colony, while Rhode Island and Connecticut were self-governing and had no direct authority.

The colonies were divided into sections: New England, Middle Colonies, and Southern Colonies. New England's economy was based on fishing and forest harvesting. The Middle Colonies had arable ground and developed a farming economy with heavy yields in wheat for export. The Southern Colonies, having a warm climate like southern Europe, with rich soil, grew crops such as tobacco, rice, and cotton. By the 1700s, the thirteen colonies were invaluable, making England much wealthier. In early years of colonization, indentured servitude provided much-needed labor. These servants pledged a certain amount of years, usually between five and seven, to pay for their passage and some land and tools to become prosperous citizens once their indentured time was completed. Initially, Africans came as indentured servants. This occurred first in Jamestown in 1619; however, by the late 1600s, slavery within all of the colonies was introduced. The bulk of African slaves were used in the Southern Colonies to work on plantations.

Founded in 1788, the British colony in Australia was originally a penal colony populated by convicts deported from Britain. Between 1788 and 1868, more than 160,000 British convicts were transported to the Australian penal colony. Criminals were used to settle the area and work the land. If they finished their sentence, they could begin to work for themselves. Many had families that were freed from forced labor. The fertile areas of Australia were used for crop raising and grazing sheep. More and more land was seized from the Aboriginal Australians for agriculture and grazing, pushing the Aboriginals into the less desirable desert region. By the mid-nineteenth century, Australia would be a desirable place for non-convicts due to numerous gold rushes and a booming agricultural industry. Established in 1841, the nearby New Zealand colonists similarly drove out the native Maori tribes and used their land to graze sheep and raise crops. Unlike Australia, New Zealand was never used as a penal colony, though some of its occupants were escaped convicts. Most settlers were former sailors, whalers, or sealers. The exportation of exotic woods, and later the capture and trade of natives into slavery in Australia, were sources of revenue for the colony.

The introduction of new diseases to the Aborigines and the Maoris decimated their numbers. The Maoris' numbers decreased significantly again when, after adopting the English musket as a method of warfare, intertribal wars led to more deadly conflicts. Like Australia, the New Zealand settlers also pushed out the native people, leading to a series of armed conflicts between 1845 and 1872, collectively known as the *New Zealand Wars*. In the end, the settlers prevailed, and the number of Maoris greatly diminished.

Attempts were made to colonize Africa, but disease, resistance, and the difficult terrain caused Europe to limit settlements to trade ports and coastal forts. However, through colonization, indigenous African civilizations were decimated by the slave trade.

From the 1500s to the 1700s, Spain and Portugal colonized the areas of Mexico, the West Indies, and places in South America. Later, the French and English would gain control of places in the Caribbean Islands and the West Indies. Unlike the thirteen colonies, Spanish rule was authoritarian and centralized, with the government having more power and fewer restrictions. The economies in Mexico, the West Indies, and Latin America were based on mining, plantations, and livestock. Slave labor was in heavy use. In no other place was the Roman Catholic Church more influential abroad than the colonies of the southern Americas. They were second only to the Spanish government, having influence politically and socially. The church owned nearly half of the land, with church officials being part of the wealthy landowning aristocracy.

The Major Causes and Consequences of Revolutions, Nationalism, and Imperialism in the Period 1750 CE to 1914 CE

While the colonies were increasing in population and production over their first 150 years, British oversight was loose, and the colonies enjoyed extensive self-government. However, in the mid-1700s, England, in need of revenue, began to enforce laws and create new ones that restricted the freedoms in trade the colonies enjoyed. Starting in 1764, the prime minister of England, Lord George Grenville, began to impose acts that the American colonies resented and protested, including the Sugar Act, the Quartering Act, and the Stamp Act. Groups were formed in protest, such as the Sons of Liberty, and even the colonial governments threatened to refuse to obey the acts. A spirit of nationalism swept through the colonies, who began to view themselves as a collective entity.

In 1765, believing that the colonies had the only right to tax colonists, nine colonies banded together to form the Stamp Act Congress, also known as the *First Congress of the American Colonies*. The Stamp Act Congress sent their grievances to King George III of England. Though the Stamp Act was repealed, Parliament issued a law making it clear that the colonies were under the British government's rule. More laws were enacted to tax the colonies, further stirring discontent in the British colonies. In an attempt to punish and subdue the American colonies, Parliament issued further acts called the *Coercive Acts,* or the *Intolerable Acts,* as they were known in America. These acts only served to unify the colonies and, as a result, the First Continental Congress in 1774 issued another formal complaint. The response from King George III and Parliament was to increase troops in the colonies. In the Second Continental Congress, the colonies again petitioned the king, sending the Olive Branch Petition to King George III. On July 4, 1776, after the failed diplomatic attempts, the Declaration of Independence was adopted, and after the war, it would herald a radical form of self-government never before seen in world history.

Unlike the United States' revolution against a ruler across the ocean, the French Revolution was an internal fight. In 1789, tension between the lower class (peasants) and middle class (bourgeois) and the extravagant wealthy upper class of France came to a head. The Old Regime, headed by the monarchy, was overthrown, and the Third Estate, made up of the bourgeois class, seized power. The American Revolution, overtaxation, years of bad harvests, drastic income inequality, and the Enlightenment influenced the French Revolution. In August 1789, the National Constituent Assembly, a democratic assembly formed during the French Revolution, passed the Declaration of the Rights of Man and of the Citizen, which defined the natural right of men to be free and equal under the law.

France radically changed the government from a monarchy to a democracy with provisions for civil rights, religious freedoms, and decriminalization of various morality crimes, like same-sex relationships. Two political powers emerged: liberal republicans called *Girondist*s and radical revolutionaries, known as *Jacobins*. Conflict between the parties resulted in the Reign of Terror—a period of mass executions— and eventually the rise of Napoleon who set up a nationalist military dictatorship. During the revolution, Napoleon Bonaparte consolidated power after becoming famous for his heroism during the revolutionary wars against Britain, Austria, and other monarchies that sought to retain their right of royal rule. However, by 1804, Napoleon declared himself emperor and remilitarized France, and he conquered most of Europe in a series of global conflicts collectively known as the *Napoleonic Wars,* starting in 1803 and continuing until Napoleon's defeat at the Battle of Waterloo in 1815.

After the chaos sparked by the French Revolution that fanned across Europe during the revolutionary wars, European powers met at the Congress of Vienna in November 1814 to June 1815 to rebalance power and restore old boundaries. The Congress of Vienna carved out new territories, changing the map of Europe. France lost all of its conquered territories, while Prussia, Austria, and Russia expanded their own. With the restoration of a balance of power, Europe enjoyed nearly fifty years of peace.

Fueled by the successful American Revolution, Napoleon's rise to power, and the writings of the Enlightenment, a spirit of revolution swept across the Americas. The French colony in Haiti was the first major revolution occurring in 1791. The Haitian Revolution was the largest slave uprising since the Roman Empire, and it holds a unique place in history because it is the only slave uprising to establish a slave-free nation ruled by nonwhites and former slaves. In 1804, the Haitians achieved independence and became the first independent nation in Latin America. When Napoleon conquered Spain in 1808, Latin American colonies refused to recognize his elder brother, Joseph Bonaparte, as the new Spanish monarch and advocated for their own independence. Known as the *Latin American Wars of Independence,* Venezuela, Colombia, Ecuador, Argentina, Uruguay, Paraguay, Chile, Peru, and Bolivia all achieved independence between 1810 and 1830. In 1824, Mexico declared itself a republic when, after several attempts by the lower classes of Mexico to revolt, the wealthier classes joined and launched a final and successful revolt. When Napoleon overtook Portugal, King John VI fled to Brazil and set up court. Later he left his son Pedro behind to rule. Pedro launched a revolution that saw him crowned emperor.

By the mid-1800s, the revolutions of Latin America ceased, and only a few areas remained under European rule. The U.S. president James Monroe issued the Monroe Doctrine, which stated that the Americas could no longer be colonized. It was an attempt to stop European nations, especially Spain, from colonizing areas or attempting to recapture areas. England's navy contributed to the success of the doctrine, as they were eager to increase trade with the Americas and establish an alliance with the United States.

Industrial Revolution

While Europe was in the midst of colonization and revolutions, they experienced an industrial revolution that would impact the social and economic fabric of life. Starting in the 1760s, with humble origins in England's textile economy, it lasted until the 1820s and changed the way people worked and lived. The revolution brought new scientific developments and improvements to agriculture and textile manufacturing. It was also a time of great invention in steam- and water-powered engines, machines, tools, chemicals, transportation, factories, lighting, glass, cement, medicines, and many more. Additional information concerning the Industrial Revolution and the Second Industrial Revolution are included in the section called "The Major Economic Transformations that Have Affected World Societies."

In some ways, it improved people's standard of living, but in many ways, it made life harder. Falling prices on goods made nutrition levels improve and allowed people more buying power. Medicines and better transportation also improved the quality of life for many. However, crowded living quarters in the booming urban centers were often appalling, as were the diseases brought on by working in factory conditions. The use of child labor eventually brought about reform, and labor unions had an effect on working conditions, but it took many years for either of these problems to be properly addressed.

Nationalism and Imperialism

With most revolutions, nationalism, or the devotion to one's country, plays a central role. The American and French revolutions, along with the revolutions of Latin America, were fought with the desire to improve the prosperity and position of its civilians. After the Napoleonic Wars and the Congress of Vienna, the years of undisturbed peace resulted in a buildup of nationalism. Countries like Italy and Poland resented Austrian and Russian rule as much as they had disliked French occupation. A rise in nationalism in Germany was a constant threat to Austria, as it tried to govern multiple cultures and languages across a wide geographic area. The precarious situation would remain hostile to some degree until the outbreak of World War I. The Industrial Revolution had made the lower and middle classes restless for change and improvements. By 1848, uprisings began to spring up all over Europe, beginning with France. Many who had nationalistic leanings toward a country that was either no longer in existence or had been forced into another country were able to separate from other nations. The Hungarians broke with Vienna, though they were forced back soon after, the Romanians split from papal power, and the Italians threatened rebellion.

The development of imperialism began in the mid-nineteenth century and lasted until the twentieth century, with much of the imperialized world gaining freedom after World Wars I and II. The spread of imperialism that was to follow the revolutions of the eighteenth and nineteenth centuries can be traced, in part, to the idea of nationalism. Some countries believed they were doing a good, and even a moral, thing by conquering and colonizing new territory to spread their culture, traditions, religion, and government. However, a darker side of nationalism—the feeling of superiority and right—caused the takeover of areas and the enforcement of foreign rules and laws.

The British Empire stretched across the world, and at one point had over 450 million people under its rule. With the loss of its American colonies, England began to focus on other areas of the world. In the mid-1700s, India was the first target of British imperialism. Opposition to the ruling Mughal Empire allowed the British army an inroad at the Battle of Plassey in 1757, where General Robert Clive and his army overtook Bengal in northeast India. Next, the British forced the Mughal emperor to give all tax-collecting rights to England. In 1784, Parliament passed the East India Company Act, also known as *Pitt's India Act,* which brought the East India Company's rule in India under control of the British government. Railway systems to expedite the shipment of goods to Great Britain were built, and a new government called the *British Raj* was established. Indians were educated to work in the government and, at first, used their education to promote reform in India. Many of these civil service workers would take on the mantle of nationalism and advocate for India's independence. Great Britain further expanded its empire into areas of Africa and solidified its rule in Australia, capitalizing on exports from Australia and Canada. It also had what is seen as an informal empire in China and other nations due to its ability to dominate trade and influence economic policy.

Imperialism was also seen in Japan, a country that moved from a primitive and feudal system to a strong empire quickly and overtook Taiwan, Korea, many islands in the Pacific Ocean, and parts of China. It was not until the end of World War II that Japan was forced to surrender control of its accumulated empire. Germany, Russia, and the Ottoman Empire also gained land through imperialism during the years before World War I, most of which was lost by the end of the Great War. The United States was initially against imperialism after having been a colony itself and even solidified these ideas in the Monroe Doctrine; however, by the late nineteenth and early twentieth centuries, the United States defeated Spain in the Spanish-American War and annexed Hawaii, Guam, and the Philippines.

The Major Ideological, Economic, and Political Causes and Consequences of the First and Second World Wars and the Cold War

First World War
The onset of World War I began with the precarious balance of power and the geographic divisions written by the Napoleonic Wars' Vienna Congress.

Austria-Hungary's large empire was diverse in culture and included various peoples of several races, languages, and beliefs. However, minorities in their lands in the Balkans grew tired of foreign control.

This was especially true in Bosnia, which was all but under control by the nationalistic secret military society, the Black Hand. This nationalistic sentiment grew until, in 1914, Gavrilo Princip, a Serb patriot and member of the Black Hand, assassinated Archduke Franz Ferdinand, heir presumptive to the throne of Austria-Hungary. In response, Emperor Franz Joseph I of Austria-Hungary declared war on the kingdom of Serbia, officially launching the First World War.

Europe had tied itself into a tangled web of alliances and mutual protection pacts. Germany and Austria-Hungary were allies. Russia promised protection to France and Serbia, and England maintained a tacit support to its past allies throughout the mainland. Each of the Allies soon mobilized to support each other. Germany had already planned for declarations of war, however, and was nervous about fighting a two-border war against both France and Russia, so it developed the Schlieffen Plan—a strategy to quickly demolish French resistance before turning around to fight Russia on the Eastern Front. However, this plan relied on the neutrality of England; after Germany invaded Belgium to attack France, England's declaration of war ensured that a long war would be inevitable.

The Great War lasted from 1914 to 1918 and was the deadliest war in European history until World War II, with approximately 16 million combatants and civilians dying in the conflict. The carnage was largely a result of technological innovation outpacing military tactics. World War I was the first military conflict to deploy millions of soldiers and the first war to involve telephones, tanks, aircrafts, chemical weapons, and heavy artillery. These twentieth-century technological innovations were deployed alongside outdated military tactics, particularly trench warfare. As a result, hundreds of thousands of troops would die during battles without achieving any meaningful strategic gains. Countries were devastated by the loss of the male population and struggled to cope with a depleted workforce, and widows and orphans struggled to regain any degree of normalcy.

Due to the high death tolls, the Allies' need of the financial support, and the anger associated with the war, the Treaty of Versailles harshly punished Germany, who the Allies blamed for the war. The Allies coerced Germany into signing the treaty that was a death sentence to their country's economy. It contained a "guilt clause," which, unlike the Congress of Vienna's terms for the similarly belligerent France, made oppressive demands on Germany. The treaty took German lands, enforced a heavy reparations debt that was impossible to pay, and stripped Germany of its colonies. After suffering enormous losses during the war itself, the Treaty of Versailles ensured that no national recovery would be possible.

In the aftermath, Russia, Italy, and Germany turned to totalitarian governments, and colonies of Europe started to have nationalistic, anticolonial movements. The Russian Revolution of 1917 led to a civil war in which the Bolsheviks, or Communists, took control under the guidance of Communist revolutionary Vladimir Lenin and established the Soviet Union. The Communist government turned into a dictatorship when Stalin emerged as leader in 1924. Stalin ruled with an iron fist and executed all of his political opponents, including the Bolsheviks. Dissatisfaction with the treaty in Italy led to the rise of fascist leader Benito Mussolini. Germany suffered through several small revolutions, splintering political parties, and class division; this, combined with wartime debt and hyperinflation—a result of the Treaty of Versailles—caused many to become desperate, especially during the throes of the Great Depression. Adolf Hitler, a popular leader in the National Socialist German Workers' Party (Nazi Party), organized street violence against Communists. In the 1932 parliamentary elections, the Nazis emerged as the largest party in the *Reichstag* (German Parliament), but the Nazis did not have enough votes to name Hitler as chancellor. The street violence against Communists and Jews continued unabated, and on January 30, 1933, political pressure led to President von Hindenburg naming Adolf Hitler the chancellor of Germany. Hitler immediately expelled Communists, the second most popular political party, from the

Reichstag, and coerced the *Reichstag* to pass the Enabling Act of 1933, effectively creating a dictatorship.

The start of decolonization in India occurred after World War I, with the Government of India Act of 1919. While the war was raging, Britain promised India more self-rule if they supported the war effort. However, the act did not grant freedom in taxation, foreign policy, or justice and only went as far as allowing local matters to be addressed by native-born citizens. For the Indian National Congress, India's largest political party, this fell short of what they had expected. In the 1920s, Mahatma Gandhi, leader of the Indian National Congress, protested using civil disobedience. In August 1947, England granted independence to India and split the British Indian Empire into India and Pakistan.

Second World War
Nazi Germany had risen to power through the 1920s and 1930s, with Hitler's belief that Germany would only recover its honor if it had a resounding military victory over Europe. Nazi ideology adhered to an extreme nationalism advocating for the superiority of the German people and the necessity of expanding their lands into an empire. Jews, Communists, and other nonconformists were banned from political and social participation.

In 1936, German troops violated the Treaty of Versailles by moving outside Germany's borders, with a remilitarization of the Rhineland. The Rome-Berlin Axis, an alliance between Germany and Italy, was forged in the same year. Germany was the only European power to support Italy's invasion and annexation of Ethiopia, and in exchange, Italy supported Germany's annexation of Austria. In 1936, a civil war broke out in Spain between Spanish nationalist rebels and the government of the Spanish Republic. Mussolini and Hitler supported the Spanish nationalist general Francisco Franco and used the Spanish Civil War as a testing ground for their new alliance. The Allies did not respond to these actions, and when Germany demanded the return of the Sudetenland, a territory in Czechoslovakia, France and Great Britain agreed in hopes of an appeasement despite the protests of the Czech government. Hitler then moved into more areas farther afield, which prompted the Soviet Union to sign a nonaggression pact with Germany. On September 1, 1939, Germany invaded Poland, and on September 3, 1939, France and Great Britain declared war on Germany, jumpstarting the deadliest conflict in world history.

Aside from the incredible casualties resulting from intense fighting and bombings of cities, World War II is marked by the worst war crimes in human history. Germany conducted a systematic genocide of six million Jewish people during the Holocaust, sending two-thirds of Europe's Jewish population to be executed in death camps. Millions of non-Jews were also exterminated during the Holocaust, including Slavs, Poles, Romani, people of color, Communists, homosexuals, and disabled people, among others. It is estimated that anywhere between six and eleven million people were executed in the Holocaust. Although less discussed than the Holocaust, the Japanese military committed similar war crimes across Asia, executing between three and ten million Chinese and Koreans, among others, between 1937 and 1945. In one event, the Rape of Nanking, Japanese soldiers captured Nanking and brutally murdered 300,000 civilians. An additional twenty thousand women, children, and elderly were raped during the massacre. Japanese newspapers closely covered a contest between two Japanese officers to see who could kill more people with a sword during the Rape of Nanking. Stalin also committed heinous war crimes during World War II, with estimates ranging from four to ten million deaths as a result of executions and sentences to the Gulag. The United States has also faced criticism for its decision to drop two nuclear bombs on the Japanese cities of Hiroshima and Nagasaki, killing more than 129,000 civilians, leveling both cities, and ending the war. The American government justified the use of nuclear weapons as the only way to avoid a ground invasion of Japan that would have cost more Japanese and American lives than the bombs.

Towns and cities had been leveled, civilian and soldier death tolls were crippling to economies, and countries struggled well into the 1950s to recover economically. It became a breeding ground for Communism, and in China, the end of the war meant a reprisal of the civil war between Mao Zedong's Communists and nationalists that had been interrupted by world war. Another result of the war was a changed map of the world, as countries were divided or newly formed, and the end of most of Britain's colonialism occurred as a result of the empire's economic and military losses. Following the war, Great Britain, France, Portugal, Belgium, Italy, the Netherlands, and Japan had either granted freedom to colonies or lost areas during the war. Many African and Middle Eastern countries would be granted their independence; however, the newly formed countries' borders were drawn according to those of the former colonies, creating ethnic and religious tensions that still exist today.

In an effort to stop a world war from occurring again, the Allies created the United Nations to be a safeguard and upholder of peace. This proved especially important, yet difficult, as the world was divided between a capitalist Western bloc and a Communist Eastern bloc. Germany was divided between the United States and Soviet Union to maintain peace and to better control the reconstruction of Germany; occupation zones were established, with East Germany occupied by the Soviet Union and West Germany occupied by Great Britain, France, and the United States.

Cold War
Within two years of World War II, the world was involved in a different kind of war—a Cold War—that pitted capitalism and Communism against each other. World War II left Europe on the brink of collapse, leaving the United States and Soviet Union as the world's undisputed remaining superpowers. The United States and its Allies embarked on a campaign of containment in an attempt to keep Communism from spreading to other countries. After World War II, the United States offered European countries the Marshall Plan—a grant of American subsidies to help Europe and Japan recover economically. The largest recipients were England, France, and West Germany. Aside from sincere humanitarian desires, the Marshall Plan also served the interests of the United States by ensuring that Europe's citizens did not resort to Communism out of desperation. In turn, the Soviet Union developed their own plan, the Molotov Plan, to help their Communist Allies' recovery.

In the 1940s, U.S. president Harry S. Truman, in an effort to contain Communism, offered U.S. military and economic protection to any nation threatened by Communist takeover. By 1949, the United States, Canada, and ten European nations agreed to the same idea in an alliance known as the *North Atlantic Treaty Organization (NATO)*. When West Germany was invited into NATO in 1955, the Soviet Union responded with a similar alliance known as the *Warsaw Pact*. The Warsaw Pact and NATO were vehicles for the United States and Soviet Union to flex their military might. In addition to conventional arms, the two superpowers competed in a nuclear arms race throughout the Cold War. The nuclear arms race created a situation where each country could destroy the world many times over at the push of a button. There were several close calls during the conflict due to mixed signals, misunderstandings, or provocation—the most notorious being the Cuban Missile Crisis when the Soviet Union placed nuclear missiles in Cuba, ninety miles away from Florida.

In China, Mao Zedong, the chairman of the Communist Party and leader of the People's Republic of China, attempted to quickly transform China into a Communist state through an ineffective and devastating economic program known as the *Great Leap Forward,* which abolished private ownership of property and featured collective communes. The Great Leap Forward caused a humanitarian disaster, resulting in tens of millions of deaths, due to inefficient economic planning under a poorly devised Communist system.

The United States fought a series of proxy wars against the Soviet Union to prevent the spread of Communism. The Korean War, 1950-1953, was an attempt to keep Communism from spreading into Korea. China and the Soviet Union joined together to fight the United States and Allies until an armistice was signed that divided Korea into a Communist North and a democratic South along the thirty-eighth parallel. The thirty-eighth parallel was an important demarcation during the war itself, as America was cautious to pursue the North Koreans back across the parallel or else risk escalating the proxy war into a conventional one against the Soviets. The Vietnam Conflict, 1955-1975, was another proxy war pitting the United States against Communism. China and the Soviet Union provided extensive aid to the Communist Viet Cong guerilla fighters and the more conventional North Vietnamese army. Although the United States was the superior conventional military force, the American military struggled mightily against the guerillas using the dense jungle as cover. As intense opposition to the war mounted in the United States, the United States withdrew after the North Vietnamese captured Saigon in April 1975. The Soviet Union similarly struggled against guerilla forces backed by the United States during the Soviet-Afghan War, which lasted between 1979 and 1989. The United States provided military and financial support to the Afghans during the conflict, many of who would later found al-Qaeda or join the Taliban to fight the United States, including Osama bin Laden.

Protests and new leaders gave some economic freedom and recovery to these European nations after WWII, but East Germany was excluded. In 1961, a wall was built to separate East and West Germany in an attempt to keep people from fleeing the Soviet-controlled East. However, in 1985, Mikhail Gorbachev became the Soviet leader and began to change politics in the Soviet Union, with *glasnost*—a policy of government transparency and openness—and *perestroika,* a government reform. He allowed the Eastern European satellite countries more economic freedom and limited self-government. The Soviet economy could not keep up with the United States, especially when President Reagan increased American military spending. Pushed to the brink of economic collapse, the Soviet Union could no longer maintain control over their satellites and Allies, who were increasingly agitated for complete autonomy. On November 9, 1989, the Soviet Union ordered the Berlin Wall to be knocked down, an important step toward thawing the Cold War. On December 26, 1991, the Soviet Union officially collapsed and broke up into fifteen distinct countries.

The Major Developments of the Post-Cold War

The collapse of the Soviet Union left the United States as the sole world superpower. In addition, Communism no longer represented a viable political ideology, cementing the market economy as the leading economic system, which is later discussed in greater detail in the section "The Major Economic Transformations that Have Affected World Societies." In the mid-1990s, the Internet emerged as a driving force in globalization, connecting people across the world and providing instantaneous access to vast stores of information. Globalization further presented itself in the form of supranational governance. In 1992, the European Union was established for the purpose of creating a common market for goods and capital. Other supranational political entities would lead the way toward the creation of a globalized economy.

Founded in 1995, the World Trade Organization is a supranational organization composed of 164 member states, and it establishes regulations, norms, and dispute resolution to govern trade agreements between countries. Trade agreements between two entities are referred to as *bilateral agreements,* and any larger type of agreement is classified as *multilateral.* The entity entering into the trade agreement can be either a single nation-state or a trade bloc—an informal group of countries who negotiate as a single entity. The most common type of trade agreement is free trade, which offers preferential treatment through the elimination of trade restrictions, like tariffs and quotas. Trade agreements force countries to rely on the economic health of their trade partners, which naturally leads to interdependence. Examples of trade agreements include the North America Free Trade Agreement and Association of Southeast Asian Nations.

Trade agreements form the basis of a globalized economy as countries seek to maximize the economic principle of economies of scale, which defines how countries can function most efficiently within markets and vis-à-vis competitors. It encourages countries to specialize in what they do best and devote the bulk of their resources to maximizing that specialty. In theory, increasing production will make the output more efficient and cost effective. Incentivizing countries to boost their production and pursue their competitive advantage inherently leads to greater economic interdependence and globalization; trading countries are necessarily dependent on their partners to meet some need. For example, in the North America Free Trade Agreement, the United States provides technology and white-collar skills, while Mexico primarily focuses on manufacturing.

Despite the trend toward supranational political and economic entities, nationalism has reemerged as a powerful force in the post-Cold War Era. Nationalism is best understood as people seeking independence for some collective reason, like geographical proximity or cultural similarities. In addition, nationalism is primarily expressed via its opposition to external influences. Just as nationalism served as a rallying cry for colonial people fighting to gain their independence, nationalism has come back into vogue as the means for people to advocate for greater local control.

The Yugoslav Wars of 1991 to 2001 and eventual collapse of Yugoslavia illustrate how ethnic nationalism exists as a powerful countervailing force to globalization trends. The former Socialist Federal Republic of Yugoslavia contained several republics that consisted of distinct ethnic groups, including Bosnia and Herzegovina, Croatia, Macedonia, Serbia, and Slovenia. Additionally, Serbia was further divided between Kosovo and Vojvodina. After the death of Yugoslavia's founding authoritarian ruler, Josip Broz Tito, the country eventually collapsed under separatist nationalist movements. Following a series of bloody wars and war crimes, collectively known as the Yugoslav Wars, seven newly independent states emerged out of Yugoslavia—Bosnia and Herzegovina, Croatia, Kosovo, Macedonia, Montenegro, Serbia, and Slovenia.

Nationalism is also on the rise in Western democracies as people grapple with the consequences of a globalized economy and greater involvement of supranational political entities beyond their control. In June 2016, the United Kingdom held a referendum on the country's membership in the European Union, and British citizens voted to withdraw, which is commonly referred to as the "Brexit" (British exit). Nationalism greatly influenced British citizens' reluctance to cede any degree of sovereignty, pay taxes, or follow regulations from the European Union. In particular, British citizens resented the quotas of Syrian refugees that the European Union required England to accommodate. A similar spirit of nationalism also carried Donald Trump to the Republican nomination in the United States during the 2016 election. Millions of Americans rejected the global economy and free trade agreement, demanding that America should come first.

Similar to nationalism, religious fundamentalism has increased dramatically in the post-Cold War Era. Specifically, the globalized economy has directly resulted in cultural clashes between the West and Islam. Islamic fundamentalism often resorts to terrorism to fight against their conventionally more powerful enemies. The most infamous modern terrorist attack occurred on September 11, 2001, when terrorists associated with al-Qaeda hijacked four commercial airliners and flew the planes into the World Trade Center and Pentagon. The 9/11 attack initially led to the United States' invasion of Afghanistan and later contributed to the decision to invade Iraq. These wars heightened the interaction between the Western and Arab worlds, and fundamentalism has increased ever since. Jihadists and religious extremists have flooded the region to defend Islam against what they perceive as the invading West. Additionally, the Arab Spring created a spirit of unrest in many Middle Eastern countries with a history of authoritarian rule. Following the Americans' withdrawal from Iraq and uprisings in neighboring Syria, the religious extremists declared an Islamic State in the region, known as the *Islamic State of Iraq and Levant,* ensuring the proliferation of Islamic fundamentalism and terrorism for the foreseeable future.

Impact of Technological Innovations and Adaptations on World Societies

Advancements in technology can have positive and negative consequences, but all change the world in some way. Examples of major innovations include the printing press, cotton gin, electricity, gunpowder, and Internet. These discoveries have laid the groundwork for numerous adaptations and new inventions.

Invented by Johannes Gutenberg around 1440, the printing press spread ideas that fueled the Reformation, the American and French revolutions, and the Enlightenment. As a cheaper and quicker way to spread information, the printing press led to an explosion in literacy. Prior to the invention of the printing press, books were handwritten; thus, few copies were available, and the copies that were available were very expensive, so only the elite could read and write. In particular, the explosion of books dramatically altered people's relationship with religion. Before Gutenberg's invention, religious scholars were the only people who could read the Bible, and religious services were the only place where people heard Christianity. After its invention, millions of people could read the Bible for themselves, directly leading to the Reformation, as people arrived at their own interpretations. Similarly, the political order was challenged, as people could more easily communicate and gather news across long distances.

Electrical energy was observed in ancient civilization, but it wasn't until after the spread of information through the printing press that electricity became studied and used. In the 1800s, electrical knowledge was furthered by numerous inventions, such as Alexander Graham Bell's telephone and Thomas Edison's light bulb and phonograph. George Westinghouse's electricity distribution system improved on Edison's direct current with alternating current, which is a much more reliable method of conducting electricity safely across long distances. Electricity completely changed the face of manufacturing and further spurred the Industrial Revolution.

The Chinese invented gunpowder in the ninth century, and the written formula appears in records of the Song dynasty in the eleventh century. Gunpowder spread along the Silk Road, from central Asia to the Middle East to Europe. Gunpowder totally changed the way war was waged, decimating nations and cultures without the technology and making empires for those who had it. Although Europeans did not start using gunpowder until the thirteenth century, gunpowder would provide the means for Europeans to quickly conquer the Americas, including toppling the powerful Incan and Aztec empires. Gunpowder naturally led to the invention of more deadly explosives. War on land, air, and sea became bloodier and more devastating.

Originally created by the United States in the 1960s to connect military networks, the Internet became available for commercial usage in the early 1990s and exponentially increased ever since. The Internet empowers people and nations in various ways. Knowledge is now available at the fingertips of anybody with a working Internet connection. The Internet is the modern-day printing press. Politicians and economists can easily share incredible amounts of technical data and information in an instant. Furthermore, the capital necessary for large-scale investment is more readily available, thanks to improvements in communication technology. Within society, the Internet increases civic engagement by expanding citizens' knowledge of public affairs and broadening political participation. People can now directly communicate with their elected representatives, and those representatives are able to modify their positions based on the will of the people. In addition, watchdog groups are capable of closely monitoring the actions of public officials. More recently, social media networks have further connected people.

Along with these inventions and adaptions, discoveries and improvements in transportation and medicine have dramatically impacted world history. The invention of the steamboat, train, automobile, and airplane allowed people to efficiently travel across long distances. Improvements to transportation would continually increase commerce and communication; however, transportation also served devastating military purposes. During World War II, tanks steamrolled through enemy lines, planes dropped millions of tons of explosives on cities, and submarines sunk unsuspecting ships. Medical improvements, such as penicillin, x-rays, and vaccinations, have saved innumerable lives. People are living longer, healthier lives with a higher standard of living. In 1900, the average life expectancy was thirty-one, and by 2010, the world average was sixty-seven. However, life expectancy is higher in the developed world relative to the developing world where medical advances have not yet fully reached.

The Roles of Major World Religions in Shaping Societies and Affecting Major Historical Turning Points

Modern world religions include Christianity, Islam, Hinduism, Buddhism, Taoism, Shinto, Sikhism, and Judaism. Christianity, Islam, and Judaism are Abrahamic religions because they all trace their origin to, or recognize the importance of, the tribal patriarch Abraham. Hinduism, Buddhism, and Sikhism are often referred to as *Dharmic* faiths because they originated in the Indian subcontinent. Taoism is one of the most popular religions practiced in China, and Shinto is the largest religion in Japan. From ancient times through modernity, religion has played an important role in world history.

Despite their considerable similarities in religious beliefs, the conflict between Christianity and Islam is one of the most fraught relationships in world history. Between 1095 CE and 1291 CE, Christians and Muslims fought a series of wars commonly referred to as the Crusades. In 1095 CE, Pope Urban II launched the First Crusade at the request of the Byzantine emperor to fight the Turks. The First Crusade ended with Christian forces massacring Muslim and Jewish inhabitants of Jerusalem. History would repeat itself from the twelfth century through the fourteenth century, as Christians fought Muslims from Jerusalem to the Rhineland to the Iberian Peninsula. Despite the rampant pillaging and bloodthirsty killing, the West gained immensely from their contact with Islamic civilizations, which were far more advanced. Christians rediscovered forgotten Greek and Roman texts in Muslim libraries and adopted advances in science, hygiene, and urban development. However, the Crusades' ultimate legacy would be to sow distrust and hostility between the world's two most popular religions. Hostility would only grow after the defeat and partition of the Ottoman Empire after World War I. Christian nations, such as France and England, colonized and occupied the Middle East until after World War II. The hostility between Christianity and Islam is particularly heightened in modern times due to the rise of Islamic fundamentalism, as discussed above.

The major division between Christianity occurred in the 1500s as a result of the Protestant Reformation. Catholics and Protestants fought several wars to decide what religion would dominate in a particular region. The wars were often for political and economic gain but fought on the basis of religion. In particular, the Thirty Years' War was the bloodiest conflict in world history until the First World War. As discussed before, the Thirty Years' War directly led to the concept of the nation-state, one of the most important developments in modern history. The need for an identifiable nation-state grew out of the need for regions to determine their own religion to prevent future conflict.

During periods of strife and persecution, different denominations of Christianity migrated to the United States, especially during the colonial period. Such groups who sought religious freedom and tolerance included the Quakers, who settled in Pennsylvania; the Dutch Anabaptists and Calvinists, who settled in New York; and the Catholics, who settled in Maryland, among others. The Great Awakening, a religious revival in colonial America during the 1730s and 1740s, contributed to the American Revolution by encouraging people to challenge authority in their pursuit of salvation. Many colonists believed that the war was just in the eyes of God, and so it gave them a moral reason to fight. Ministers, like Jonathan Mayhew, who coined the phrase "No taxation without representation," preached that the revolution was a religious crusade and that it was the Christian's duty to do battle against tyrants and oppressors. Religion would later play a critical role in the American Civil War as both sides supported their causes with Christian arguments. In North America, Quakers and Protestant evangelicals crusaded against slavery, considering the practice to be the young nation's greatest sin. In contrast, American Southerners defended slavery as a practice recognized in the Bible and argued that it was their duty to baptize and convert their slaves.

Throughout most of world history, the Jewish people have faced anti-Semitism, but nothing compares to the Holocaust, the worst genocide in human history. Adolf Hitler's Nazi Party systematically executed 6 million European Jews, more than two-thirds of the European Jewish population. Following World War II, Great Britain withdrew from Palestine, and the United Nations passed a mandate to create a Jewish state in the region. On May 14, 1948, David Ben-Gurion declared the establishment of the State of Israel. The creation of a Jewish state is one of the most important events in modern history due to the ensuing conflict between Israel and the Muslim world. In fact, one day after Israel declared independence, the Arab League invaded the fledgling Jewish state and launched the 1948 Arab-Israeli War. Israel would again fight and defeat Arab countries in the Six-Day War and the 1973 Arab-Israeli War. A close ally to the United States, Israel plays an integral role in the West's foreign policy.

Religion has a long history of influencing the ruling dynasties until the Chinese Communist Revolution. Confucianism, Buddhism, and Taoism, collectively referred to as *the three teachings,* contributed to many golden ages of Chinese culture. In fact, Chinese emperors justified their right to rule based on the Mandate of Heaven, declaring that the gods had hand selected the emperor to rule. The legendary scholar Confucius developed a set of philosophy based on humanism and rationalism. Confucianism heavily influenced the Sui dynasty's imperial examination system, which established an efficient meritocracy within the civil service. During the Han dynasty, Taoism and Buddhism emerged as popular religions and added a spiritual element to Chinese religious practice. This spiritual melting pot would last until Mao Zedong's Communist forces overthrew the government. Communism is unique in its opposition to religious practice. As was the case in the Soviet Union, Mao Zedong would outlaw religious practice and oppress all spiritual movements.

The Role of Trade and Other Forms of Economic Exchange Both Within Societies and in Contacts Between Societies

Trade between nations was prominent in ancient civilizations; however, the method was slow and focused on a few types of goods, with a few routes and ports. China and India did not seek out goods and services from Europe and Africa, but Europe's desire for silk and spices caused an influx of imports and few exports. As lands were conquered, trade became insular. Certain empires began to lessen their dependence on imports with the additional incorporation of land plentiful with these goods. This was the impetus for the control of India's food production by the British and the Japanese desire for Manchuria, which yielded abundances of natural resources.

Many nations still participate in gift giving to other nations to show goodwill or friendship. The idea of giving tribute was often seen as a way to keep barbarians and other outside attackers from taking over nations. China gave many tributes to the Mongols to stave off invasions. Similarly, in the British Isles, the Vikings and Celts exacted tribute from neighboring tribes. Often this type of tribute did not keep the peace long. Aside from money, tribute could take the form of goods, lands, or people. Tributary states are often allowed self-government if tribute is paid to a larger nation. In addition, tribute might be given to gain access to a resource or land. For example, from the early sixteenth century until the nineteenth century, the Barbary pirates held ports in North Africa and patrolled the surrounding waters, referred to as the *Barbary Coast*. European countries often paid tribute in the form of money, goods, or ships in order to secure safe passage through those waters. Tribute was also used to free European and Christian slaves that the Barbary pirates would capture and sell to the Ottoman Empire.

In the early age of trade, the Silk Road, which connected Europe, northern Africa, the Middle East, India, and China, was the main way to trade. Starting around 114 BCE, the Silk Road constitutes the first interaction between the East and West. From 114 BCE until 1450 CE, Chinese, Arab, Turkish, Indian, Persian, Greek, Syrian, Roman, Georgian, and Armenian traders would travel the Silk Road and trade for the precious silk. In addition to goods, the travelers also engaged in cultural exchange. Religions, disease, and technologies were easily spread through trade. Examples include Christianity, Buddhism, Islam, the Black Plague, and naval navigational techniques.

Today, countries primarily trade within the parameters of mutually agreed-upon trade agreements, which are discussed above. These trade agreements theoretically increase the performance of every trade partner's economy by allowing countries to specialize in their strengths and trade for what they do not produce. However, people in developed countries often fear that manufacturing and other traditionally "blue collar" work will be lost to less developed countries. Similarly, people in less developed countries often criticize the agreements for mandating investment in lower-paying jobs. Thus, even as greater wealth is accumulated, free trade agreements can cause conflict within society. Modern trade commonly involves questions concerning who is the true beneficiary of trade.

The Major Political Ideologies that Have Influences on the Organization of Societies in the Modern World

Communism is a radical political ideology that seeks to establish common ownership over production and abolish social status and money. Communists believe that the world is split between two social classes, capitalists and the working class, often referred to as the *proletariat*. Political philosophers Karl Marx and Friedrich Engels argued that Communism is society's destiny because capitalism will ultimately collapse. During the 1917 October Revolution in Russia, the Bolsheviks overthrew the monarchy and became the first Communist party to rule a country. The collapse of the Soviet Union weakened Communism across the world. Currently, China, Cuba, Laos, North Korea, and Vietnam are the only remaining Communist states.

Socialism is a political ideology that prioritizes the public collective over the individual, as characterized by collective ownership of the means of production. Consequently, Socialism is closely tied to an economic system. Under the political philosopher Karl Marx, Socialism is the transitional stage between capitalism and Communism. In general, Socialism is less extreme than Communism. While Communists believe that capitalists must be overthrown by whatever means are necessary, Socialists are more willing to work within the framework of democracy to elect Socialist policies. Most modern countries include some degree of Socialism, such as progressive taxation and welfare systems. The Scandinavian countries of Denmark, Finland, Sweden, and Norway are the most successful modern-day Socialist countries.

Liberalism developed during the Age of Enlightenment in opposition to absolute monarchy, royal privilege, and state religion. In general, liberalism emphasizes liberty and equality, freedom of speech, freedom of religion, free markets, civil rights, democracy, gender equality, and secular governance. Liberal political philosophy heavily influenced the revolutionaries in the Glorious Revolution in England, American Revolution, and French Revolution. Social liberalism is intrinsically tied with the modern welfare state as established in Europe and North America.

Conservatism is a political ideology that prioritizes traditional institutions within a culture and civilization. In general, conservatives oppose modern developments and value stability. Since conservatism depends on the traditional institution, this ideology differs greatly from country to country. Conservatives often emphasize the traditional family structure and emphasize the importance of individual self-reliance. Fiscal conservatism is one of the most common variants, and in general, the proponents of fiscal conservatism oppose government spending and public debt. Other forms of conservatism include libertarian conservatism, national conservatism, social conservatism, religious conservatism, and liberal conservatism.

Totalitarianism is a political ideology where the state controls all aspects of public and private life. It is an extreme version of authoritarianism, which is only concerned with the state consolidating political power and retaining dominance over the political system. In contrast, totalitarianism utilizes extensive propaganda, surveillance, and state-controlled mass media to dictate all aspects of life within the country. Totalitarianism often involves a single political party led by a dictator, oppression of political opponents, state monopoly over weapons and communication, centralized political direction and economic control, and the use of terror, such as a secret police. Fascism is a form of totalitarianism that became popular in Europe after World War I. Fascists advocated for an all-powerful government led by a strong dictator that would be prepared for total war and the mass mobilization of resources for the benefit of the state. Fascism is often tied with nationalism, which is discussed below. Adolf Hitler's Nazi Party is the most infamous example of a fascist totalitarian government.

The simplest political spectrum orders political ideologies on a left-to-right axis. The far left and far right represent the most extreme political ideologies, while the center is more moderate. The political spectrum is most useful to gain a basic understanding of how ideologies relate to each other; however, it should be noted that the terminology and positions of ideologies within a specific country will be more nuanced.

Nationalism is an ideology that prioritizes a loyalty and devotion to the home country. Typically, nationalists exalt their country over all others; thus, nationalism prioritizes promoting its own culture over all other cultures and foreign interests. Nationalism developed alongside the growth of the European nation-state during the nineteenth century. Unlike the ideologies discussed above, nationalism does not promote any single type of political system. For example, nationalists can be on the far right or far left. Nationalism is a powerful unifying force within a country or region. For instance, a spirit of nationalism developed in colonies like India and the United States as the local people united against their rulers. However, nationalism can also be a source of conflict, because it is essentially insular and opposed to foreign entities. As an example, imperial powers justified their conquest of foreign people based on the need to spread their superior culture. In modern times, nationalist groups oppose globalism, such as free trade agreements and supranational political entities, viewing global cooperation as a threat to their national culture.

The Major Economic Transformations that Have Affected World Societies

The world industrialized at different rates and at different times. Industrialization occurs when countries develop from a primarily agricultural society to an industrial economy. Beginning in Great Britain around 1760, the first Industrial Revolution spread throughout Europe until 1840. With the improvement of technologies discovered during this time period, the second Industrial Revolution took place from 1840 to 1870. Important technological innovations occurred in textiles, steam power, and iron making. The Industrial Revolution reached the United States shortly after the Civil War. During industrialization, the standard of living rose significantly, as did the discovery of new medicines, causing life expectancy to increase. Sanitation, improved living conditions, electricity, and education were all expanded as urbanization occurred. Over time, other areas of the world became industrialized, including East Asia during the late 1800s and early 1900s.

During the nineteenth century, Europe experienced what is known as the *Great Divergence*—a time of great economic growth in Europe. It was significant because Europe moved rapidly from a primitive economy to wealth surpassing the much larger, more established, and more sophisticated economies in East Asia, the Middle East, and the Indian subcontinent. The timing coincided with the establishment of colonies and the solidification of trade routes. Europe maintained its economic dominance by embracing technology and transportation, like railroads and steamboats. In addition, mining technology brought greater wealth to European countries, and advances in agriculture allowed countries to support larger populations, even in new urban areas. Countries used their wealth to improve roads and sanitation and to fund education and medical advancement.

Types of market economies, or economies based on supply and demand, are capitalistic in nature and include laissez-faire, free market, and welfare capitalism. Laissez-faire is a set of economic principles that promote private interaction free from any government interference on the economy, like regulations, tariffs, subsidies, and taxes. Laissez-faire is more theoretical than an actual economic system. A free market economy curtails government intervention, allowing the forces of supply and demand to move the market. The free market economy promotes many laissez-faire principles, like individualism, freedom, and competition. Welfare capitalism is a type of free market in which the government places taxes on goods and services to pay for social services. Welfare capitalism is also referred to as a *mixed economy*. Welfare capitalism is common in Europe, especially in Scandinavia; however, all modern-day economies incorporate some form of welfare, such as social security and disability. The basic principles of market economies have been the most successful in history due to their superior production. The primacy of the market economy became entrenched after the collapse of the Soviet Union, the leading Communist economic system. Currently, China remains the only powerful Communist country, but the Chinese government has adopted numerous free market reforms in recent years.

The Major Differences and Similarities in Family Structure and Gender Roles Across Societies

Traditional family structure includes a man, a woman, and one or more children who are either biological or adopted. This is also referred to as a *nuclear family*. In most of human history, the extended family, which includes grandparents, aunts, uncles, and cousins, would live in the same area and work together. The idea of an extended family living and working together broke with the rise of individualism and financial stability in the United States and Europe after World War II. In the modern-day West, the nuclear family is the most common family structure. In addition, the traditional family in the West has grown to include cohabitation families, single-parent families, and same-sex families.

In the Middle East, Africa, Asia, and India, it is still common to have multigenerational households and extended family networks living in close proximity. It is also common to pass down a trade or family business, like a restaurant or masonry business. The role of women is more domestic in these areas. In contrast, women in the United States and Europe more commonly participate in the workforce. In many societies, the wealthier classes educated woman in music and arts but did not encourage much education in mathematics and science. For the most part, the Middle East, Africa, Asia, and India have remained more constant in their family structure and gender roles, while Europe and the United States have seen the most changes in family structure. Examples include divorce and remarriage, evolution of the nuclear family, and change in traditional gender roles.

Until the modern age, girls of the higher classes were often taught housekeeping skills, music, drawing, needlework, and languages. These were often discouraged after marriage, apart from housekeeping, which became a woman's main duties along with childrearing. Boys in the wealthiest class were often educated at elite schools, and though some managed their estates or were members of government, most were expected to use and enjoy their wealth and status without laboring at a job.

Boys of the middle class would seek a profession such as a lawyer, teacher, or minister, often with some college training. Some would be apprenticed to a trade or learn the family business. Girls in the middle class were trained to manage a household, including preparing meals and balancing the family budget, while the higher-class girls focused more on how to entertain guests and manage servants.

Many of the lowest class and orphans, both boys and girls, were used in factory and coalmining work, where quick hands and nimble bodies were useful. For the lower classes, education was not common until the late 1800s. Previously, the wealthier classes suppressed literacy and education for the lower classes, finding it to be a good way of controlling the social and financial status quo. However, girls who received any form of education usually learned domestic skills, simple math, and needlework. Boys of the lower classes would follow the men of their family into whatever work they did, such as coalmining, farming, or factory work.

Nobility and landowners, until World War I, sought to preserve their lineage and wealth through a single male line. The wealth of this class and many of the male heirs were lost in World Wars I and II. Often primogeniture, or the inheritance of an intact estate with all the land, wealth, and titles, was legally passed to the firstborn son. A daughter would only inherit if no male heir was available.

The Roles of Both Conflict and Cooperation in Shaping and Transforming Societies

Conflict and cooperation have transformed societies throughout history. Conflict often results in power shifting between countries. Typically, after a conflict, some of the countries emerge with more territory and greater global influence, while others dissolve into fragmented or diminished entities. In addition, conflict can force countries into adopting internal reforms, such as a new system of government. Cooperation between countries generally strengthens their countries' economy and military. Examples of cooperation between countries include military alliances and trade agreements. Cooperation can also result in countries ceding some of their sovereignty to create more global forms of governance.

Examples of conflict exist from ancient societies through the modern day. As discussed above, armed rebellion led to the fall of the Roman Empire, arguably the strongest political entity in human empires. That conflict led to the Byzantine Empire consolidating power in the East, while the West became fragmented and power became localized. World War I was one of the most significant conflicts in modern history due to the unprecedented deaths and destruction. Approximately 14 million soldiers and civilians lost their lives during World War I, and the Great War cost the participants more than $300 billion. In addition, the conflict's political consequences cannot be overstated. The aftermath caused the collapse of four powerful monarchies—Russia, Austria-Hungary, Germany, and Turkey—and it led to the end of colonialism. The world would suffer an even more horrific and transformative conflict only a few decades later in World War II.

Examples of cooperation in recent history have roots in the aftermath of World War II. Immediately following the war, the United States created the Marshall Plan, which gave Western Europe more than $12 billion to rebuild the shattered region. In addition to financial aid, the United States and Western Europe formed NATO, a defensive pact formed in 1949 to counter the power of the Soviet Union and prevent the further spread of Communism. Signatory countries pledged to come to any member's defense in the event of an attack by a foreign power. Similarly, the Soviet Union created the Warsaw Pact to facilitate cooperation between territories held by the Soviets following World War II. These military alliances amplified the power of the two superpowers and provided protection against another global conflict by creating a powerful deterrent. Military alliances continue to be an important part of cooperation between nations.

In addition to military alliances, countries often cooperate with trade agreements. Not only does creating these economic ties benefit the participants' internal economies, but trade agreements also serve as a deterrent against conflict. The role of trade is discussed in greater detail in the section, "The Role of Trade and Other Forms of Economic Exchange Both Within Societies and in Contacts Between Societies."

Other examples of modern cooperation between countries are illustrated by the creation of supranational political entities, like the United Nation and European Union. The United Nations was established on October 24, 1945, for the primary purpose of preventing a third disastrous global conflict. It is the most inclusive political organization in the world, consisting of 193 member states. Currently, the United Nations primarily works to maintain global peace and security, promote human rights, facilitate economic development, and provide humanitarian aid during natural disasters and armed conflict. The modern European Union was later formally established in 1992. The European Union's primary purpose is to establish a common internal market to ensure the free movement of goods, capital, and services.

Understands the Major Demographic Trends in World History and their Effects

One of the most significant demographic trends in world history is the increase in populations, which began to increase exponentially in the twentieth century. Before the 1800s, it took thousands of years to reach 1 billion people in the world. However, by 1999, the world population had increased to more than 6 billion people. As of 2016, the world population is 7.4 billion, and it is estimated that the population will increase to more than 11 billion by 2100. This is largely a result of a lower child mortality rate and higher life expectancy due to scientific progress. The effects of having a larger population are most visible in Africa and Asia, especially in India and China. Although larger populations provide for a larger workforce, they also put strain on the economy because more young people require employment.

The mortality rate for infants has dropped significantly due to improvements in medicine, nutrition, infant care, and education. In modern times, the overwhelming source of infant deaths occurs in developing countries, where medical assistance is low and many live in poverty. The same factors can be attributed to the longer life expectancies of people living in developed countries. The populations of developed countries benefit from adults who have been able to live longer due to medicine and improved living conditions, effectively creating a more stable economy. However, the populations of developing countries are rapidly increasing, causing many to immigrate to developed nations.

Immigration has changed the demographics of countries and can have positive and negative effects. Migration and immigration have occurred due to famine, warfare, and lack of economic prospects. Immigration can aid countries struggling to maintain a workforce, and it can also bring in needed medical professionals, scientists, and others with special training. However, immigration also puts strain on developed economies to support migrants who arrive without the necessary education and training to thrive in the advanced economies. Until recently, immigrants were encouraged, or in some cases, forced to assimilate and take on the customs and culture of their new country. For example, in the United States, legislation was passed to force German immigrants to learn English. More recently, developed countries have struggled to assimilate new arrivals to their countries, such as the recent surge of refugees into Europe. Unfortunately, the failure to adequately assimilate immigrants has created greater inequality and prevalence of radical behavior.

Practice Questions

1. Which of the following civilizations developed the first democratic form of government?
    a. Roman Empire
    b. Ancient Greece
    c. Achaemenid Empire
    d. Zhou dynasty

2. Which of the following statements most accurately describes the Achaemenid Empire in Persia until the fourth century BCE?
    a. Islam was the official religion.
    b. Achaemenid emperors constructed the entire Silk Road network.
    c. The Achaemenid Empire successfully conquered Greece.
    d. None of the above

3. The Silk Roads had which of the following results?
    a. Spread of Buddhism from India to China
    b. Resulted in the devastation of European economies
    c. Introduction of the Bubonic Plague to the New World
    d. Resulted in the Great War

4. What caused the end of the Western Roman Empire in 476 CE?
    a. Invasions by Germanic tribes
    b. The Mongol invasion
    c. The assassination of Julius Caesar
    d. Introduction of Taoism in Rome

5. Which of the following statements most accurately describes the Mongol Empire?
    a. The Mongol army was largely a cavalry force.
    b. Mongol rulers did not tolerate other religions.
    c. Mongol rulers neglected foreign trade.
    d. The Mongol Empire is known for its discouragement of literacy and the arts.

6. What social consequence(s) did the Black Death have in Europe?
    a. It gave birth to the concept of absolute monarchy.
    b. It ignited the Protestant Reformation.
    c. It eroded serfdom.
    d. It gave rise to Child Labor Laws in England.

7. Renaissance scholars and artists were inspired by which classical civilization?
    a. Ancient Greece
    b. Ancient Egypt
    c. The Zhou dynasty
    c. The Ottoman Empire

8. Nicolaus Copernicus was a key figure in which cultural phenomena?
    a. The Scientific Revolution
    b. The Age of Enlightenment
    c. The Renaissance
    d. The Protestant Reformation

9. Which of the following statements best describes King Louis XIV of France?
    a. He abdicated his throne during the French Revolution.
    b. He supported the American Revolution.
    c. He was the ultimate example of an absolute monarch.
    d. He created the concept of the Mandate of Heaven.

10. Which of the following resulted from the Age of Enlightenment?
    a. The discovery of the heliocentric theory
    b. The birth of Lutheranism
    c. The American Revolution
    d. The Renaissance

11. Which of the following consequences did NOT result from the discovery of the New World in 1492 CE?
    a. Proof that the world was round instead of flat
    b. The deaths of millions of Native Americans
    c. Biological exchange between Europe and the New World
    d. The creation of new syncretic religions

12. Which of the following statements best describes the relationship, if any, between the revolutions in America and France?
    a. The French Revolution inspired the American Revolution.
    b. The American Revolution inspired the French Revolution.
    c. They both occurred simultaneously.
    d. There was no connection between the French and American revolutions.

13. Which of the following was a consequence of industrialization in Europe during the 1800s?
    a. The birth of the working class
    b. The expansion of European empires in Africa and Asia
    c. Improved transportation and economic efficiency
    d. All of the above

14. Which of the following was a consequence of increasing nationalism in Europe in the 1800s?
    a. The unification of Spain
    b. The unification of France
    c. Increasing competition and tension between European powers
    d. More efficient trade between nations

15. Which of the following military technologies did NOT play a role in World War I from 1914 to 1918?
    a. The atomic bomb
    b. Poison gas
    c. Armored tanks
    d. Aircraft

16. Which of the following statements best describes international affairs between World War I and World War II?

    a. A lenient World War I peace treaty for Germany delayed the start of World War II.

    b. The policy of appeasement only encouraged further aggression by Hitler.

    c. A powerful League of Nations fostered increased cooperation and negotiation.

    d. Tensions grew between Germany and Japan.

17. Which of the following was a consequence of World War II?

    a. The collapse of British and French empires in Asia and Africa

    b. A Communist revolution in Russia

    c. The end of the Cold War

    d. The death of Franz Ferdinand, the Archduke of Austria

18. Which of the following trends did NOT occur after the end of the Cold War in 1991?

    a. A decrease in nationalistic tension

    b. An increase in cultural and economic globalization

    c. An increase in religious fundamentalism

    d. An increase in environmentalism

19. What impact, if any, did the introduction of the movable type printing press have in Europe?

    a. It increased the cost of books because the process was labor intensive.

    b. It led to an increase in literacy.

    c. The Catholic Church used it to effectively suppress the Protestant Reformation.

    d. It led to the Dark Ages.

20. In which phase(s) of the Space Race did the United States achieve victory over the USSR?

    a. Putting the first satellite into orbit

    b. Putting the first man into space

    c. Putting the first man on the moon

    d. All of the above

21. Which of the following is NOT a sect of Islam?

    a. Shinto

    b. Sunni

    c. Shi'a

    d. Sufi

22. Which form of economic exchange allowed the Chinese to maintain political control over their empire?

    a. Potlatches

    b. Tribute

    c. Bartering

    d. All of the above

23. Which of the following statements best describes the ideological relationship, if any, between liberalism and totalitarianism?

    a. Liberalism and totalitarianism are very similar.

    b. Liberalism and totalitarianism are diametrically opposed.

    c. Liberalism and totalitarianism share some similarities as well as differences.

    d. They are completely unrelated.

24. Which of the following statements accurately describes patriarchal societies?
    a. They forbid divorce.
    b. Women have more power and prestige.
    c. Men have more power and prestige.
    d. No one group of people has more power and prestige; everyone chooses their own roles.

25. Which of the following statements accurately describes the European Union?
    a. It was formed in 1945 after World War II.
    b. It was founded as a result of the Paris Peace Conference that ended the first World War.
    c. It aims to ensure free movement of people, goods, services and capital within the internal market.
    d. It was founded to avoid the repetitions of the Great War.

26. Which of the following statements best describes world demographic trends in the late twentieth and early twenty-first century?
    a. Population growth has important environmental consequences.
    b. More developed regions are experiencing little or no population growth.
    c. Youth make up a larger part of the population in less developed regions.
    d. All of the above

Answer Explanations

1. B: Ancient Greeks created many of the cultural and political institutions that form the basis of modern western civilization. Athens was an important Greek democracy, and all adult men could participate in politics after they had completed their military service. The Roman Empire, Choice *A,* evolved from the Roman Republic, but it was not democratic. The Achaemenid Empire and Zhou Dynasty, Choices *C* and *D,* were imperial monarchies that did not allow citizens to have much, if any, political voice.

2. D: During the Achaemenid Empire, Persians practiced the Zoroastrian faith and worshipped two gods. Islam only came about one thousand years later. The Achaemenids built a Royal Road that stretched across their empire, but the Silk Roads expanded throughout Asia. The Achaemenids twice tried to conquer Greece but failed both times.

3. A: The Silk Roads were a network of trade routes between Asia and the Mediterranean. Merchants and Pilgrims traveled along the Silk Roads and brought new ideas and technologies, as well as trade goods. For example, Buddhism spread from India to China. Chinese technologies also spread westward, including gunpowder and the printing press. The Silk Roads also spread the Bubonic Plague to Europe, but it did not arrive in the New World until Columbus landed there in 1492.

4. A: Invasions by Germanic tribes. Large numbers of Franks, Goths, Vandals, and other Germanic peoples began moving south in the fifth century CE. They conquered Rome twice, and the Western Roman Empire finally disintegrated. The Mongol invasion, Choice *B,* pushed westward in the thirteenth century, long after the western Roman Empire was gone. The assassination of Julius Caesar, Choice *C,* led to the end of the Roman Republic and the birth of the Roman Empire. Taoism never spread to Rome, making Choice *D* incorrect.

5. A: The Mongol army was largely a cavalry force. The Mongols were a nomadic people who trained as horsemen from a young age. They used their highly mobile army to build a huge empire in Asia, the Middle East, and Eastern Europe. Mongol rulers were relatively tolerant of other religions because they wanted to reduce conflict within their empire, making Choice *B* incorrect. They also encouraged trade because they produced few of their own goods, making Choice *C* incorrect. The Mongol rulers also encouraged literacy and appreciated visual art, making Choice *D* incorrect.

6. C: It eroded serfdom. Millions of people died during the Black Death, but those who survived found that their standard of living had improved, especially serfs. Before the Black Death, serfs had few rights and were expected to work without pay for their lord. Because labor was in such short supply after the Black Death, serfs found they were in a much better bargaining position. The Protestant Reformation was a cultural phenomenon, and the rise of absolutism was a political change. Neither had any connection to the Black Death, making Choices *A* and *B* incorrect. Choice *D* is also incorrect; although Child Labor Laws came after the Black Death in the early 1800s, they weren't a direct result of the Black Death.

7. A: Renaissance scholars and artists sought to emulate classical Greek and Roman culture. They translated Greek and Roman political philosophers and literature. They also copied classical architecture. Europeans had little direct contact with China until the thirteenth century, which was long after the Zhou Dynasty collapsed, making Choice *C* incorrect.

8. A: Copernicus exemplified the key techniques of the Scientific Revolution, including an emphasis on empirical data and the scientific method. He carefully observed the movement of the planets and found that his data did not match the contemporary geocentric theory, which stated that the earth was the center of the universe. He found that his data indicated that the planets revolved around the sun instead.

9. C: Louis the XIV was an absolute monarch who ruled during the sixteenth century. He concentrated power on the throne by forcing nobles to spend most of their time at the royal court. The French Revolution occurred about two hundred years after he died. Absolute monarchs like Louis the XIV bolstered their prestige by claiming they were appointed by God. The Mandate of Heaven was a similar concept, but it was developed by the Zhou Dynasty in China about two thousand years before Louis XIV was born.

10. C: The Age of Enlightenment in the eighteenth century focused on political and economic philosophy as opposed to scientific discoveries. English philosopher John Locke introduced the concept of a social contract between the ruler and his subjects. His ideas helped inspire revolutions in the British colonies in North America and later France. Choice *A* is incorrect; the discovery of the heliocentric theory happened in 1543. Luther began to criticize the Catholic Church about two hundred years before the Age of Enlightenment began, making Choice *B* incorrect. Choice *D* is also incorrect, as the Renaissance happened before the Age of Enlightenment from approximately 1300-1600.

11. A: Most scholars already knew the world was round by 1492. On the other hand, the arrival of Europeans in North and South America introduced deadly diseases that killed millions of native peoples. Europeans had developed immunity to diseases such as smallpox, while Native Americans had not. In addition, Europeans introduced a number of new plants and animals to the New World, but they also adopted many new foods as well, including potatoes, tomatoes, chocolate, and tobacco. Finally, Europeans tried to convert Native Americans to Christianity, but Indians did not completely give up their traditional beliefs. Instead, they blended Christianity with indigenous and African beliefs to create new syncretic religions.

12. B: The American Revolution occurred first in 1775, and a number of European soldiers fought for the patriots. The American Revolution, in part, inspired the French Revolution. The Marquis de Lafayette came to America in 1777 and was wounded during the Battle of Brandywine. He returned to France after the American Revolution and became a leader in the French Revolution in 1789.

13. D: The Industrial Revolution is probably one of the most important turning points in world history. The United States and Western Europe, especially Britain, were the first areas to industrialize. Steam engines were used to improve economic and transportation efficiency. They also gave western empires a military advantage over less developed countries in Asia and Africa. Finally, industrialization required large amounts of unskilled labor, which created the working class.

14. C: In the 1800s, nationalists in different parts of Europe encouraged their countrymen to take pride in their shared backgrounds. This led to tension between different nations, as each sought to increase its status and prestige. The French and British nearly came to blows in Africa, and nationalism ultimately led to World War I in 1914. However, France and Spain were unified several centuries before the 1800s.

15. A: The atomic bomb was created during World War II (1939-1945). Scientists and engineers did develop a number of other weapons in order to break through the heavily entrenched front lines during World War I. Poison gas killed or injured millions of men between 1914 and 1918. Aircraft were used to observe enemy positions and bombard enemy troops. Armored tanks were able to crush barbed wire fences and deflected machine gun bullets.

16. B: Eager to avoid another global conflict, European leaders tried to appease Hitler by letting him occupy Austria and Czechoslovakia. This policy failed because it only emboldened Hitler, and he invaded Poland in 1939. Rather than receiving leniency after World War I, Germany was forced to sign a humiliating peace treaty. Furthermore, the League of Nations failed to prevent conflict because it lacked any real power. This encouraged continued aggression from Italy, Germany, and Japan, which culminated in World War II.

17. A: Devastated by World War II, Britain and France were unable to maintain their empires. Japan and Germany were also weak, which left only the United States and USSR as superpowers. The Russian Revolution had occurred during World War I, in 1917, making Choice *B* incorrect. Ideological and economic conflict between the U.S. and the USSR led to the start of the Cold War shortly after World War II ended, making Choice *C* incorrect. Choice *D* is also incorrect; the death of Franz Ferdinand marked the beginning of World War I.

18. A: Nationalism remains a powerful force to this day. Nationalism drove conflict in Ireland, Spain, Yugoslavia, and elsewhere. However, the end of the Cold War removed many of the political barriers that had prevented interaction between the western and Communist blocs. In addition, religious fundamentalism became an increasingly common response to the rapid changes that occurred during the late twentieth and early twenty-first centuries. There was also a rise in cultural and economic globalization, as well as in environmentalism.

19. B: The printing press was much more efficient than previous methods, which required a single scribe to copy text by hand. This made books much more affordable and encouraged the growing middle class to read. No church or organization had a monopoly on the technology, so many different writers used it to spread the ideas of the Reformation, as well as the Renaissance, Scientific Revolution, and Age of Enlightenment.

20. C: The USSR put Sputnik, the first satellite into orbit, in 1951. They also claimed victory when the Soviet cosmonaut Yuri Gagarin went into space in 1961. The United States only surpassed the USSR by sending the Apollo 11 crew to the moon in 1969.

21. A: The schism between Sunnis and Shi'as began shortly after the Islamic prophet Muhammad died in 632 CE. Sunnis and Shi'a disagreed over who should have become Muhammad's successor. Sufism emerged about eighty years after Muhammad died, and they focused on perfecting their faith through meditation. Shintoism is a traditional polytheistic faith that is practiced mainly in Japan.

22. B: The Chinese required other countries to pay tribute in order to establish trade relations. Foreign emissaries also had to prostrate themselves before the Chinese emperor. Potlatches, Choice *A*, were a Native American form of gift giving. Bartering, Choice *C*, was a common form of economic exchange, but it had no political significance.

23. B: Liberalism and totalitarianism were antithetical ideologies. Liberal activists demanded that the government give up some powers and allow individuals to have more political rights. On the other hand, totalitarian regimes, such Nazi Germany, exerted control over all aspects of private life.

24. C: Patriarchal societies value men highly and usually give women fewer rights. On the other hand, matriarchal societies place women at the head of the household. Divorce is legal in most societies, regardless of whether they are patriarchal or matriarchal.

25. C: The European Union aims to ensure free movement of people, goods, services, and capital within the internal market. The United Nations was formed in 1945 after World War II, making Choice *A* incorrect. The League of Nations was founded as a result of the Paris Peace Conference that ended the first World War and was also founded to avoid the repetitions of the first World War, making Choices *B* and *D* incorrect.

26. D: A number of scientific and technical advances have improved life expectancy and agricultural productivity. As a result, the world population has been growing rapidly for the last two hundred years, and especially since World War II. The increasing population has led to more competition for natural resources. However, the population growth has been most pronounced in less developed regions where fertility rates are higher. More developed regions have older populations and a lower fertility rate.

Government/Civics/Political Science

Political Theory

<u>Major Political Concepts</u>
Politics is the process of governance, typically exercised through the enactment and enforcement of laws, over a community, most commonly a state. Political theory involves the study of politics, especially concerning the efficacy and legitimacy of those responsible for governance. The major concepts in political theory include *power* and *authority*. The concepts of power and authority are closely related but possess certain significant distinctions.

Power is the ability of a ruling body or political entity to influence the actions, behavior, and attitude of a person or group of people; in short, power implies a degree of control over a human community. In order to possess *authority*, the ruling body or political entity must be recognized as having the right and justification to exercise power. This is commonly referred to as *legitimacy*. In representative governments, authority is garnered from the citizens through democratic processes, but in more autocratic regimes, influential elites grant that authority. In some cases, a ruling body or political entity may possess authority recognized by its citizens or influential elites but lack the power to influence those citizens and political entities or effect change within the system of governance. When power and authority are not properly aligned, governments are extremely weak, often deadlocked, and at risk of collapse or revolution.

Government is the result of the decisions made by a society during the political process and is a physical manifestation of the political entity or ruling body. The government determines and enforces the power of the state. A government includes the formal institutions of a society with the power and authority to enact, enforce, and interpret laws. The many different forms of government are determined based on this delegation of power between those institutions. Government encompasses the functions of *law*, *order*, and *justice* and is responsible for maintaining the society.

Sovereignty refers to a political entity's right and power to self-govern, including enacting and enforcing its own taxes and laws without interference from external forces. A political entity may possess varying degrees of sovereignty, as some sovereign states may still be subject to influence by outside political entities. For example, the members of the European Union cede some sovereignty in order to enjoy membership. A state's sovereignty is legitimate when outside political entities recognize the right of the state to self-govern. Both sovereignty and legitimacy are requirements to form a state.

The terms *nation* and *state* are often used interchangeably, but in political theory, they are two very distinct concepts. *Nation* refers to a people's cultural identity, while *state* refers to a territory's political organization and government.

Unlike states, there are no definitive requirements to be a nation; the nation just needs to include a group that is bound together by some shared defining characteristics such as the following:

- Language
- Culture and traditions
- Beliefs and religion
- Homeland
- Ethnicity
- History
- Mythology

The term *state* is commonly used to reference a nation-state, especially in regard to their government. There are four requirements for a political entity to be recognized as a state:

- Territory: a clearly defined geographic area with distinct borders

- Population: citizens and noncitizens living within the borders of the territory with some degree of permanence

- Legitimacy: legal authority to rule that is recognized by the citizens of the state and by other states

- Sovereignty: a political entity's right and power to self-govern without interference from external forces

Nation-state is the term used to describe a political entity with both a clearly defined nation and state. In a nation-state, the majority population of the state is a nation that identifies the territory as their homeland and shares a common history and culture. It is also possible to have several nations in the same nation-state. For example, there are Canadians in Canada and nations of Aboriginal peoples. The presence of multiple nations raises issues related to sovereignty.

Example of a nation: Sikhs in India

Example of a state: Vatican City

Example of a nation-state: Germany

Liberty and Freedom
Governments provide different *liberty* and *freedom*, depending on the form of government that, in turn, is influenced by the states' shared history and culture. Philosophers started articulating defined rights and liberties and arguing for their adoption and protection by the government during the Enlightenment. Liberalism advocates for increasing liberty and freedom in society and economics, while authoritarian regimes offer considerably less protection. The terms liberty and freedom both reference the same thing in society. Examples of liberty and freedom relate to speech, religion, press, economic pursuits, etc. The degrees and breadth of protections are context dependent, and they might be fluid and influenced by the political process. Many states delineate liberty and freedoms in their constitution. Rights and privileges are different because they involve something that is legal to do or possible according to the government sanctioning the action; thus, rights and privileges are typically more easily revoked from both specific individuals and larger communities.

Rights and Privileges

A *right* is a freedom, protection, or entitlement afforded to a person. In political theory, a right or *privilege* specifically refers to that which is granted to the citizens of a political territory according to the legal system or the social conventions of the society. Rights and privileges typically cannot be removed without due process under the law, although this depends on the form of government. Like the distinction between liberty and freedom, the difference between rights and privileges is indistinguishable. They are often the concrete representations of liberty and freedom in a society; as rights and privileges grow in number and strength, the society enjoys more liberty and freedom. Rights are the privileges provided by the government; however, the term right is commonly used to refer to a privilege of higher status that receives more scrutiny and protection from the state, usually requiring more due process to revoke or alter.

Example of a right: the right to vote

Example of a privilege: the privilege to receive a driver's license

Law, Order, and Justice

Governments must establish *law*, *order*, and *justice* through the government's political institutions. Protecting citizens' rights under the systems of laws, as well as effectively punishing the violators, is one of government's foundational responsibilities. Establishing law, order, and justice is an exercise in sovereignty—states that do not impose law and order under a reasonable standard of justice risk public unrest and challenges to the regime's legitimacy.

Law is the system of rules, policies, and regulations that govern behavior that is enacted by a political entity and enforced by the formal institutions created by the political entity. *Order* refers to each citizen, institution, and political entity acting as the law. Political entities secure order through the execution of laws through its enforcing institutions, like the police and justice system.

The term *justice* often refers to the fairness in the political entity's treatment of its citizens. When discussing its relation to law and order, justice refers to the necessary, agreed-upon consequences for failure to act according to the law. In political theory, justice is the social contract between the political entity and its citizens in which all parties involved have agreed upon what is considered "fair" in a society and what the consequences of acting contrary to the law should be.

Citizenship and Nationality

Citizenship is the political term referring to the legal status of an individual recognized by the state or government as a protected member. *Citizens* are subject to the laws of their state and granted the rights and liberties afforded by that state, including the right to vote and be elected to office.

Citizenship does not necessarily denote *nationality*, which refers to the relationship between an individual and a nation, rather than a legal status. Nationality is a component of citizenship, but nationality does not afford an individual any of the rights associated with citizenship of a state without official sanction from the state.

Major Political Theorists

Aristotle, 384 BC to 322 BC

A student of Plato, Aristotle was a Greek philosopher best known for his theories of rationality and ethics. In *Politics*, Aristotle asserted that "man is a political animal" and that man must actively participate in politics to further the political well-being of the city-state. He believed that man could only attain the happy life that nature intended through noble acts that bettered the community in which they lived. To this end, he envisioned an ideal society in which the most virtuous and knowledgeable men ruled and the citizens lived virtuous lives in the service of their city-state. Aristotle is one of the leading contributors to Western philosophy and, later, Liberalism. The Roman Republic applied much of his theories on ethics and civics to their government.

Niccolo Machiavelli, 1469-1527

Machiavelli was an Italian diplomat, politician, and historian during the Italian Renaissance. He is most known for his infamous political treatise, *The Prince,* which inspired the political philosophy known as Machiavellianism. In *The Prince,* Machiavelli instructed rulers that it is "better to be feared than to be loved" and asserted that a ruler must be willing to commit any acts necessary to maintain power and establish the stability of their society. He advocated violence, deceit, and immoral acts and advised rulers to seek out and eliminate any potential political rivals within the community. Machiavellianism prioritizes maintaining and consolidating power over all else.

Thomas Hobbes, 1588-1679

Thomas Hobbes was an English philosopher most notable as being the founder of social contract theory. In his 1651 book, *Leviathan,* Hobbes stated that without a strong central authority, the people would live in constant fear; they would go without industry, knowledge, or commodities if there was no system for enforcing good behavior As such, he asserted that the people enacted social contracts with ruling bodies, in which the people agreed to submit to the laws and limitations imposed by the ruling body in exchange for the protection and quality of life afforded to them. Hobbes was responsible for founding many of the fundamentals of liberal thought, stating that all men are naturally equal and that a ruling body may only gain legitimacy through the consent of the people.

John Locke, 1632-1704

John Locke was an English philosopher influenced by Thomas Hobbes' social contract theory. Though he agreed with the theory on some points, he argued against Hobbes' assertion that man requires protection from a ruling body in order to maintain a civilized society, Instead, Locke believed that men are rational and tolerant beings by nature. Locke is considered the "Father of Liberalism." His works on political theory include the famous *Two Treatises on Government*, which contributed significantly to modern ideals of liberal theory, including espousing the need to protect the right to life, liberty, health, and possessions. Locke's philosophy on rights and self-government influenced the writers of the Declaration of Independence.

Jean-Jacques Rousseau, 1712-1778

Jean-Jacques Rousseau was a philosopher, writer, and composer during the Enlightenment in France whose political writings, *Discourse on Equality* and *The Social Contract,* influenced aspects of the French Revolutionary War and many modern political theories. Rousseau thought man was free in the more primitive stage, and this freedom could only be maintained in a state if the people remained sovereign through representative government. He advocated for religious equality and argued that the people are sovereign, rather than a divinely empowered monarch, and that the people should have the right to rule themselves. His work was banned in France, but his ideals influenced the people and inspired many of the political reforms that led to the Revolutionary War.

Immanuel Kant, 1724-1804

A German philosopher, Kant is best known for the set of ideas known as Kantianism, which states that individuals possess dignity and deserve respect. Although more famous for his philosophy, Kant discussed political theory in his essay, *Perpetual Peace: A Philosophical Sketch,* where he argued that world peace may be achieved through universal democracy and international cooperation. In this work, he explained that, in order to end all wars and create lasting peace, all states must form constitutional republics in which elected officials adhere to the rule of the constitutional law to govern the state.

John Stuart Mills, 1806-1873

John Stuart Mills, an English philosopher and political economist, was considered the "most influential English-speaking philosopher of the nineteenth century" and was best known for being the first member of Parliament to advocate women's suffrage. His book *On Liberty* promoted utilitarianism, which advocates that people should always make decisions based on what would be the most net positive. In his work, Mills sought to limit the power exercised upon the individual by any ruling body and stated that moral actions are those that promote utility and increase individuals' and society's well-being. He called for limited constraints upon individual behavior that only restrict those actions that cause harm to others.

Karl Marx, 1818-1883

Karl Marx, a philosopher, social scientist, historian, and revolutionary, is considered one of the most influential Socialist thinkers of the nineteenth century. His ideas became known as Marxism, and Marx heavily influenced powerful Socialist and Communist leaders, such as Vladimir Lenin, with his 1848 pamphlet *The Communist Manifesto.* In this pamphlet, he explained that, in a capitalist society, perpetual "class struggle" exists in which a ruling class (bourgeois) controls the means of production and exploits the working class (proletariat), who are forced to sell labor for wages. He advocated for the working class to rebel against the ruling class and establish a classless society with collective ownership of the means of production. He envisioned world history as a series of stages in which capitalism eventually collapses into Communism.

Vladimir Lenin, 1870-1924

As a leading figure in the Russian Revolution and eventual founding of the Soviet Union, Lenin was one of the most controversial and influential political figures in the international Communist movement. Strongly influenced by Karl Marx, Lenin established the one-party system of government, which advocates pure Communism: a classless, egalitarian society in which the people abide by one rule—from "each according to his ability, to each according to his needs," a slogan coined by Marx. Lenin led the Bolsheviks into power after the Russian Revolution, and his Communist Party dominated the centralized one-party system. Lenin redistributed land among the peasants and nationalized most private industries, and he suppressed all political opposition with aggression, most notably during the Red Terror. Lenin advocated for Communist revolution across the world. Joseph Stalin, who further consolidated power of the increasingly authoritarian centralized government, succeeded Lenin as head of the Soviet Union.

Political Orientations

A *political orientation* is a set of ideals, principles, and doctrines that inform how government should be organized, specifically the balance between individual rights, government power, and economic policy. Thus, the country's dominant orientation will largely shape the state form of government. Orientations are also known as political ideologies and are commonly plotted on a political system to provide a visual representation for comparative purposes. The simplest political spectrum orders political orientations on a left-to-right axis. The far left and far right represent the most extreme political orientations, while the center is more moderate.

Left Axis

In general, the orientations on the left emphasize social and economic equality and advocate for government intervention to achieve it. Examples of "leftist" ideologies include Communism, Socialism, Progressivism, and Liberalism.

Communism

Communism is a radical political ideology that seeks to establish common ownership over production and abolish social status and money. Communists believe that the world is split between two social classes—capitalists and the working class (often referred to as the proletariat). Communist politics assert that conflict arises from the inequality between the ruling class and the working class; thus, Communism favors a classless society. Political philosophers Karl Marx and Friedrich Engels argued that Communism is society's destiny since capitalism would ultimately collapse. The collapse of the Soviet Union weakened Communism across the world.

Socialism

Socialists prioritize the health of the community over the rights of individuals, seeking collective and equitable ownership over the means of production. Consequently, Socialism is closely tied to an economic system. Under the political philosopher Karl Marx, Socialism is the transitional stage between capitalism and Communism. In general, Socialism is less extreme than Communism. Socialists are more willing to work within the framework of democracy to elect Socialist policies, like social security, universal health care, unemployment benefits, and other programs related to building a societal safety net. Most modern countries include some degree of Socialism, such as progressive taxation and welfare systems. The Scandinavian countries of Denmark, Finland, Sweden, and Norway are examples of countries with a socialized welfare system.

Progressivism

Progressive ideals maintain that progress in the form of scientific and technological advancement, social change, and economic development improve the quality of human life. Progressive ideals include the view that the political and economic interests of the ruling class suppress progress, which results in perpetual social and economic inequality.

Liberalism

Liberalism developed during the Age of Enlightenment in opposition to absolute monarchy, royal privilege, and state religion. In general, Liberalism emphasizes liberty and equality, and liberals support freedom of speech, freedom of religion, free markets, civil rights, gender equality, and secular governance. Liberals support government intervention into private matters to further social justice and fight inequality; thus, liberals often favor social welfare organizations and economic safety nets to combat income inequality. A popular form of Liberalism is Populism, which advocates for incorporating advances in technology, social organization, science, and economics into the government to benefit society.

Right Axis

Orientations on the right of the spectrum generally value the existing and historical political institutions and oppose government intervention, especially in regard to the economy. Examples include Conservatism, Libertarianism, and Fascism.

Conservatism

Conservatism is a political ideology that prioritizes traditional institutions within a culture and civilization. In general, Conservatives oppose modern developments and value stability. Since

Conservatism depends on the traditional institution, this ideology differs greatly from country to country. Conservatives often emphasize the traditional family structure and the importance of individual self-reliance. Fiscal Conservatism is one of the most common variants, and in general, the proponents of fiscal Conservatism oppose government spending and public debt.

Libertarianism
Libertarianism opposes state intervention on society and the economy. Libertarians advocate for a weak central government, favoring more local rule, and seek to maximize personal autonomy and protect personal freedom. Libertarians often follow a conservative approach to government, especially in the context of power and intervention, but favor a progressive approach to rights and freedom, especially those tied to personal liberty, like freedom of speech.

Fascism
Fascism is a form of totalitarianism that became popular in Europe after World War I. Fascists advocate for a centralized government led by an all-powerful dictator, tasked with preparing for total war and mobilizing all resources to benefit the state. This orientation's distinguishing features include a consolidated and centralized government. In addition, Fascists show more willingness to use violence as a means to accomplish state goals. Popular support for Fascism fell drastically after World War II. There is widespread disagreement among historians, political theorists, and other commentators as to whether governments or political movements qualify as Fascist regimes. Kim Jong-un's status as the supreme leader of North Korea is often cited as a Fascist regime due to the extreme consolidation of totalitarian power. Similarly, Vladimir Putin's Russia is often characterized as Fascist. There are also many European political parties—typically, nationalist parties that oppose immigration and international governance—that advocate for policies widely considered to be Fascist, like the Golden Dawn in Greece. However, few modern movements and regimes would describe themselves as Fascist. Fascism implies some comfort with totalitarian government, and it is most closely associated with the Fascist regimes during World War II, especially Adolf Hitler's Nazi Party.

Off the Spectrum
Some political orientations do not fit within the political spectrum because they can fit alongside other orientations and ideologies. For example, Nazism is both a Fascist and nationalist ideology. Examples include nationalism, internationalism, and anarchism.

Nationalism
Nationalism is an ideology that prioritizes a loyalty and devotion to the home country. Typically, nationalists exalt their country over all others; thus, nationalism prioritizes promoting its own culture over all other cultures and foreign interests. Nationalism developed alongside the growth of the European nation-state during the nineteenth century. Nationalists can be on the far right or far left. Nationalism is a powerful unifying force within a country or region. In modern times, nationalist groups oppose globalism, such as free trade agreements and supranational political entities, viewing global cooperation as a threat to their national culture.

Internationalism
Internationalist ideals support strong social, political, and economic unity among the states, nations, and people of the world. Internationalists value political institutions on an international level, commonly referred to as supranational political entities. Member states cede some degree of sovereignty to the international entity and receive the associated benefits. Internationalism advocates for free trade and globalism. Nongovernmental organizations play an important role in internationalism's approach to

global problems. Examples of supranational organizations include the United Nations, European Union, North Atlantic Treaty Organization (NATO), and World Trade Organization (WTO).

Anarchism

Anarchism is a radical political orientation that advocates for self-government and abolishment of existing political institutions; instead, society would be based on voluntary institutions. Anarchists oppose the state, arguing that political institutions organize society hierarchically, which creates the conflict. Thus, law and order is then accomplished by freeing the people from the state's corruption.

United States Government and Politics

Constitutional Underpinnings

The role of government is to maintain a society and provide public services through its formal institutions, protect the citizens of the state, and regulate the economic system. To determine how a government should perform these functions and to protect the rights and liberties of the citizens, states enact a *constitution*, a written document that typically establishes the form of government and delegation of powers within the government, delineates limits on government, and defines protected rights, liberties, and privileges.

The many underpinnings, or foundations, upon which the *Constitution* of the United States was founded include:

Articles of Confederation (1781-1789)

The Articles of Confederation established a formal agreement or confederation between the original thirteen states. The Articles of Confederation established a central government composed of a unicameral legislative assembly in which each state was granted a single representative. Passing a bill required votes from nine of the thirteen representatives. Under the Articles of Confederation, the centralized government, the Continental Congress, was granted very limited powers, rendering it largely ineffective. Those powers included:

- Borrowing money from states or foreign government
- Creating post offices
- Appointing military offices
- Declaring war
- Signing treaties with foreign states

The weak central government established under the Articles of Confederation lacked the power to impose taxes, enforce a draft to staff the new army and navy, regulate trade, or enforce the laws enacted in Congress. As such, the sovereignty remained primarily with the states. Under the Articles, the states reserved the powers to impose taxes upon each other and the citizens of their states, regulate trade within their states, coin and print money, and sign treaties with foreign states. The states also often ignored the laws enacted by the Congress because there was no executive branch to enforce the law.

This imbalance of power between the central government and the states led to crisis within the states, resulting in economic difficulties and violence. The lack of common currency and investment in interstate infrastructure greatly hindered economic growth. In the years 1786 and 1787, farmers in several states staged a series of protests over local tax and debt collection imposed on struggling farms, commonly known as Shay's Rebellion.

Constitutional Convention, 1787
The failures of the Articles of Confederation to effectively govern on a national level directly led to the Constitutional Convention, and those experiences influenced the founders' decision to include a more robust federal government in the United States Constitution. The Constitutional Convention faced several challenges, including disputes over representation between large and small states, tension between the southern and northern states over slavery, differing visions of how power would be delegated within the government, and opposition to ceding states' sovereignty to a national federal government.

New Jersey Plan
Led by William Patterson, the New Jersey Plan called for a unicameral legislature that would grant each state a single vote. It proposed a plural executive power selected by the legislature, which would possess no veto power over the legislature, as well as judges appointed by the executive power for the duration of their lives.

The Virginia Plan
Drafted by James Madison, the Virginia Plan featured a bicameral legislature with two houses. The representatives of the lower house were to be selected by the people, and then the lower house would elect the upper house. The number of representatives of each house would be based upon population or the amount of money contributed to the federal government by each state; thus, large states supported the Virginia Plan. In this plan, the legislature could appoint judges and select a single executive with veto power.

Compromises
Connecticut Compromise
This compromise included aspects of both the New Jersey Plan and Virginia Plan in a bicameral legislature. Representation in the House of Representatives was proportional to a state's population, and in the Senate, states enjoyed equal representation with two senators per state.

Slavery Compromises
Several other compromises were made during the Convention, including the *Three-Fifths Compromise,* which, in an effort to appease both the South states who wanted slaves to be counted as part of the population for the purpose of representation but not counted for the purpose of taxes, and the North, who demanded slaves be counted for taxes but not representation, the framers of the Constitution determined that three-fifths of the slave population of each state would be counted for the purpose of both taxes and representation. In an additional compromise called the *Commerce and Slave Trade Compromise,* Congress agreed not to tax exports from states or ban the trading of slaves for twenty years. This eased Southerners' fears that if the Northern states controlled the federal government, then they could enforce antislavery policies.

Constitution vs. Articles of Confederation
The Constitution addressed the weaknesses of the Articles of Confederation in the following ways:

- Unlike the sovereign states under the Articles of Confederation, the people are now the sovereign, and they bestow sovereignty to both the states and federal government, according to principles of Federalism.

- The Constitution creates a robust central government with many specific and implied powers.

- The Constitution empowers the federal government to levy taxes against the states.

- The Constitution establishes an executive branch of the federal government to enforce the laws; it is led by a president who serves as the commander-in-chief.

- The Constitution establishes a federal judiciary branch with a Supreme Court and lower courts to interpret the laws enacted by the legislative branch.

- The Constitution removes the states' power to coin and print money and establishes a national currency; Congress may regulate interstate and international commerce.

- The Constitution specifies representation in Congress based on population and equal representation for each state in the Senate.

- The Constitution requires a simple majority in both houses to enact laws rather than a vote of at least nine out of thirteen, as specified in the Articles of Confederation. In addition, senators vote separately under the Constitution, while states vote as a single bloc in the Constitution.

- The Constitution requires a two-thirds majority vote in the House of Representatives and a two-thirds majority in the Senate to amend the Constitution, while the Articles of Confederation required a unanimous vote.

Federalism

To strengthen the central government, while still appeasing the individual states who preferred to remain sovereign over their territories, the framers of the Constitution based the new government upon the principles of *Federalism*—a compound government system that divides powers between a central government and various regional governments. The Constitution clearly defined the roles of both the state governments and the new federal government, specifying the limited power of the federal government and reserving all other powers not restricted by the Constitution to the states in the Tenth Amendment to the Constitution, commonly referred to as the Reservation Clause.

The Constitution establishes the specific powers granted to the federal and state governments.

- Delegated powers: the specific powers granted to the federal government by the Constitution
- Implied powers: the unstated powers that can be reasonably inferred from the Constitution
- Inherent powers: the reasonable powers required by the government to manage the nation's affairs and maintain sovereignty
- Reserved powers: the unspecified powers belonging to the state that are not expressly granted to the federal government or denied to the state by the Constitution
- Concurrent powers: the powers shared between the federal and state governments

The Constitution would delegate the following expanded powers to the federal government:

- Coin money
- Declare war
- Establish lower federal courts
- Sign foreign treaties
- Expand the territories of the United States, and admit new states into the union
- Regulate immigration
- Regulate interstate commerce

The following powers were reserved for the states:

- Establish local governments
- Hold elections
- Implement welfare and benefit programs
- Create public school systems
- Establish licensing standards and requirements
- Regulate state corporations
- Regulate commerce within the state

The *concurrent* powers granted to both the federal and state governments in the Constitution include:

- The power to levy taxes
- The power to borrow money
- The power to charter incorporations

Ratifying the Constitution
The framers of the Constitution signed the Constitution on September 17, 1787, but the Articles of Confederation required nine of the thirteen states to ratify the document. Conventions were held in all thirteen states and sparked heated debates between those who supported and those who opposed the new system of government. The Federalists supported the expansion of the federal government, and the anti-Federalists feared that a stronger central government would weaken the states. The anti-Federalists also sought additional protection for civil liberties. The debates between these two parties continued for two years and inspired a series of essays known as the *Federalist Papers* and *Anti-Federalist Papers* authored anonymously by leaders of their respective party.

Notable Federalists and authors of the *Federalist Papers* include:

- Alexander Hamilton: founder of the Federalist Party and advocate for a centralized financial system

- George Washington: commander-in-chief of the Continental Army and future first president of the United States

- James Madison: one of the primary drafters of the Constitution and the future fourth president of the United States

- John Jay: president of the Continental Congress and future first chief justice of the United States

- John Adams: future second president of the United States

Notable anti-Federalists and authors of the *Anti-Federalist Papers* include:

- Thomas Jefferson: primary author of the Declaration of Independence and future third president of the United States

- Patrick Henry: governor of Virginia (1776-1779, 1784-1786)

- Samuel Adams: governor of Massachusetts (1794-1797), lieutenant governor of Massachusetts (1789-1794), and president of the Massachusetts Senate (1782-1785, 1787-1788)

- George Mason: one of only three delegates who did not sign the Constitution at the Constitutional Convention and author of Objections to This Constitution of Government (1787) and the Virginia Declaration of Rights of 1776, which served as the basis for the Bill of Rights

The first state to ratify the Constitution was Delaware in a unanimous vote on December 7, 1787. Several other states followed, and eventually, after ten months, New Hampshire became the ninth state to ratify the Constitution in June 1788. However, some states still remained divided between Federalist and anti-Federalist sentiments and had yet to approve the document, including the two most populous states, Virginia and New York. To reconcile their differing views, the Federalists agreed to include a bill of rights if anti-Federalists supported the new Constitution. Federalist sentiment prevailed, and the remaining states approved the document. On May 29, 1790, the last holdout, Rhode Island, ratified the Constitution by two votes. As promised, the Bill of Rights—the first 10 amendments to the Constitution—was added in 1791, providing expanded civil liberty protection and due process of law.

Powers, Structure, and Processes of National Political Institutions

A *political institution* is an organization created by the government to enact and enforce laws, act as a mediator during conflict, create economic policy, establish social systems, and carry out some power. These institutions maintain a rigid structure of internal rules and oversight, especially if the power is delegated, like agencies under the executive branch.

The Constitution established a federal government divided into three branches: legislative, executive, and judicial.

The Three Branches of the U.S. Government

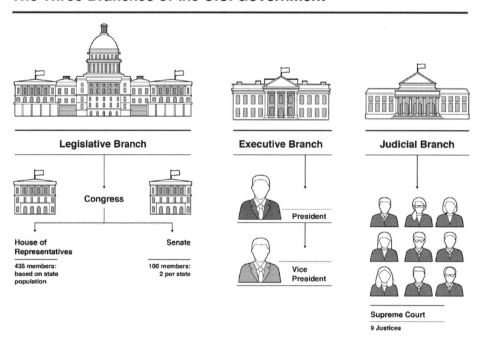

Executive Branch

The executive branch is responsible for enforcing the laws. The executive branch consists of the president, the vice president, the president's cabinet, and federal agencies created by Congress to execute some delegated.

The president of the United States:

- Serves a four-year term and is limited to two terms in office
- Is the chief executive officer of the United States and commander-in-chief of the armed forces
- Is elected by the Electoral College
- Appoints cabinet members, federal judges, and the heads of federal agencies
- Vetoes or signs bills into law
- Handles foreign affairs, including appointing diplomats and negotiating treaties
- Must be thirty-five years old, a natural-born U.S. citizen, and have lived in the United States for at least fourteen years

The vice president:

- Serves four-year terms alongside and at the will of the president
- Acts as president of the Senate
- Assumes the presidency if the president is incapacitated
- Assumes any additional duties assigned by the president

The cabinet members:

- Are appointed by the president
- Act as heads for the fifteen executive departments
- Advise the president in matters relating to their departments and carry out delegated power

Note that the president can only sign and veto laws and cannot initiate them himself. As head of the executive branch, it is the responsibility of the president to execute and enforce the laws passed by the legislative branch.

Although Congress delegates their legislative authority to agencies in an enabling statute, they are located in the executive branch because they are tasked with executing their delegating authority. The president enjoys the power of appointment and removal over all federal agency workers, except those tasked with quasi-legislative or quasi-judicial powers.

Legislative Branch

The legislative branch is responsible for enacting federal laws. This branch possesses the power to declare war, regulate interstate commerce, approve or reject presidential appointments, and investigate the other branches. The legislative branch is *bicameral*, meaning it consists of two houses: the lower house, called the House of Representatives, and the upper house, known as the Senate. Both houses are elected by popular vote.

Members of both houses are intended to represent the interests of the constituents in their home states and to bring their concerns to a national level. Ideas for laws, called bills, are proposed in one chamber and then are voted upon according to the body's rules; should the bill pass the first round of voting, the other legislative chamber must approve it before it can be sent to the president.

The two houses (or chambers) are similar though they differ on some procedures such as how debates on bills take place.

House of Representatives
The House of Representatives is responsible for enacting bills relating to revenue, impeaching federal officers including the president and Supreme Court justices, and electing the president in the case of no candidate reaching a majority in the Electoral College.

In the House of Representatives:

- Each state's representation in the House of Representatives is determined proportionally by population, with the total number of voting seats limited to 435.

- There are six nonvoting members from Washington, D.C., Puerto Rico, American Samoa, Guam, Northern Mariana Islands, and the U.S. Virgin Islands.

- The Speaker of the House is elected by the other representatives and is responsible for presiding over the House. In the event that the president and vice president are unable to fulfill their duties, the Speaker of the House will succeed to the presidency.

- The representatives of the House serve two-year terms.

- The requirements for eligibility in the House include:

    o Must be twenty-five years of age
    o Must have been a U.S. citizen for at least seven years
    o Must be a resident of the state they are representing by the time of the election

Senate
The Senate has the exclusive powers to confirm or reject all presidential appointments, ratify treaties, and try impeachment cases initiated by the House of Representatives.

In the Senate:

- The number of representatives is one hundred, with two representatives from each state.
- The vice president presides over the Senate and breaks the tie, if necessary.
- The representatives serve six-year terms.
- The requirements for eligibility in the Senate include:
    o Must be thirty years of age
    o Must have been a U.S. citizen for the past nine years
    o Must be a resident of the state they are representing at the time of their election

Legislative Process
Although all members of the houses make the final voting, the senators and representatives serve on committees and subcommittees dedicated to specific areas of policy. These committees are responsible for debating the merit of bills, revising bills, and passing or killing bills that are assigned to their committee. If it passes, they then present the bill to the entire Senate or House of Representatives (depending on which they are a part of). In most cases, a bill can be introduced in either the Senate or the House, but a majority vote of both houses is required to approve a new bill before the president may sign the bill into law.

Judicial Branch

The *judicial branch*, though it cannot pass laws itself, is tasked with interpreting the law and ensuring citizens receive due process under the law. The judicial branch consists of the Supreme Court, the highest court in the country, overseeing all federal and state courts. Lower federal courts are the district courts and court of appeals.

The Supreme Court:

- Judges are appointed by the president and confirmed by the Senate.
- Judges serve until retirement, death, or impeachment.
- Judges possess sole power to judge the constitutionality of a law.
- Judges set precedents for lower courts based on their decisions.
- Judges try appeals that have proceeded from the lower district courts.

Checks and Balances

Notice that a system of checks and balances between the branches exists. This is to ensure that no branch oversteps its authority. They include:

- Checks on the Legislative Branch:
  - The president can veto bills passed by Congress.
  - The president can call special sessions of Congress.
  - The judicial branch can rule legislation unconstitutional.
- Checks on the Executive Branch:
  - Congress has the power to override presidential vetoes by a two-thirds majority vote.
  - Congress can impeach or remove a president, and the chief justice of the Supreme Court presides over impeachment proceedings.
  - Congress can refuse to approve presidential appointments or ratify treaties.
- Checks on the Judicial Branch:
  - The president appoints justices to the Supreme Court, as well as district court and court of appeals judges.
  - The president can pardon federal prisoners.
  - The executive branch can refuse to enforce court decisions.
  - Congress can create federal courts below the Supreme Court.
  - Congress can determine the number of Supreme Court justices.
  - Congress can set the salaries of federal judges.
  - Congress can refuse to approve presidential appointments of judges.
  - Congress can impeach and convict federal judges.

The three branches of government operate separately, but they must rely on each other to create, enforce, and interpret the laws of the United States.

Checks and Balances

Executive Branch

Appoint Justices to the Supreme Court and Pardon Federal Prisoners

Override Presidential Vetoes by 2/3 vote and Impeach the President

Preside Over Impeachment Proceedings

Legislative Branch

Judicial Branch

Create Federal Courts Below the Supreme Court and Impeach Federal Judges

Rule Legislation Unconstitutional

How Laws are Enacted and Enforced

To enact a new law:

- The bill is introduced to Congress.
- The bill is sent to the appropriate committee for review and revision.
- The approved bill is sent to the Speaker of the House and the majority party leader of the Senate, who places the bill on the calendar for review.
- The houses debate the merits of the bill and recommend amendments.

    o   In the House of Representatives, those who wish to debate about a bill are allowed only a few minutes to speak, and amendments to the bill are limited.

    o   In the Senate, debates and amendments are unlimited, and those who wish to postpone a vote may do so by filibuster, refusing to stop speaking.

- The approved bill is revised in both houses to ensure identical wording in both bills.
- The revised bill is returned to both houses for final approval.
- The bill is sent to the president, who may

    o   Sign the bill into law

    o   Veto the bill

    o   Take no action, resulting in the bill becoming law if Congress remains in session for ten days or dying if Congress adjourns before ten days have passed

The Role of State Government

While the federal government manages the nation as a whole, state governments address issues pertaining to their specific territory. In the past, states claimed the right, known as nullification, to refuse to enforce federal laws that they considered unconstitutional. However, conflicts between state and federal authority, particularly in the South in regard to first, slavery, and later, discrimination, have led to increased federal power, and states cannot defy federal laws. Even so, the Tenth Amendment limits federal power to those powers specifically granted in the Constitution, and the rest of the powers are retained by the states and citizens. Therefore, individual state governments are left in charge of decisions with immediate effects on their citizens, such as state laws and taxes.

In this way, the powers of government are separated both horizontally between the three branches of government (executive, legislative, and judicial) and vertically between the levels of government (federal, state, and local).

Like the federal government, state governments consist of executive, judicial, and legislative branches, but the exact configuration of those branches varies between states. For example, while most states follow the bicameral structure of Congress, Nebraska has only a single legislative chamber. Additionally, requirements to run for office, length of terms, and other details vary from state to state. State governments have considerable authority within their states, but they cannot impose their power on other states.

Separation of Powers

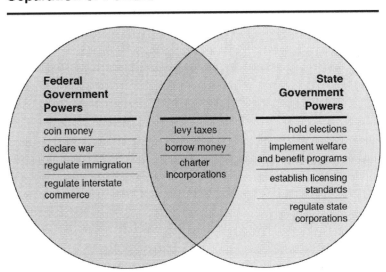

Civil Liberties and Civil Rights

The protection of *civil liberties* is one of the most important political values upon which American society is based. Though the terms *civil liberties* and *civil rights* are commonly used interchangeably, they describe two very distinct types of protections. Civil liberties refer to the legal protections afforded to U.S. citizens against government action, while civil rights refer to equal treatment under the law, especially in relation to minority groups, like women, African Americans, and Hispanics.

Civil Liberties

A civil liberty is a protection from legal action by the government. Civil liberties are granted by the Constitution in the first ten amendments, collectively known as the Bill of Rights, which were added to the Constitution in 1791. Civil liberties are conditional and do not afford protection from government action in every scenario. They can be restricted when they infringe on the rights of others; for example, with defamation, child pornography, or "fighting words." They also may be suspended with just cause, such as in the case of limiting the freedom of press to protect national security.

The Bill of Rights

The first ten amendments of the Constitution are called the Bill of Rights. They were passed to win over anti-Federalists during the ratification of the Constitution. Anti-Federalists wanted assurances that the federal government would protect certain fundamental civil liberties. The Bill of Rights includes:

- Amendment I: Establishes freedom of religion, speech, and press; the right to assemble in peaceful protest; and the right to petition the government without fear of reprisal

- Amendment II: Establishes the right to bear arms

- Amendment III: Establishes the right to refuse to quarter, or house, soldiers in time of war

- Amendment IV: Establishes protection against unreasonable search and seizure and requires a warrant based on probable cause supported by specific information

- Amendment V: Protects against self-incrimination in criminal trials, except in cases of military court martial; protects against being tried more than once for the same crime, known as double jeopardy; and protects against seizure of private property for public use without compensation

- Amendment VI: Establishes extensive set of rights to protect defendants in a criminal trial—the right to a speedy and timely trial before a judge and impartial jury of peers, the right to be informed of criminal accusations, the right to present and compel witnesses in defense of the accused, the right to confront witnesses against the accused, and the right to assistance of counsel

- Amendment VII: Protects the right to a trial by jury in civil cases exceeding a dollar amount of $20

- Amendment VIII: Protects against cruel and unusual punishment and excessive fines

- Amendment IX: Establishes the existence of additional fundamental rights unnamed in the Constitution; protects those rights that are not enumerated

- Amendment X: Reserves all powers that are not specified to the federal government or prohibited to the states or the people, establishing the principles of separation of powers and Federalism

Civil Rights

Civil rights concern who is protected, while *civil liberties* concern what is protected. Civil rights refer to protection against unfair treatment based on characteristics such as gender, race, ethnicity, religion, sexual orientation, and disability. The struggle for civil rights has a long history in the United States. Following the Civil War, the ratification of three amendments—Thirteenth, Fourteenth, and Fifteenth, collectively known as the Reconstruction Amendments—expanded the constitutional protection of equal civil rights.

The Thirteenth Amendment abolished slavery and involuntary servitude, except as punishment for a crime. The issue of slavery was no longer in the states' hands. Although the Emancipation Proclamation freed slaves in the Confederacy, the status of former slaves remained uncertain as the war neared its conclusion. Many Northerners did not hold strong views on slavery, but most wanted to punish the South and resolve the primary cause of the bloody Civil War. The Northern states all immediately ratified the amendment, and in December 1865, enough reconstructed Southern states ratified the amendment for it to be adopted into law.

The Fourteenth Amendment prohibited states from depriving life, liberty, or property without due process and from violating equal protection based on race, color, or previous condition of servitude. Now, all persons born or naturalized in the United States were considered legal citizens. Although revolutionary for the theoretical rights of all American citizens, newly freed or otherwise, the Fourteenth Amendment did not provide actual federally enforced equal protection until the Civil Rights Act of 1964.

The Fifteenth Amendment prohibits the government from denying a citizen the right to vote for reasons of race, color, or previous condition of servitude. Adopted in 1870, the last of the Reconstruction Amendments, the Fifteenth Amendment sought to protect newly freed slaves' right to vote. As discussed below, most states interpreted the amendment to only apply to male suffrage. In addition, Southern states passed a series of laws to systematically disenfranchise African Americans, like poll taxes, literacy tests, and residency rules. The use of violence and intimidation for political purpose was also common. Meaningful change did not occur until the Civil Rights Movement, nearly one hundred years later. In 1964, the Twenty-Fourth Amendment prohibited the states and federal government from charging a poll tax or fee to vote. Later, the Voting Rights Act of 1965 empowered the federal government to enforce the Fifteenth Amendment on the states for the first time.

Women's Suffrage
The Fourteenth Amendment specified equal treatment for all citizens; however, it did not establish women's right to vote in elections, known as women's suffrage. Although landowning women were allowed to vote in New Jersey in the late eighteenth century, the right was removed in 1807. The fight for women's suffrage continued in the middle of the nineteenth century. Famous women's rights activists include Susan B. Anthony, Lucy Stone, and Elizabeth Cady Stanton, who authored the *Declaration of Rights and Sentiments*, which demanded access to the civil liberties granted to all men. Women gained the right to vote in 1869 in Wyoming and 1870 in Utah.

The women's suffrage movement gained momentum in the early twentieth century after their increased participation in the economy during World War I when much of the workforce went overseas to fight. The National Women's Party picketed outside the White House and led a series of protests in Washington, resulting in the imprisonment of the party's leader, Alice Paul. In 1918, Woodrow Wilson declared his support for women's suffrage despite earlier opposition, and in 1920, Congress passed the Nineteenth Amendment, which made it illegal for states to withhold voting rights based on gender.

Jim Crow Laws
Southern states circumvented the Fourteenth Amendment and imposed what were referred to as Jim Crow laws, which established racial segregation of public facilities. These "separate but equal" facilities included the military, workplaces, public schools, restaurants, restrooms, transportation, and

recreational facilities. Despite the label of "separate but equal," most facilities reserved for African Americans were considerably inferior.

In 1896, the Supreme Court handed down a decision in the case of *Plessy vs. Ferguson*, in which Homer Plessy, a Louisiana man of mixed race, attempted to board a railway car reserved for "whites only" and was charged for violating the separate car law. Plessy subsequently filed suit against the state, claiming they violated his Fourteenth Amendment rights. The Supreme Court decided in favor of the state, ruling that the law was not unconstitutional. The Supreme Court upheld separate but equal laws until the 1954 case of *Brown vs. the Board of Education of Topeka* where the Supreme Court ruled that racial segregation of public schools violated the Fourteenth Amendment.

Civil Rights Movement

Brown vs. the Board of Education prohibited segregation in 1954, but the Civil Rights Movement, led by the National Association for the Advancement of Colored People (NAACP) and such famous activists as Martin Luther King Jr. and Malcolm X, did not secure the enforcement of the Fourteenth Amendment until the passage of the Civil Rights Act of 1964, which outlawed discrimination based on gender, race, ethnicity, and religion. African American and Native American women, however, did not gain the right to vote until the Voting Rights Act of 1965, which enforced the voting rights articulated in the Fourteenth Amendment and Fifteenth Amendment. Section 5 of the Voting Rights Act prevented states with a history of discrimination from altering their voting laws without getting approval from the attorney general or a federal district court.

Political Beliefs and Behaviors

Political beliefs are the beliefs held by the citizens of a nation about the government, leaders, policies, and the related political issues of their state. Political beliefs differ among individual citizens, but in America, a strong basis of democracy shapes the political beliefs, behaviors, and attitudes.

Democratic Values

The foundation of democratic values upon which the United States is based include:

- The people are sovereign, and they elect a representative government to exercise that sovereignty.
- The citizens of the nation are equal under the law.
- The peaceful transition of power is valued regardless of election results.
- The private property of individuals cannot be taken by force by the government without due process or fair compensation.
- The civil liberties of the citizens of the state cannot be abridged or violated by the government without due process.
- The government should be accountable to the citizenry.

Political Socialization

American citizens undergo a process of *political socialization* from early childhood to adulthood during which they develop their individual sense of political identity and civic pride. Children learn about politics in the home from an early age, whether from the views, opinions, and facts of family and friends, or through the media to which they are exposed.

In school, they learn about the nation's political history, basic politics, and democratic values, as well as the ideals of patriotism and the processes of government. As they grow older, they join interest groups, labor unions, religious groups, and political organizations that further influence their political beliefs.

This socialization shapes not only the political beliefs and values of individual citizens and groups but the political ideals of the nation and public opinion.

Public Opinion
Public opinion is the shared political ideals, opinions, and attitudes of the people of a state regarding the politics, current events, and social issues that influence policy and shape the political atmosphere of a state. Public opinion is the result of political beliefs, socialization, and current events. Political scientists measure public opinion through:

- Distribution of opinion across demographics such as age, race, gender, and religion
- Strength of the opinion
- Stability of the opinion over time

Public opinion refers to the majority opinion in a democratic state. Citizens express public opinion through the interest groups they join, the media they consume and interact with, and the leaders they elect. To measure public opinion, scientists use polls to gather data. Accurate polling requires:

- Random sampling of representative populations
- Unbiased questions
- Clear instructions for how to answer questions
- Controlled procedures such as the use of telephone, mail, Internet, or in-person interviews with an unbiased pollster
- Accurate reporting of the results, including information about methods, inconsistencies, respondents, and possible sources and degree of error

Political Participation
Citizens express their political beliefs and public opinion through participation in politics. The conventional ways citizens can participate in politics in a democratic state include:

- Obeying laws
- Voting in elections
- Running for public office
- Staying interested and informed of current events
- Learning U.S. history
- Attending public hearings to be informed and to express their opinions on issues, especially on the local level
- Forming interest groups to promote their common goals
- Forming political action committees (PACs) that raise money to influence policy decisions
- Petitioning government to create awareness of issues
- Campaigning for a candidate
- Contributing to campaigns
- Using mass media to express political ideas, opinions, and grievances

Voting
In a democratic state, the most common way to participate in politics is by voting for candidates in an election. Voting allows the citizens of a state to influence policy by selecting the candidates who share their views and make policy decisions that best suit their interests, or candidates who they believe are most capable of leading the country. In the United States, all citizens—regardless of gender, race, or

religion—are allowed to vote unless they have lost their right to vote through due process, such as felons.

Since the Progressive movement and the increased social activism of the 1890s to the 1920s that sought to eliminate corruption in government, direct participation in politics through voting has increased. Citizens can participate by voting in the following types of elections:

- Direct primaries: Citizens can nominate candidates for public office.

- National, state, and municipal elections: Citizens elect their representatives in government.

- Recall elections: Citizens can petition the government to vote an official out of office before their term ends.

- Referendums: Citizens can vote directly on proposed laws or amendments to the state constitution.

- Voter initiatives: Citizens can petition their local or state government to propose laws that will be approved or rejected by voters.

Electoral Process, Political Parties, Interest Groups, and Mass Media

As members of a Constitutional Republic with certain aspects of a *democracy*, U.S. citizens are empowered to elect most government leaders, but the process varies between branch and level of government. Presidential elections at the national level use the *Electoral College* system. Rather than electing the president directly, citizens cast their ballots to select *electors* that represent each state in the college.

Legislative branches at the federal and state level are also determined by elections. In some areas, judges are elected, but in other states judges are appointed by elected officials. The U.S. has a *two-party system*, meaning that most government control is under two major parties: the Republican Party and the Democratic Party. It should be noted that the two-party system was not designed by the Constitution but gradually emerged over time.

Electoral Process

During the *electoral process*, the citizens of a state decide who will represent them at the local, state, and federal level. Different political officials that citizens elect through popular vote include but are not limited to:

- City mayor
- City council members
- State representative
- State governor
- State senator
- House member
- U.S. Senator
- President

The Constitution grants the states the power to hold their own elections, and the voting process often varies from city to city and state to state.

While a popular vote decides nearly all local and state elections, the president of the United States is elected by the *Electoral College*, rather than by popular vote. Presidential elections occur every four years on the first Tuesday after the first Monday in November.

The electoral process for the president of the United States includes:

Primary Elections and Caucuses
In a presidential election, *nominees* from the two major parties, as well as some third parties, run against each other. To determine who will win the nomination from each party, the states hold *primary elections* or *caucuses*.

During the primary elections, the states vote for who they want to win their party's nomination. In some states, primary elections are closed, meaning voters may only vote for candidates from their registered party, but other states hold *open primaries* in which voters may vote in either party's primary.

Some states hold *caucuses* in which the members of a political party meet in small groups, and the decisions of those groups determine the party's candidate.

Each state holds a number of delegates proportional to its population, and the candidate with the most delegate votes receives the domination. Some states give all of their delegates (*winner-take-all*) to the primary or caucus winner, while some others split the votes more proportionally.

Conventions
The two major parties hold national conventions to determine who will be the nominee to run for president from each party. The *delegates* each candidate won in the primary elections or caucuses are the voters who represent their states at the national conventions. The candidate who wins the most delegate votes is given the nomination. Political parties establish their own internal requirements and procedures for how a nominee is nominated.

Conventions are typically spread across several days, and leaders of the party give speeches, culminating with the candidate accepting the nomination at the end.

Campaigning
Once the nominees are selected from each party, they continue campaigning into the national election. Prior to the mid-1800s, candidates did not actively campaign for themselves, considering it dishonorable to the office, but campaigning is now rampant. Modern campaigning includes, but is not limited to:

- Raising money
- Meeting with citizens and public officials around the country
- Giving speeches
- Issuing policy proposals
- Running internal polls to determine strategy
- Organizing strategic voter outreach in important districts
- Participating in debates organized by a third-party private debate commission
- Advertising on television, through mail, or on the Internet

General Election
On the first Tuesday after the first Monday in November of an election year, every four years, the people cast their votes by secret ballot for president in a *general election*. Voters may vote for any

candidate, regardless of their party affiliation. The outcome of the popular vote does not decide the election; instead, the winner is determined by the Electoral College.

Electoral College

When the people cast their votes for president in the general election, they are casting their votes for the *electors* from the *Electoral College* who will elect the president. In order to win the presidential election, a nominee must win 270 of the 538 electoral votes. The number of electors is equal to the total number of senators and representatives from each state plus three electoral votes for Washington D.C. which does not have any voting members in the legislative branch.

The electors typically vote based on the popular vote from their states. Although the Constitution does not require electors to vote for the popular vote winner, no elector voting against the popular vote has ever changed the outcome of an election. Due to the Electoral College, a nominee may win the popular vote and still lose the election.

For example, let's imagine that there only two states, Wyoming and Nebraska, in a presidential election. Wyoming has three electoral votes and awards them all to the winner of the election by majority vote. Nebraska has five electoral votes and also awards them all to the winner of the election by majority vote. If 500,000 people in Wyoming vote and the Republican candidate wins by a vote of 300,000 to 200,000, the Republican candidate will win the three electoral votes for the state. If the same number of people vote in Nebraska, but the Republican candidate loses the state by a vote of 249,000 to 251,000, the Democratic candidate wins the five electoral votes from that state. This means the Republican candidate will have received 549,000 popular votes but only three electoral votes, while the Democratic candidate will have received 451,000 popular votes but will have won five electoral votes. Thus, the Republican won the popular vote by a considerable margin, but the Democratic candidate will have been awarded more electoral votes, which are the only ones that matter.

	Wyoming	Nebraska	Total # of Votes
Republican Votes	300,000	249,000	**549,000**
Democratic Votes	200,000	251,000	**451,000**
Republican Electoral Votes	3	0	**3**
Democratic Electoral Votes	0	5	**5**

If no one wins the majority of electoral votes in the presidential election, the House of Representatives decides the presidency, as required by the Twelfth Amendment. They may only vote for the top three candidates, and each state delegation votes as a single bloc. Twenty-six votes, a simple majority, are required to elect the president. The House has only elected the president twice, in 1801 and 1825.

Here how many electoral votes each state and the District of Columbia have:

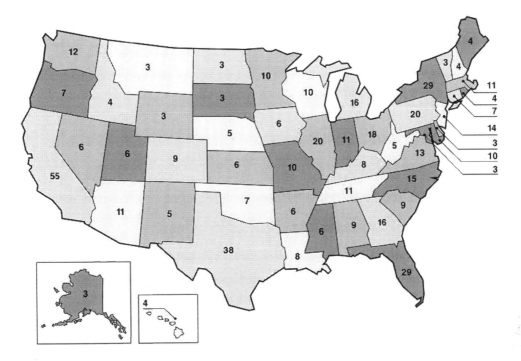

Political Parties

A *political party* is an organized group of voters who share the same political values and support or oppose the same policies. Members of a political party vote for the candidates from their party who they believe share their values and will approve or reject the policies they support or oppose. Political parties often determine the positions party members take on issues of policy, such as the economy, taxation, and social services.

The Founding Fathers of the United States opposed the divisiveness they associated with political parties, and President George Washington railed against the evil of political parties in his Farewell Address. However, the ratification of the Constitution led to the creation of the first two American political parties, the Federalists and the anti-Federalist Democratic-Republican Party. When Andrew Jackson became the fourth president of the United States as a Democrat, his opposition organized under the Whig Party. The Whigs asserted Congress' supremacy over the president and primarily focused on economic concerns, like banking and violations.

Slavery divided the nation and created unrest among the political parties, as members took opposing views and splintered into separate sects of the party or started new parties with members who shared their views. The Whig Party, so divided by the differing views of the members, collapsed. Former Whigs joined or formed the following parties:

- Constitutional Union Party: Devoted itself to a single-issue platform of preserving the Union and recognizing the Constitution as the supreme rule of law. The party did not take a firm issue on slavery, but vigorously opposed secession.

- Democratic Party: Divided into northern and southern factions over slavery, but the Democrats sought to compromise and remain unified.

- Know-Nothing Party: Advocated for an anti-immigration single-party platform, especially immigrants from Catholic countries.

- Republican Party: Formed in response to the Kansas-Nebraska Act, which threatened to extend slavery into new territories, called for the abolition of slavery and argued for a more modernized economy.

Modern Political Parties

The defeat of the South in the Civil War resulted in the Republicans holding power until the 1930s, when Franklin D. Roosevelt, a Democrat, was elected president. Roosevelt instituted the New Deal, which included many social policies that built an expansive social welfare program to provide financial support to citizens during the Great Depression. The Republican Party opposed this interference by the government, and the two parties became more strongly divided. The political landscape again shifted during the Civil Rights Movement, as Southern Democrats fled to the Republican Party over their opposition to enforcing federal civil rights onto states. This strengthened the modern coalition between economic conservatives and social conservatives.

Today, the Democrats and Republicans are still the two major parties, though many third parties have emerged. The Republicans and Democrats hold opposing views on the degree of state intervention into private business, taxation, states' rights, and government assistance. The ideals of these parties include:

Republican (or the Grand Old Party [GOP])
- Founded by abolitionists
- Support capitalism, free enterprise, and a policy of noninterference by the government
- Support strong national defense
- Support deregulation and restrictions of labor unions
- Advocate for states' rights
- Oppose abortion
- Support traditional values, often based on Judeo-Christian foundations, including considerable opposition to same-sex marriage

Democrat
- Founded by anti-Federalists and rooted in classical Liberalism
- Promote civil rights, equal opportunity and protection under the law, and social justice
- Support government-instituted social programs and safety nets
- Support environmental issues
- Support government intervention and regulation, and advocate for labor unions
- Support universal health care

Some prominent third parties include:

- Reform Party: support political reform of the two-party system
- Green Party: support environmental causes
- Libertarian Party: support a radical policy of nonintervention and small, localized government

Interest Groups

An *interest group* is an organization with members who share similar social concerns or political interests. Members of political interest groups work together to influence policy decisions that benefit a particular segment of society or cause. Interest groups might include:

- Activist groups, like the NAACP, American Civil Liberties Union (ACLU), or People for the Ethical Treatment of Animals (PETA)
- Corporations, like pharmaceutical companies or banks
- Small-business advocates
- Religious groups, like the Concerned Women PAC and the Muslim Public Affairs Council
- Unions, such as the Association of Teacher Educators and International Brotherhood of Electrical Workers

Lobbyists

To promote their causes and influence policy in their favor, many interest groups employ *lobbyists*, paid advocates who work to influence lawmakers. Lobbying is a controversial practice, but it is sanctioned and protected as free speech. Lobbying from interest groups has a powerful impact on many policy decisions made in the United States. Examples of lobbyist groups include American Israel Public Affairs Committee (AIPAC) and Pharmaceutical Research and Manufacturers of America.

Mass Media

Mass media refers to the various methods by which the majority of the general public receives news and information. Mass media includes television, newspapers, radio, magazines, online news outlets, and social media networks. The general public relies on mass media for political knowledge and cultural socialization, as well as the majority of their knowledge of current events, social issues, and political news.

Evolution of Mass Media

- Until the end of the nineteenth century, print media such as newspapers and magazines was the only form of mass communication.

- In the 1890s, after the invention of the radio, broadcast media become a popular form of communication, particularly among illiterate people.

- In the 1940s, television superseded both print and broadcast media as the most popular form of mass media.

- In 1947, President Harry Truman gave the first political speech on television.

- In 1952, Dwight Eisenhower was the first political candidate to air campaign ads on television.

- Today, the Internet is the most widespread mass media technology, and citizens have instant access to news and information, as well as interactive platforms on which they can communicate directly with political leaders or share their views through social media, blogs, and independent news sites.

Influence of Mass Media on Politics

Mass media has a powerful effect on public opinion and politics. Mass media:

- Shapes public interests

- Enables candidates to reach voters wherever they are
- Determines what is and is not considered important in society based on how it prioritizes events and issues
- Provides the context in which to report events
- Is paid for by advertisers who may pressure news outlets to suppress or report information in their own interests

Comparative Politics and International Relations

Government is the physical manifestation of the political entity or ruling body of a state. It includes the formal institutions that operate to manage and maintain a society. The form of government does not determine the state's *economic system*, though these concepts are often closely tied. Many forms of government are based on a society's economic system. However, while the form of government refers to the methods by which a society is managed, the term *economy* refers to the management of resources in a society. Many forms of government exist, often as hybrids of two or more forms of government or economic systems. Forms of government can be distinguished based on protection of civil liberties, protection of rights, distribution of power, power of government, and principles of Federalism.

Regime is the term used to describe the political conditions under which the citizens live under the ruling body. A regime is defined by the amount of power the government exerts over the people and the number of people who comprise the ruling body. It is closely related to the form of government because the form of government largely creates the political conditions. Regimes are governmental bodies that control both the form and the limit of term of their office. For example, authoritarianism is an example of a form of government and type of regime. A regime is considered to be ongoing until the culture, priorities, and values of the government are altered, ranging from the peaceful transitions of power between democratic political parties to the violent overthrow of the current regime.

The forms of government operated by regimes of government include:

Aristocracy
An *aristocracy* is a form of government composed of a small group of wealthy rulers, either holding hereditary titles of nobility or membership in a higher class. Variations of aristocratic governments include:

- Oligarchy: form of government where political power is consolidated in the hands of a small group of people

- Plutocracy: type of oligarchy where a wealthy elite class dominates the state and society

Though no aristocratic governments exist today, it was the dominant form of government during ancient times, including the:

- Vassals and lords during the Middle Ages, especially in relation to feudalism
- City-state of Sparta in ancient Greece

Authoritarian
An authoritarian state is one in which a single party rules indefinitely. The ruling body operates with unrivaled control and complete power to make policy decisions, including the restriction of denying civil liberties such as freedom of speech, press, religion, and protest. Forms of authoritarian governments

include *autocracy*, *dictatorship*, and *totalitarian*—states or societies ruled by a single person with complete power over society.

Examples of states with authoritarian governments:

- Soviet Union
- Nazi Germany
- Modern-day North Korea

<u>Democracy</u>
Democracy is a form of government in which the people act as the ruling body by electing representatives to voice their views. Forms of democratic governments include:

- Direct democracy: democratic government in which the people make direct decisions on specific policies by majority vote of all eligible voters, like in ancient Athens

- Representative democracy: democratic government in which the people elect representatives to vote in a legislative body. This form of soft government providing for the election of representatives is also known as representative republic or indirect democracy. Representative democracy is currently the most popular form of government in the world.

The presidential and parliamentary systems are the most common forms of representative democracy. In the presidential system, the executive operates in its own distinct branch. Although the executive and legislative branches might enjoy powers checking each other, as in the American presidential system, the two functions are clearly separated. In addition, the president is typically both the head of state and head of government. Examples of presidential systems include Brazil, Nigeria, and the United States.

In the parliamentary system, the prime minister serves as the head of the government. The legislative branch, typically a parliament, elects the prime minister; thus, unlike in the presidential system, the parliament can replace the prime minister with a vote of no confidence. This practically means that the parliament has considerable influence over the office of prime minister. Parliamentary systems often include a president as the head of state, but the office is mostly ceremonial, functioning like a figurehead. Examples of parliamentary systems include Germany, Australia, and Pakistan.

The presidential system is a form of government better designed to distribute power between separate branches of government. This theoretically provides more stability. The president serves for a limited term of years, while prime ministers serve until replaced after receiving a vote of no confidence.

In the parliamentary system, the interdependence and interconnectedness between the parliament and prime minister facilitates efficient and timely governance, capable of adjusting to developing and fluid situations. In contrast, the presidential system is more prone to political gridlock because there is no direct connection between the legislative and executive branches. The legislature in a presidential system cannot replace the executive, like in the parliamentary system. The separation of powers in a presidential system can lead to disagreement between the executive and legislature, causing gridlock and other delays in governance.

Federalism is a set of principles that divides power between a central government and regional governments. Sovereign states often combine into a federation, and to do so, they cede some degree of sovereignty to establish a functional central government to handle broad national policies. The United

States Constitution structures the central government according to principles of Federalism. Canada is another example of a form of government with a Federalist structure.

Monarchy

Monarchy is a form of government in which the state is ruled by a *monarch*, typically a hereditary ruler. Monarchs have often justified their power due to some divine right to rule. Types of monarchies include:

- Absolute monarchy: a monarchy in which the monarch has complete power over the people and the state

- Constitutional monarchy: a type of monarchy in which the citizens of the state are protected by a constitution, and a separate branch, typically a parliament, makes legislative decisions. The monarch and legislature share power.

- Crowned republic: a type of monarchy in which the monarch holds only a ceremonial position and the people hold sovereignty over the state. It is defined by the monarch's lack of executive power.

Examples of monarchies:

- Kingdom of Saudi Arabia is an absolute monarchy.
- Australia is a crowned republic.

Major Types of Electoral Systems

An *electoral system* defines the procedures by which voters make decisions regarding who will rule a state and how those elected officials will make policy decisions for the state. Electoral systems dictate how the members of the ruling body are selected, how votes translate into positions, and how seats are filled in the political offices at each level of government. States use three types of electoral systems to determine the outcomes of elections: plurality, majority, and proportional representation.

Plurality

In a *plurality* electoral system, a candidate must receive a plurality, or highest percent, of votes in order to win a political seat. For example, if three candidates are running for election to a single-seat political office and Candidate A receives 37 percent, Candidate B receives 39 percent, and Candidate C receives 24 percent, Candidate B will win the seat, even though the majority of the electorate actually voted *against* them.

One benefit of a plurality electoral system is that additional rounds of voting are not required if none of the candidates receive a majority vote. However, a plurality does not reflect the majority opinion, as in the example above, where most voters voted against the winner. Plurality electoral systems often lead to a wide variety of political parties because it is possible to win without a majority.

Majority

In a majority electoral system, a candidate must receive a majority of votes in order to be awarded a seat. If none of the candidates hit the mark, another round of voting is called, also referred to as a runoff. Some states only include the two candidates with the most votes to participate in the second round, while other states only require a candidate to reach a certain threshold of votes (for example, 15 percent) in order to be included as a candidate in the second round of voting.

A benefit of majority electoral systems is that they are more representative of public opinion than a plurality, as no candidate may win if the majority has voted against them. However, until a candidate receives a vote of 50 percent plus 1, additional rounds of voting must occur, which can lead to confusion. In addition, the second round of voting can lead to the less popular candidate winning. The Twelfth Amendment of the United States mandates that if no presidential candidate wins a majority of electoral delegates, then the House determines the winner by majority vote. The House could then elect a candidate that received considerably less support in the first round, such as a third-party candidate.

Proportional Representation
A proportional representation electoral system is often used for elections in which more than one seat in a legislative body is open. Proportional representation awards seats in proportion to the percent of votes each party receives. It is most common in parliamentary systems. For example, if there are ten seats and Party A receives 40 percent, Party B receives 20 percent, Party C receives 30 percent, and Party D receives 10 percent, Party A is awarded four seats, Party B is awarded two, Party C is awarded three, and Party D is awarded one.

A benefit of proportional representation is that it is the most representative of the people. However, it requires complex procedures and formulas to allocate votes and award seats, causing some confusion in the process. There are two types of proportional representation electoral systems—party list systems and single transferable systems.

Party List Systems: This method employs the *highest average method,* in which the votes received by each party are divided based on a formula (for example, the number of seats), and the highest quotient values are used to determine which parties receive a seat. In some party list systems, the voters directly select a political party, while others pool the total vote of the candidates from the party. The political parties typically issue lists of candidates that would serve in the government if their political party wins the seats.

Single Transferable Systems: In this method, voters rank the candidates in order of preference. To determine the number of votes to qualify, a candidate must receive a number of votes equal to $[v/(s + 1)] + 1$ in which v represents the number of votes and s represents the number of seats.

The number 1 rankings are counted first, and the first candidate to receive the required votes is awarded a seat. Any further votes that ranked that candidate number 1 will instead be awarded to the candidate ranked number 2. When a second candidate receives the required votes, any votes for them will be transferred to the next candidate on the list, and so on, until all the seats are filled. In this system, if no one receives the required number of votes, the candidate with the lowest number of #1 ranking votes is dropped, and the process begins again.

Countries that use proportional representation electoral systems:

- Ireland
- Belgium

Foreign Policy
Foreign policy refers to a state's international policy governing and informing their interactions with other states. A state's foreign policy typically defines the methods they employ to safeguard the state against foreign states, the social and economic goals of the state, and how the state will achieve these goals in the global arena through their relations with foreign states. Foreign policy is typically an executive function, either through the head of state or delegated to the foreign minister.

A state's foreign policy is influenced by several factors, including:

- Public opinion
- Economic and domestic stability
- Current events
- Social and humanitarian interests

The foreign policy of the United States has changed dramatically since the Founding Fathers established a policy of isolationism, which persisted well into the nineteenth century. After World War II, the United States emerged alongside the Soviet Union as the lone remaining global support powers. The United States led Europe and her allies during the Cold War's fight against the spread of Communism. When the Cold War ended after the collapse of the Soviet Union, the United States was left as the only true superpower, enjoying an unrivaled military and one of the world's most productive economies. American foreign policy shifted toward funding sustainable development economic projects in struggling countries and supporting democracy across the globe. The United States remains the leader of the NATO and has entered into several free trade agreements, most notably the North American Free Trade Association between Mexico, America, and Canada.

The president and secretary of state of the United States determine and enforce the U.S. foreign policy. The goals of U.S. foreign policy include:

- Maintain national security
- Promote world peace
- Promote civil rights and democracy
- Ally with other states to solve international problems
- Promote global cooperation and trade

To accomplish these goals, the State Department:

- Employs foreign diplomats to meet and talk with officials from foreign countries
- Maintains U.S. embassies in foreign nations from which to practice diplomacy
- Joins and supports international organizations such as:
  - NATO
  - WTO
  - United Nations

Theories of International Relations
The study of international relations involves analyzing the methods and effectiveness of different countries' approaches to international relations. Those approaches are informed by theories of international relations. The foundational theories of international relations are Realism and Liberalism.

Realism
Realism believes that states' foreign policy is guided by principles of "realpolitik"—the idea that states' politics and foreign relations are based primarily on the specific circumstances and factors. Realism advocates for studying international relations through the inevitable conflict between states pursuing power. There are four basic tenets common to all schools of Realism.

1. States are the central actors, not individuals or international institutions.
2. There is no supreme authority guiding international relations, so the system is anarchic.

3. States act rationally to advance their self-interest.
4. All states are interested in maintaining or expanding their power as a means to self-preservation.

Liberalism
Liberalism has roots dating back to the Enlightenment, advocating for equality between states of the world. Liberals assert that global cooperation and interdependence is a force of world peace. Liberals seek to form international organizations to respond to international issues. There are three foundational principles common to all schools of Liberalism.

1. Rejects realpolitik and the assumption that conflict is the inevitable outcome for international relations

2. Supports international cooperation for the states' mutual benefit

3. Seeks to establish international organizations and nongovernmental organizations to influence states' policy decisions and respond to international issues

International Relations in Practice
Examples of practices related to the execution of states' foreign policy, and the subject of the study of international relations, include diplomacy, conflict, treaties, and cooperation.

Diplomacy is the act of meeting with officials from foreign states to:

- Discuss matters of international interest
- Foster harmonious relationships
- Organize international partnerships
- Broker agreements
- Resolve disputes

States conduct diplomacy to negotiate compromises between states; accomplish militaristic, economic, environmental, and humanitarian goals; and garner allies in case of future crisis or conflict.

Conflict
International *conflict* refers to disputes between states. If not defused with international intervention and diplomacy, conflicts often lead to violence and armed conflict. The causes of international conflict might include:

- Territorial disputes
- Economic interests
- Religious or cultural tensions
- Social or humanitarian interests
- Political differences
- Civil rights and liberties
- Struggle for power

Treaties

To promote harmonious international relations, solve disputes, or protect against foreign invasions, states enter into *treaties* with other states. Treaties resolve armed conflict, establish trade agreements, or form defense alliances by:

- Creating compromises between the states for mutual benefit because treaties are invalid when signed under coercion
- Outlining the responsibilities and benefits of membership
- Limiting the actions of the states
- Describing the consequences of breaking the treaty agreement

Cooperation

To achieve common goals, states *cooperate*, or work together. When states cooperate, they form military alliances to protect each other against other states and make trade agreements that outline how trade is conducted fairly between the states to benefit both states' economies. States form international organizations that regulate military action and trade between states. Some of the most powerful of these include:

- United Nations: a global organization created after World War II in an effort to prevent another world war, foster cooperation among the nations of the world, and protect human rights across the world

- WTO: a global organization created to encourage, regulate, and promote fair trade among the nations of the world

- NATO: an organization of states from North America and Europe, led by the United States, formed after the end of World War II to counter the Soviet Union and Warsaw Pact's efforts to spread Communism across the world

Power and Problems of International Organizations and International Law

States form *international organizations* to foster cooperation among the nations of the world. These include organizations that are dedicated to regulating trade, outlining rules for dealing with conflict among states, settling territory disputes, solving global problems, and promoting social or humanitarian efforts around the world. International organizations also develop the body of *international laws*—the rules and regulations for interactions between the states. International organizations are important for the enforcement of international agreements and treaties. Without these organizations, there would be no way to enforce obligations and rights, effectively rendering those agreements useless.

Benefits of international organizations:

- States gain a forum to discuss matters of international politics and peacefully settle disputes.

- States increase their political power and wealth by combining their power with other powerful nations.

- States collaborate to solve global issues.

- States protect each other against more powerful foreign enemies; conflict is less likely due to the threat of stronger collective action.

Problems of International Law Enforcement

International laws enacted by international organizations are difficult to enforce, as no international enforcement agency exists to ensure states abide by the rules and regulations agreed upon by the organization. As such, states are bound only by the understanding that it is in their best interest to comply with the rules of the organization, rather than out of fear of retaliation from other states, except in the most extreme cases. There are also issues related to the balance of sovereignty between international organizations and states.

The methods by which organizations can punish state members who fail to follow the rules of the organization include:

- Reciprocal action: If a state acts against another state, the offended state may reciprocate the act.

- Economic boycott: If a state fails to comply with the organization's rules, the other states may refuse to trade with the offending state.

- Damaged reputation: If a state fails to follow the rules, the organization speaks out publicly to shame the offending state; thus, other states are less likely to do future business with the violating state.

- Collective military action: If a state violates the rules of the organization to an extreme extent, such as by committing government-sanctioned genocide or interfering with the territorial integrity of another state, states and international organizations may use military force to punish the offending state.

Practice Questions

1. Which political concept describes a ruling body's ability to influence the actions, behaviors, or attitudes of a person or community?
    a. Authority
    b. Sovereignty
    c. Power
    d. Legitimacy

2. Which feature differentiates a state from a nation?
    a. Shared history
    b. Common language
    c. Population
    d. Sovereignty

3. Which political theorist considered violence necessary in order for a ruler to maintain political power and stability?
    a. John Locke
    b. Jean-Jacques Rousseau
    c. Karl Marx
    d. Niccolo Machiavelli

4. Which political theorist is considered the father of the social contract theory?
    a. John Stuart Mills
    b. Thomas Hobbes
    c. Aristotle
    d. Immanuel Kant

5. Which political orientation emphasizes maintaining traditions and stability over progress and change?
    a. Socialism
    b. Liberalism
    c. Conservatism
    d. Libertarianism

6. Which political orientation supports cooperation between states as a means to improve the quality of life for all states, nations, and people?
    a. Fascism
    b. Conservatism
    c. Anarchism
    d. Internationalism

7. Which political orientation emphasizes a strong central government and promotes violence as a means of suppressing dissent?
    a. Communism
    b. Socialism
    c. Nationalism
    d. Fascism

8. After the ratification of the Constitution, which power held by the states under the Articles of Confederation was ceded to the federal government?
    a. Power to levy taxes
    b. Power to establish courts
    c. Power to coin money
    d. Power to regulate trade

9. Under Federalism, which is considered a concurrent power held by both the states and the federal government?
    a. Hold elections
    b. Regulate immigration
    c. Expand the territories of a state
    d. Pass and enforce laws

10. Which check does the legislative branch possess over the judicial branch?
    a. Appoint judges
    b. Call special sessions of Congress
    c. Rule legislation unconstitutional
    d. Determine the number of Supreme Court judges

11. Which part of the legislative process differs in the House and the Senate?
    a. Who may introduce the bill
    b. How debates about a bill are conducted
    c. Who may veto the bill
    d. What wording the bill contains

12. Which of the following is NOT included in the Bill of Rights?
    a. Freedom to assemble
    b. Freedom against unlawful search
    c. Freedom to vote
    d. Reservation of non-enumerated powers to the states or the people

13. Which political party was founded to advocate for the abolition of slavery?
    a. Constitutional Union
    b. Southern Democrat
    c. Republican
    d. Libertarian

14. What is NOT a common characteristic of an interest group?
    a. Seeks to influence public policy
    b. Employs lobbyists
    c. Regulates trade
    d. Benefits a specific segment of society

15. Which of the following is NOT a power of the mass media?
    a. Ability to shape public opinion
    b. Ability to regulate communications
    c. Ability to influence the importance of events in society
    d. Ability to determine the context in which to report events

16. Which form of government divides power between a regional and central government?
    a. Democracy
    b. Constitutional monarchy
    c. Federalism
    d. Feudalism

17. Which form of government most limits the civil liberties of the people?
    a. Authoritarianism
    b. Communism
    c. Socialism
    d. Federal monarchy

18. Which type of electoral system is considered the most proportionate?
    a. Majority
    b. Electoral College
    c. Plurality
    d. Single transferable vote

19. The U.S. foreign policy currently includes all but which of the following goals?
    a. Prevent the spread of Communism
    b. Solve international problems
    c. Promote global cooperation
    d. Maintain national security

20. Which theory of international relations suggests that international relations are primarily influenced by states' perceptions of history, culture, and relations with foreign countries?
    a. Realism
    b. Institutionalism
    c. Liberalism
    d. Constructivism

21. Which practice of international relations most limits the sovereignty of a state?
    a. Diplomacy
    b. Foreign aid
    c. Treaty
    d. Cooperation

22. The presidential and parliamentary systems differ in which of the following ways?
    a. The presidential system establishes a separation of powers.
    b. The legislature elects the chief executive in a presidential system.
    c. Voters directly elect the prime minister in a parliamentary system.
    d. The parliamentary system never includes a president.

23. Which of the following best describes a principle of Realism in international relations?
    a. It supports international cooperation for mutual benefit.
    b. It seeks to establish international organizations and values the contributions of nongovernmental organizations.
    c. All states are interested in advancing their self-interests by expanding their power.
    d. It seeks to reduce the net conflict in the world.

24. Which of the following is NOT required to be a recognized state?
    a. A clearly defined territory with distinct borders
    b. A representative government
    c. A population with some degree of permanence
    d. A legitimate claim of authority to rule

25. The United States elects the president by which of the following ways?
    a. Popular majority vote
    b. Plurality vote
    c. Electoral College
    d. Party list system

26. In the American election system, where do the candidates ultimately receive the nomination from their party?
    a. At the primary
    b. At the caucus
    c. At the debates
    d. At the party convention

Answer Explanations

1. C: Power is the ability of a ruling body or political entity to influence the actions, behavior, and attitude of a person or group of people. Authority, Choice *A*, is the right and justification of the government to exercise power as recognized by the citizens or influential elites. Similarly, legitimacy, Choice *D*, is another way of expressing the concept of authority. Sovereignty, Choice *B*, refers to the ability of a state to determine and control their territory without foreign interference.

2. D: Sovereignty is the feature that differentiates a state from a nation. Nations have no sovereignty, as they are unable to enact and enforce laws independently of their state. A state must possess sovereignty over the population of a territory in order to be legitimized as a state. Both a nation and a state must have a population, Choice *C*. Although sometimes present, shared history and common language are not requirements for a state, making Choices *A* and *B* incorrect.

3. D: In his book, *The Prince*, Niccolo Machiavelli advocated that a ruler should be prepared to do whatever is necessary to remain in power, including using violence and political deception as a means to coerce the people of a state or eliminate political rivals. John Locke, Choice *A*, contributed and advocated liberal principles, most prominently the right to life, liberty, and health. Jean-Jacques Rousseau, Choice *B*, heavily influenced the French Revolution and American Revolution by advocating individual equality, self-rule, and religious freedom. Karl Marx, Choice *C*, wrote that the struggle between the bourgeois (ruling class) and the proletariat (working class) would result in a classless society in which all citizens commonly owned the means of production.

4. B: Thomas Hobbes is considered the father of social contract theory. In his book *Leviathan,* Hobbes advocated for a strong central government and posited that the citizens of a state make a social contract with the government to allow it to rule them in exchange for protection and security. John Stuart Mills, Choice *A*, is most commonly associated with the political philosophy of utilitarianism. Aristotle, Choice *C*, believed that man could only achieve happiness by bettering their community through noble acts, while Immanuel Kant, Choice *D*, promoted democracy and asserted that states could only achieve lasting global peace through international cooperation.

5. C: Conservatism emphasizes maintaining traditions and believes political and social stability is more important than progress and reform. In general, Socialism, Choice *A*, seeks to establish a democratically elected government that owns the means of production, regulates the exchange of commodities, and distributes the wealth equally among citizens. Liberalism, Choice *B*, is based on individualism and equality, supporting the freedoms of speech, press, and religion, while Libertarian ideals, Choice *D*, emphasize individual liberties and freedom from government interference.

6. D: Internationalism promotes global cooperation and supports strong unity between the states in order to achieve world peace and improve quality of life for all global citizens. Fascism, Choice *A*, values the strength of a state over all foreign powers and emphasizes the state over individual liberties, and Fascists typically establish an authoritarian government and consider violence necessary to suppress dissent and revitalize a struggling nation. Conservatism, Choice *B*, is focused on maintaining the traditions and political institutions within a single country. Anarchism, Choice *C*, favors a completely free society ruled by a government composed of only voluntary institutions.

7. D: Fascism considers a strong central government, martial law, and violent coercion as necessary means to maintain political stability and strengthen the state. Neither the politics of Communism, a society in which the people own the means of production, nor Socialism, a society in which the government owns the means of production, promote violence but instead advocate a classless society that eliminates the class struggle. Thus, Choices *A* and *B* are incorrect. Nationalism, Choice *C*, emphasizes preserving a nation's culture, often to the exclusion of other cultures, but violence is not officially promoted as a means for suppressing dissent, as is the case with Fascism.

8. C: Under the Constitution, the power to coin money is designated exclusively to the federal government, but both the states and the federal government maintain the power to collect taxes from the citizens under their jurisdictions and establish courts lower than the Supreme Court, though states may only establish regional courts within their states. The states reserve the right to regulate trade within their states (intrastate), while the federal government maintains the power to regulate trade between states (interstate).

9. D: Both the states and the federal government may propose, enact, and enforce laws. States pass legislation that concerns the states in their state legislative houses, while the federal government passes federal laws in Congress. Only states may hold elections and determine voting procedures, even for federal offices such as the president of the United States, and only the federal government may expand any state territory, change state lines, admit new states into the nation, or regulate immigration and pass laws regarding naturalization of citizens.

10. D: The Constitution granted Congress the power to decide how many justices should be on the court, and Congress first decided on six judges in the Judiciary Act of 1789. The Constitution granted the power to appoint judges and to call special sessions of Congress to the president. Only the Supreme Court may interpret the laws enacted by Congress and rule a law unconstitutional and subsequently overturn the law.

11. B: The process by which the House and Senate may debate a bill differs. In the House, how long a speaker may debate a bill is limited, while in the Senate, speakers may debate the bill indefinitely and delay voting on the bill by filibuster—a practice in which a speaker refuses to stop speaking until a majority vote stops the filibuster or the time for the vote passes. In both the House and the Senate, anyone may introduce a bill. Only the president of the United States may veto the bill, so neither the House nor Senate holds that power. Before the bill may be presented to the president to be signed, the wording of the bill must be identical in both houses. Another procedural difference is that the number of amendments is limited in the House but not the Senate; however, this does not appear as an answer choice.

12. C: The first ten amendments to the Constitution are collectively referred to as the Bill of Rights. The Founding Fathers did not support universal suffrage, and as such, the Bill of Rights did not encompass the freedom to vote. The Fifteenth Amendment provided that the right to vote shall not be denied on the basis of race, color, or previous condition of servitude, and women did not receive the right to vote until passage of the Nineteenth Amendment. The other three answer choices are included in the Bill of Rights—the freedom to assembly is established in the First Amendment; the freedom against unlawful search is established in the Fourth Amendment; and the reservation of non-enumerated powers to the states or the people is established in the Tenth Amendment.

13. C: The Republican Party emerged as the abolitionist party during the antebellum period and succeeded in abolishing slavery after the North's victory in the Civil War. The Constitutional Union Party supported slavery but opposed Southern secession, while the Southern Democrats supported slavery and secession. The Whig Party splintered in the 1850s as a result of tension over slavery, leading to the creation of the Republican Party and Constitutional Union Party.

14. C: While interest groups attempt to influence the legislation and organizations that regulate trade, they do not possess the authority to enact or enforce laws necessary to regulate trade. However, they may influence policy through the use of petitions, civil suits against the government, and by the practice of lobbying, in which paid lobbyists put pressure on lawmaking bodies. Interest groups form due to a common connection between the members of a group attempting to bring about change that benefits a specific segment of society, such as teachers or pharmaceutical corporations.

15. B: The mass media does not have the ability to regulate communications. The mass media has the ability to shape public opinion, making Choice *A* incorrect. Mass media selects which events to report on and thereby influences the perceived importance of events in society and determines the context in which to report events, making Choices *C* and *D* incorrect. Only the federal government may regulate communications through agencies such as the Federal Communications Commission (FCC).

16. C: Federalism divides power between regional and federal governments, and it is the form of government upon which the United States is structured, according to the Tenth Amendment. While a constitutional monarchy, Choice *B*, is typically divided between a monarch, the head of state, and a legislative body, usually a parliament, power is not reserved to the regional government. A democratic government, Choice *A*, is a government ruled by the people and does not specify division of powers. Feudalism, Choice *D*, is an economic system popular in medieval Europe where the monarchy granted the nobility land in exchange for military service, and the nobility allowed serfs to live on their land in exchange for labor or percentage of crops.

17. A: An authoritarian government is ruled by a single party that holds complete control over the powerful central government. Authoritarian governments limit political freedom and civil liberties to diminish any opposition. Communism, Choice *B*, is one in which the class struggle between the ruling and working classes is eliminated because the means of production belongs to the people. Similarly, Socialism, Choice *C*, is classless, but in this type of government, the government owns the means of production and is often democratic. Unlike a regular monarchy, a federal monarchy, Choice *D*, is a federal government in which political power is divided between the monarch (head of state) and regional governments, resulting in checks and balances of power.

18. D: Proportional electoral systems reflect the divisions in an electorate proportionately in the elected body. In single transferable vote systems, voters rank individual candidates by their preference, and the top candidates' votes are transferred to the second-place candidate, and so on, once a candidate receives the minimum votes to win a seat in the election; thus, the single transferable vote system is the most proportionate electoral system. The Electoral College is the method of electing the president of the United States. Although the Electoral College apportions a number of electors to each state according to the number of congressional seats in the state, it is not a proportional electoral system. To win a majority vote, a candidate must receive 50 percent plus 1 of the vote, so the minority's preferences are not proportionally reflected in the body. Similarly, a plurality only requires the highest percent of votes among any number of candidates, which often results in most voters voting *against* the winning candidate.

19. A: Since the Cold War ended, the U.S. foreign policy no longer centers on preventing the spread of Communism but instead focuses on promoting the ideals of democracy, promoting global cooperation through diplomacy and international organizations, and solving international problems through those channels. The U.S. foreign policy considers national security as the nation's most important goal.

20. D: The theory of constructivism is similar to Realism in that it supports the idea that a state will conduct international relations based upon their own self-interests but also posits that a state's perceptions of shared history, culture, and friends and enemies influence international relations, as well as nonofficial actors and public influence. Realism, in addition to asserting that states will act rationally to preserve their self-interest, asserts that states may only accomplish their goals by possessing superior military, economic, and political power. Institutional theory also supports the idea that states possess self-interest but believes that states may cooperate to mutually benefit each other's interests through international organizations, like the United Nations. Similarly, Liberalism focuses on how states mutually benefit through international cooperation, especially as a result of participation in international and nongovernmental organizations, and the theory rejects political power as the sole possible outcome of international relations.

21. C: A treaty is an agreement between states or groups of states that functions like a contract by binding the participants to the agreed-upon terms. Examples of treaties include peace treaties, trade agreements, and military defense pacts. Participating states give up some degree of sovereignty, as they are bound to the terms of the treaty until it's revoked, in exchange for the desired benefit. Cooperation and diplomacy, Choices *A* and *D*, are essential for the formation of treaties, but they do not involve the same degree of limiting the ability to govern within the state. Foreign aid, Choice *B*, is a voluntary transfer of resources between countries. Although the foreign aid might be attached to terms restricting the aid beneficiary's government, treaties always involve exchanging some degree of internal sovereignty for the treaty's intended mutual benefit; thus, treaties is the best answer.

22. A: The presidential system establishes a separation of powers. In the presidential system, voters directly elect the chief executive, and the presidential system establishes a separation of powers between different branches of government. In contrast, the parliament elects the chief executive, and the increased collaboration and dependency creates a more responsive government. Choices *B* and *C* confuse how the executive is elected in each system. Choice *D* is incorrect because many parliamentary systems include a president, though the status of head of state is often purely ceremonial.

23. C: Realism focuses on how states pursue their self-interest and asserts that the international system inevitably leads to conflict. Realism necessarily assumes that all states are interested in advancing their self-interests by expanding their power. In contrast, Liberalism advocates for equality between states and supports international and nongovernmental organizations' role in international relations. Choices *A* and *B* describe principles of Liberalism. Choice *D* is factually incorrect and more closely associated with Liberalism.

24. B: There are four requirements for a political entity to be recognized as a state—territory, population, legitimacy, and sovereignty. Choices *A, B,* and *D* accurately assert requirements for statehood. Although representative government is the most common form of government in states, it is not a requirement to be a state. Some form of government is required to meet the legitimacy and sovereignty criteria, but it does not necessarily need to be representative.

25. C: The president of the United States is elected by the Electoral College. The number of electors for each state depends on the state's total number of senators and representatives. The president must receive a majority (270) of the electoral votes (538), and if this doesn't occur, the Twelfth Amendment empowers the House of Representatives to elect the president. Choices *A, B,* and *C* are different methods for electing candidates.

26. D: The two major political parties hold conventions to nominate their presidential candidate. The delegates are awarded based on candidates' performance in the primary elections or caucuses vote at the party convention to select the nominee. Primaries and caucuses are the democratic contests held by each state to award their delegates. The candidates participate in debates on the campaign issues, but they do not receive the nomination at debates.

Geography

Map Types and Projections

Geographers utilize a variety of different maps in their study of the spatial world. Projections are maps that represent the entire world (which is spherical) on a flat surface. *Conformal projections* preserve angles locally, maintaining the shape of a small area in infinitesimal circles of varying sizes on a two-dimensional map. Conformal projections tend to possess inherent flaws due to their two-dimensional nature. For example, the most well-known projection, the *Mercator projection*, drastically distorts the size of land areas at the poles. In this particular map, Antarctica, one of the smallest continents, appears massive, almost rivaling the size of North America. In contrast to the poles, the areas closer to the central portion of the globe are more accurate. Other projections attempt to lessen the amount of distortion; the *Equal-area projection*, for example, attempts to equally represent the size of landforms on the globe. Nevertheless, equal-area projections like the *Lambert projection* also inherently alter the size of continents, islands, and other landforms, both close to Earth's center and near the poles. Other projections are a hybrid of the two primary models. For example, the *Robinson projection*, also referred to as the *Goode's homolosine projection*, tries to balance form and area in order to create a more visually accurate representation of the spatial world. Despite the efforts to maintain consistency with shapes, projections cannot provide accurate representations of the Earth's surface, due to their flat, two-dimensional nature. In this sense, projections are useful symbols of space, but they do not always provide the most accurate portrayal of spatial reality.

Unlike projections, *topographic maps* display contour lines, which represent the relative elevation of a particular place and are very useful for surveyors, engineers, and/or travelers. Hikers of the Appalachian Trail or Pacific Crest Trail, for instance, may call upon topographic maps to calculate their daily climbs.

Thematic maps are also quite useful to geographers because they use two-dimensional surfaces to convey complex political, physical, social, cultural, economic, or historical themes.

Thematic maps can be broken down into different subgroups: *dot-density maps* and *flow-line maps*. A *dot-density map* is a type of thematic map that illustrates the volume and density in a particular area. Although most dots on these maps represent the number of people in an area, they don't always have to do that. Instead, these maps may represent the number of events, such as lightning strikes, that have taken place in an area. *Flow-line maps* are another type of thematic map, which utilize both thin and thick lines to illustrate the movement of goods, people, or even animals between two places. The thicker the line, the greater the number of moving elements; a thinner line would, of course, represent a smaller number.

Similar to topographic maps, an *isoline map* is also useful for calculating data and differentiating between the characteristics of two places. In an *isoline map*, symbols represent values, and lines can be drawn between two points in order to determine differences. For example, average temperature is commonly measured on isoline maps. Point A, which is high in the mountains, may have a value of 33 degrees, while point B, which is in the middle of the Mojave Desert, may have a value of 105 degrees. Using the different values, it is easy to determine that temperatures in the mountains are 72 degrees cooler than in the desert. Additionally, isoline maps help geographers study the world by creating questions. For example, is it only elevation that is responsible for the differences in temperature? If not, what other factors could cause such a wide disparity in the two values? Utilizing these, and other sorts of maps, is essential in the study of geography.

Using Mental Maps to Organize Spatial Information

Mental maps are exactly what they sound like—maps that exist within someone's mind. The cognitive image of a particular place may differ from person to person, but the concept of remembering important places does not. For example, the commonalities usually emerge relative to the knowledge of one's workplace, school, home, or favorite restaurants. Furthermore, mental maps also embody the means of travelling from point A to point B. One may know the best route on public transit, the least hilly bike path, or the roadways that have the least amount of traffic. In places where someone has very little interaction, mental maps usually tend to be minimally informative, due to the absence of any personal experience in a particular place.

Maps are also organized through scale. Scale is simply the ratio of a distance on the ground to the corresponding distance on paper. Geographers and cartographers attempt to make the image on paper representative of the actual place. For example, the United States Geological Survey (USGS) utilizes the mathematical ratio of 1/24,000 in all of its topographical maps. This scale means that one inch on the map is equivalent to 24,000 inches—or nearly two-thirds of a mile—on the ground. The two primary types of maps, *large scale* and *small scale*, essentially serve the same purpose, but for two different types of places. Large-scale maps represent a much smaller area with greater detail, while small-scale maps are representative of much larger areas with less detail.

Recognizing and Interpreting Spatial Patterns Presented at Different Scales from Local to Global

Two primary realms exist within the study of geography. The first realm, *physical geography*, essentially correlates with the land, water, and foliage of the Earth. The second realm, *human geography*, is the study of the Earth's people and how they interact with their environment. Like land and water on Earth, humans are also impacted by different forces such as culture, history, sociology, technological advancement and changes, and access to natural resources. For example, human populations tend to be higher around more reliable sources of fresh water. The metropolitan area of New York City, which has abundant freshwater resources, is home to nearly 20 million people, whereas Australia, both a continent and a country, has almost the same population. Although water isn't the only factor in this disparity, it certainly plays a role in a place's *population density*—the total number of people in a particular place divided by the total land area, usually square miles or square kilometers. Australia's population density stands at 8.13 people per square mile, while the most densely populated nation on Earth, Bangladesh, is home to 2,894 people per square mile.

Population density can have a devastating impact on both the physical environment/ecosystem and the humans who live within the environment/ecosystem of a particular place. For example, Delhi, one of India's most populated cities, is home to nearly five million gasoline-powered vehicles. Each day, those vehicles emit an enormous amount of carbon monoxide into the atmosphere, which directly affects the quality of life of Delhi's citizens. In fact, the problem of the smog and pollution has gotten so severe that many drivers are unable to see fifty feet in front of them. Additionally, densely populated areas within third-world nations, or developing nations, struggle significantly in their quest to balance the demands of the modern economy with their nation's lack of infrastructure. For example, nearly as many automobiles operate every day in major American cities like New York and Los Angeles as they do in Delhi, but they create significantly less pollution due to cleaner burning engines, better fuels, and governmental emission regulations.

Although it's a significant factor, population density is not the only source of strain on the resources of a particular place. Historical forces such as civil war, religious conflict, genocide, and government corruption can also alter the lives of a nation's citizens in a profound manner. For example, the war-torn nation on the Horn of Africa, Somalia, has not had a functioning government for nearly three decades. As a result, the nation's citizens have virtually no access to hospital care, vaccinations, or proper facilities for childbirth. Due to these and other factors, the nation's *infant mortality rate*, or the total number of child deaths per 1,000 live births, stands at a whopping 98.39/1000. When compared to Iceland's 1.82/1000, it's quite evident that Somalia struggles to provide basic services in the realm of childbirth and there is a dire need for humanitarian assistance.

Literacy rates, like the infant mortality rate, are also an excellent indicator of the relative level of development in a particular place. Like Somalia, other developing nations have both economic and social factors that hinder their ability to educate their own citizens. Due to radical religious factions within some nations like Afghanistan and Pakistan, girls are often denied the ability to attend school, which further reduces the nation's overall literacy rate. For example, girls in Afghanistan, which spent decades under Taliban control, have a 24.2 percent literacy rate, one of the lowest rates of any nation on Earth that keeps records (Somalia's government is so dysfunctional records don't exist). Although literacy rates are useful in determining a nation's development level, high literacy rates do exist within developing nations. For example, Suriname, which has a significantly lower GDP (Gross Domestic Product) than Afghanistan, enjoys a nearly 96 percent literacy rate among both sexes. Utilizing this and other data, geographers can create questions regarding how such phenomena occur. How is Suriname able to educate its population more effectively with fewer financial resources? Is it something inherent within their culture? Demographic data, such as population density, the infant mortality rate, and the literacy rate all provide insight into the characteristics of a particular place and help geographers better understand the spatial world.

Locating and Using Sources of Geographic Data

Geographic data is essential to fully understanding both the spatial and human realms of geography. In reference to the human population, different factors affect the quality of life one experiences during their lifetime. Geographers attempt to understand why those differences exist through data utilization and comparative analysis. For example, as has been previously mentioned, population density, infant mortality rates, and literacy rates are all useful tools in analyzing human characteristics of a place; however, those are not the only tools geographers utilize. In fact, organizations such as the *Population Reference Bureau* and the *Central Intelligence Agency* both provide an incredible amount of *demographic* data useful to researchers, students, or really anyone curious about the world in which they live.

The *CIA World Factbook* is an indispensable resource for anyone interested in the field of human or physical geography. Providing information such as land area, literacy rates, birth rate, and economic data, this resource is one of the most comprehensive on the Internet. In addition to the CIA World Factbook, the *Population Reference Bureau* (PRB) also provides students of geography with an abundant supply of information. In contrast to the CIA source, the *PRB* provides a treasure trove of analyses related to human populations including HIV rates, immigration rates, poverty rates, etc.

In addition to the aforementioned sources, the *United States Census Bureau* provides similar information about the dynamics of the American population. Not only does this source focus on the data geographers need to understand the world, but it also provides information about upcoming classes, online workshops, and even includes an online library of resources for both students and teachers.

Websites for each source can be found below:

- Population Reference Bureau: www.prb.org
- United States Census Bureau: www.census.gov
- CIA World Factbook: https://www.cia.gov/library/publications/the-world-factbook/

Spatial Concepts

Location is the central theme in understanding spatial concepts. In geography, there are two primary types of locations that people utilize on a daily basis. The first type, *relative location*, is used frequently and involves locating objects by notating their proximity to another, better known object. For example, directions from person to person may relate directly to massive shopping centers, major highways, or well-known intersections. Although relative location is important, in the modern world, it's common to use digital satellite-based technologies, which rely on *GPS (Global Positioning System)*. To determine *Absolute Location*, or the exact latitudinal and longitudinal position on the globe, GPS uses sensors that interact with satellites orbiting the Earth. *Coordinates* correspond with the positions on a manmade grid system using imaginary lines known as *latitude* (also known as *parallels*) and *longitude* (also known as *meridians*).

In order to understand latitude and longitude, one should think of a simple X and Y-axis. The *equator* serves as the X-axis at zero degrees, and measures distance from north to south. The Y-axis is at zero degrees and is represented by the *Prime Meridian*.

In addition to anchoring the grid system to create the basis for absolute location, these major lines of latitude and longitude also divide the Earth into *hemispheres*. The Equator divides the Earth into the northern and southern hemispheres, while the Prime Meridian establishes the eastern and western hemispheres. Coordinates are always expressed in the following format:

Degrees north or south, degrees east or west, or 40°N, 50°E. Since lines of latitude and longitude are great distance from one another, absolute locations are often found in between two lines. In those cases, degrees are broken down into *minutes* and *seconds*, which are expressed in this manner: (40° 53' 44" N, 50° 22' 65" E).

In addition to the Equator and the Prime Meridian, other major lines of latitude and longitude exist to divide the world into regions relative to the direct rays of the sun. These lines correspond with the

Earth's *tilt*, and are responsible for the seasons. For example, the northern hemisphere is tilted directly toward the sun from June 22 to September 23, which creates the summer season in that part of the world. Conversely, the southern hemisphere is tilted away from the direct rays of the sun and experiences winter during those same months.

The transitions from season to season involve two factors: the 23 ½ degree tilt of the Earth and the movement of the direct rays of the sun relative to the Earth's revolution. To clarify, the area between the *Tropic of Cancer* (23 ½ degrees north) and the *Tropic of Capricorn* (23 ½ degrees south) can be envisioned as the playing field for the direct rays of the sun. These rays never leave the playing field, and, as a result, the area between those two lines of latitude—the *tropics*—tends to be warmer and experience fewer variations in seasonal temperatures. In contrast, the area between the Tropic of Cancer and the *Arctic Circle* (66 ½ degrees north) is in the *middle latitudes*—the region where most of the Earth's population resides. In the Southern Hemisphere, the middle latitudes exist between the Tropic of Capricorn and the *Antarctic Circle* (66 ½ degrees south). In both of these places, indirect rays of the sun strike the Earth, so seasons are more pronounced and milder temperatures generally prevail. The final region, known as the *high latitudes*, is found north of the Arctic Circle and south of the Antarctic Circle. These regions generally tend to be cold all year, and experience nearly twenty-four hours of sunlight during their respective *summer solstice* and twenty-four hours of darkness during the *winter solstice*.

Regarding the seasons, it is important to understand that those in the Southern Hemispheres are opposite of those in the Northern Hemisphere, due to the position of the direct rays of the sun. When the sun's direct rays are over the Equator, it is known as an *equinox*, and day and night are almost of equal length throughout the world. Equinoxes occur twice a year; the fall, or autumnal equinox, occurs on September 22nd, while the spring equinox occurs on March 20th. Obviously, if seasons are opposite of one another depending on the hemisphere, the corresponding names flip-flop depending on one's location (i.e. when the Northern Hemisphere is experiencing summer, it is winter in the Southern Hemisphere).

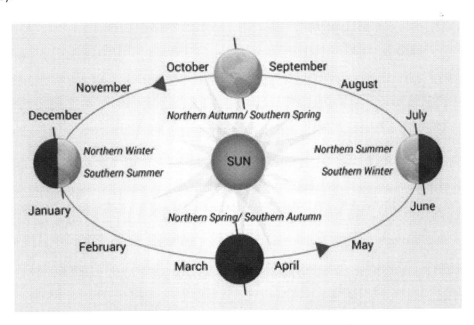

Place

Both absolute and relative location help humans understand their sense of place. Place is a simple concept that helps to define the characteristics of the world around us. For example, people may create *toponyms* to further define and orient themselves with their sense of place. Toponyms are simply names given to locations to help develop familiarity within a certain location. Although not always the case, toponyms generally utilize geographical features, important people in an area, or even wildlife commonly found in a general location. For example, many cities in the state of Texas are named in honor of military leaders who fought in the Texas Revolution of 1836 (such as Houston and Austin), while other places, such as Mississippi and Alabama, utilize Native American toponyms to define their sense of place.

Regions

In addition to location and place, geographers also divide the world into regions in order to more fully understand differences inherent with the world, its people, and its environment. As mentioned previously, lines of latitude such as the Equator, the Tropics, and the Arctic and Antarctic Circles already divide the Earth into solar regions relative to the amount of either direct or indirect sunlight that they receive. Although not the same throughout, the middle latitudes generally have a milder climate than areas found within the tropics. Furthermore, tropical locations are usually warmer than places in the middle latitudes, but that is not always the case. For example, the lowest place in the United States—Death Valley, California—is also home to the nation's highest-ever recorded temperature. Likewise, the Andes Mountains in Peru and Ecuador, although found near the Equator, are also home to heavy snow, low temperatures, and dry conditions, due to their elevation.

Formal regions are spatially defined areas that have overarching similarities or some level of *homogeneity* or *uniformity*. Although not exactly alike, a formal region generally has at least one characteristic that is consistent throughout the entire area. For example, the United States could be broken down into one massive formal region due to the fact that in all fifty states, English is the primary language. Of course, English isn't the only language spoken in the United States, but throughout that nation, English is heavily used. As a result, geographers are able to classify the United States as a formal region; but, more specifically, the United States is a *linguistic region*—a place where everyone generally speaks the same language.

Functional regions are similar to formal regions in that they have similar characteristics, but they do not have clear boundaries. The best way to understand these sorts of regions is to consider large cities. Each large city encompasses a large *market area,* whereby people in its vicinity generally travel there to conduct business, go out to eat, or watch a professional sporting event. However, once anyone travels farther away from that *primate city*, they transition to a different, more accessible city for their needs. The functional region, or *area of influence*, for that city, town, or sports team transitions, depending upon the availability of other primate cities. For example, New York City has two primary professional baseball, basketball, and football teams. As a result, its citizens may have affinities for different teams even though they live in the same city. Conversely, a citizen in rural Idaho may cheer for the Seattle Seahawks, even though they live over 500 miles from Seattle, due to the lack of a closer primate city.

Effects of Physical Processes, Climate Patterns, and Natural Hazards on Human Societies

The Earth's surface, like many other things in the broader universe, does not remain the same for long; in fact, it changes from day to day. The Earth's surface is subject to a variety of physical processes that continue to shape its appearance. In each process, water, wind, temperature, or sunlight play a role in continually altering the Earth's surface.

Erosion can be caused by a variety of different stimuli including ice, snow, water, wind, and ocean waves. *Wind erosion* is a specific phenomenon that occurs in generally flat, dry areas with loose topsoil. Over time, the persistent winds can dislodge significant amounts of soil into the air, reshaping the land and wreaking havoc on those who depend on agriculture for their livelihoods. Erosion can also be caused by water and is responsible for changing landscapes as well. For example, the Grand Canyon was carved over thousands of years by the constant movement of the Colorado River. Over time, the river moved millions of tons of soil, cutting a huge gorge in the Earth along the way. In all cases, erosion involves the movement of soil from one place to another. In water erosion, material carried by the water is referred to as *sediment*. With time, some sediment can collect at the mouths of rivers, forming *deltas*, which become small islands of fertile soil. This process of detaching loose soils and transporting them to a different location where they remain for an extended period of time is referred to as *deposition*, and is the end result of the erosion process.

In contrast to erosion, *weathering* does not involve the movement of any outside stimuli. In this physical process, the surface of the Earth is either broken down physically or chemically. *Physical weathering* involves the effects of atmospheric conditions such as water, ice, heat, or pressure. Through the process of weathering over the course of centuries, large rocks can be broken down with the effects of icy conditions. *Chemical weathering* generally occurs in warmer climates and involves organic material that breaks down rocks, minerals, or soil. This process is what scientists believe led to the creation of fossil fuels such as oil, coal, and natural gas.

Climate Patterns

Weather is defined as the condition of the Earth's atmosphere at a particular time. *Climate* is different; instead of focusing on one particular day, climate is the relative pattern of weather in a place for an extended period of time. For example, the city of Atlanta is in the American South and generally has a humid subtropical climate; however, Atlanta also occasionally experiences snowstorms in the winter months. Despite the occasional snow and sleet storm, over time, geographers, meteorologists, and other Earth scientists have determined the patterns that are indicative to north Georgia, where Atlanta is located. Almost all parts of the world have predictable climate patterns, which are influenced by the surrounding geography.

The Central Coast of California is an example of a place with a predictable climate pattern. Santa Barbara, California, one of the region's larger cities, has almost the same temperature for most of the summer, spring, and fall, with only minimal fluctuation during the winter months. The temperatures there, which average between 75 and 65 degrees Fahrenheit daily regardless as to the time of year, are influenced by a variety of different climatological factors including elevation, location relative to the mountains and ocean, and ocean currents. In the case of Santa Barbara, the city's location on the Pacific Coast and its position near mountains heavily influences its climate. The cold California current, which sweeps down the west coast of the United States, causes the air near the city to be temperate, while the mountains trap cool air over the city and the surrounding area. This pattern, known as the *orographic effect*, or *rain shadow*, also affects temperatures on the leeward side of the mountains by blocking most of the cool air and causing dry conditions to dominate. Temperatures can fluctuate by more than 20 degrees Fahrenheit on opposite sides of the mountain.

Other factors affecting climate include elevation, prevailing winds, vegetation, and latitudinal position on the globe.

Like climate, *natural hazards* also affect human societies. In tropical and subtropical climates, hurricanes and typhoons form over warm water and can have devastating effects. Additionally, tornadoes, which are powerful cyclonic windstorms, also are responsible for widespread destruction in many parts of the United States and in other parts of the world. Like storms, earthquakes, usually caused by shifting plates along faults deep below the Earth's surface, also cause widespread devastation, particularly in nations with a poor or crumbling infrastructure. For example, San Francisco, which experiences earthquakes regularly due to its position near the San Andreas Fault, saw relatively little destruction and deaths (67 total) as a result of the last major earthquake to strike there. However, in 2010, an earthquake of similar magnitude reportedly killed over 200,000 people in the western hemisphere's poorest nation, Haiti. Although a variety of factors may be responsible for the disparity, modern engineering methods and better building materials most likely helped to minimize destruction in San Francisco. Other natural hazards, such as tsunamis, mudslides, avalanches, forest fires, dust storms, flooding, volcanic eruptions, and blizzards, also affect human societies throughout the world.

Characteristics and Spatial Distribution of Earth's Ecosystems

Earth is an incredibly large place filled with a variety of different land and water *ecosystems*. *Marine ecosystems* cover over 75 percent of the Earth's surface and contain over 95 percent of the Earth's water. Marine ecosystems can be broken down into two primary subgroups: *freshwater ecosystems*, which only encompass around 2 percent of the earth's surface; and *ocean ecosystems*, which make up over 70 percent. On land, *terrestrial ecosystems* vary depending on a variety of factors, including latitudinal distance from the equator, elevation, and proximity to mountains or bodies of water. For example, in the high latitudinal regions north of the Arctic Circle and south of the Antarctic Circle, frozen *tundra* dominates. Tundra, which is characterized by low temperatures, short growing seasons, and minimal vegetation, is only found in regions that are far away from the direct rays of the sun.

In contrast, *deserts* can be found throughout the globe and are created by different ecological factors. For example, the world's largest desert, the Sahara, is almost entirely within the tropics; however, other deserts like the Gobi in China, the Mojave in the United States, and the Atacama in Chile, are the result of the orographic effect and their close proximity to high mountain ranges such as the Himalayas, the Sierra Nevada, and the Andes, respectively. In the Middle Latitudes, greater varieties of climatological zones are more common due to fluctuations in temperatures relative to the sun's rays, coupled with the particular local topography. In the Continental United States, *temperate deciduous forest* dominates the southeastern portion of the country. However, the Midwestern states such as Nebraska, Kansas, and the Dakotas, are primarily *grasslands*. Additionally, the states of the Rocky Mountains can have decidedly different climates relative to elevation. In Colorado, Denver, also known as the "Mile High City," will often see snowfalls well into late April or early May due to colder temperatures, whereas towns and cities in the eastern part of the state, with much lower elevations, may see their last significant snowfall in March.

In the tropics, which are situated between the Tropics of Cancer and Capricorn, temperatures are generally warmer, due to the direct rays of the sun's persistence. However, like most of the world, the tropics also experience a variety of climatological regions. In Brazil, Southeast Asia, Central America, and even Northern Australia, tropical rainforests are common. These forests, which are known for abundant vegetation, daily rainfall, and a wide variety of animal life, are absolutely essential to the health of the world's ecosystems. For example, the *Amazon Rain Forest* is also referred to as "the lungs of the world," as its billions of trees produce substantial amounts of oxygen and absorb an equivalent amount of carbon dioxide—the substance that many climatologists assert is causing climate change or *global warming*. Unlike temperate deciduous forests whose trees lose their leaves during the fall and winter months, *tropical rain forests* are always lush, green, and warm. In fact, some rainforests are so dense with vegetation that a few indigenous tribes have managed to exist within them without being influenced by any sort of modern technology, virtually maintaining their ancient way of life in the modern era.

The world's largest ecosystem, the *taiga*, is found primarily in high latitudinal areas, which receive very little of the sun's indirect rays. These forests are generally made up of *coniferous* trees, which do not lose their leaves at any point during the year as *deciduous* trees do. Taigas are cold-climate regions that make up almost 30 percent of the world's land area. These forests dominate the northern regions of Canada, Scandinavia, and Russia, and provide the vast majority of the world's lumber.

Overall, it is important to remember that climates are influenced by five major factors: elevation, latitude, proximity to mountains, ocean currents, and wind patterns. For example, the cold currents off the coast of California provide the West Coast of the United States with pleasant year-round temperatures. Conversely, Western Europe, which is at the nearly the same latitude as most of Canada, is influenced by the warm waters of the *Gulf Stream*, an ocean current that acts as a conveyor belt, moving warm tropical waters to the icy north. In fact, the Gulf Stream's influence is so profound that it even keeps Iceland—an island nation in the far North Atlantic—relatively warm.

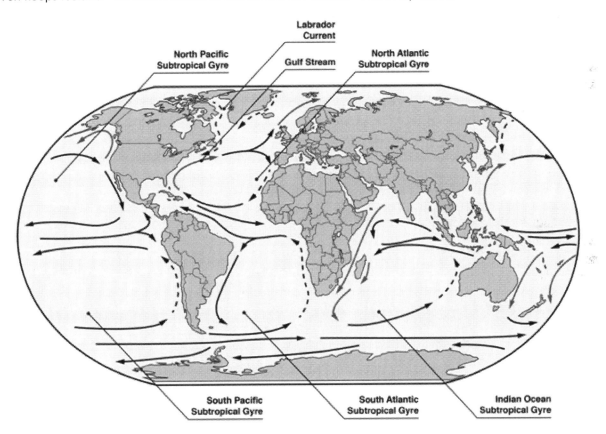

Interrelationships Between Humans and Their Environment

Like any other animal, humans adapt to their environment; but, unlike other animals, humans also adapt their environment to suit their needs. For example, human social systems are created around the goal of providing people with access to what they need to live more productive, fulfilling, and meaningful lives. Sometimes, humans create systems that are destructive, but generally speaking, humans tend to use their environment to make their lives easier. For example, in warmer climates, people tend to wear more comfortable clothing such as shorts, linen shirts, and hats. Additionally, in the excessively sun-drenched nations of the Middle East, both men and women wear flowing white clothing complete with both a head and neck covering, in order to prevent the blistering effects of sun exposure to the skin. Likewise, the native Inuit peoples of northern Canada and Alaska use the thick furs from the animals they kill to insulate their bodies against the bitter cold.

Humans also adapt to their environment to ensure that they have access to enough food and water for survival. Irrigation, or the process of moving water from its natural location to where it's needed, is an example of how humans change their environment in order to survive. For example, the city of Los Angeles, America's second most populous city, did not have adequate freshwater resources to sustain its population. However, city and state officials realized that abundant water resources existed approximately three hundred miles to the east. Rather than relocating some of its population to areas with more abundant water resources, the State of California undertook one of the largest construction projects in the history of the world, the Los Angeles Aqueduct, which is a massive concrete irrigation ditch connecting water-rich areas with the thirsty citizens of Los Angeles.

The Los Angeles Aqueduct is just one example of a human-environment interaction. In other cases, humans utilize what nature provides in close proximity. For example, the very first permanent British Colony in North America, Jamestown, VA, was heavily influenced by its environment. In contrast to the Pilgrims who settled in Plymouth, Massachusetts, Jamestown settlers found themselves in a hot, humid climate with fertile soil. Consequently, its inhabitants engaged in agriculture for both food and profit. Twelve years after Jamestown's foundation in 1607, it was producing millions of dollars of tobacco each year. In order to sustain this booming industry, over time, millions of African slaves and indentured servants from Europe were imported to provide labor. Conversely, the poor soils around Plymouth did not allow for widespread cash crop production, and the settlers in New England generally only grew enough food for themselves on small subsistence farms. Furthermore, slavery failed to take a strong foothold in the New England states, thus creating significantly different cultures within the same country, all due in part to human interaction with the environment.

Renewable and Nonrenewable Resources

When gas prices are high, prices on virtually everything increase. After all, there are very few products that humans can buy that are not transported by either a gasoline- or diesel-powered engine. As a result, an increase in fuel prices leads to an increase in the price of food, goods, or other cargo. Recently, there has been considerable debate regarding the reliance on *nonrenewable resources* like oil, natural gas, and coal. These resources, which are also known as *fossil fuels*, are quite common throughout the world and are generally abundant, and cheaper to use than *renewable resources* like solar, wind, and geothermal energy. While solar energy is everywhere, the actual means to convert the sun's rays into energy is not. Conversely, coal-fired power plants and gasoline-powered engines, which are older technologies in use during the industrial revolution, remain quite common throughout the world. In fact, reliance on non-renewable resources continues to grow, due to the availability coupled with the existing infrastructure. However, use of renewable energy is increasing, as it becomes more economically competitive with nonrenewable resources.

In addition to sources of energy, nonrenewable resources also include anything that can be exhausted. These can include precious metals like gold, silver, and platinum, freshwater underground aquifers, and precious stones such as diamonds, emeralds, and opals. Although abundant, most nonrenewable sources of energy are not sustainable because their creation takes millions of years and can therefore not be reproduced. Renewable resources are sustainable, but must be properly overseen so that they remain renewable. For example, the beautiful African island of Madagascar is home to some of the most amazing rainforest trees in the world. As a result, logging companies cut, milled, and sold thousands of them in order to make quick profits without planning how to ensure the continued health of the forests. As a result of severe deforestation on the island, mudslides became more and more common as the forests gradually shrank from widespread logging. In this case, renewable resources were mismanaged, and thus essentially became nonrenewable, due to the length of time for growth for the replacement of rainforest trees. In the United States, paper companies harvest pine trees to create paper; and because it can take almost twenty years for a pine tree to reach maturity, most of the companies utilize planning techniques to ensure that mature pine trees will always be available. In this manner, these resources remain renewable for human use in a sustainable fashion.

Renewable sources of energy are relatively new in the modern economy. Even though electric cars, wind turbines, and solar panels are becoming more common, they still do not provide enough energy to power the world's economy. As a result, reliance on older, reliable forms of energy continues, which has a devastating effect on the environment. Beijing, China, which has seen a massive boom in industrial jobs, is also one of the most polluted places on Earth. Furthermore, developing nations with very little modern infrastructure also rely heavily on fossil fuels, due to the ease in which they are converted into usable energy. Even the United States, which has one of the most developed infrastructures in the world, still relies almost exclusively on fossil fuels, with only ten percent of the required energy coming from renewable sources.

Spatial Patterns of Cultural and Economic Activities

Spatial patterns refer to where things are in the world. Biomes, regions, and landforms all have spatial patterns regarding where they exist. Additionally, elements of *human geography*—the study of human culture and its effect on the world—also have certain patterns regarding where they appear on Earth.

Ethnicity

An ethnic group, or ethnicity, is essentially a group of people with a common language, society, culture, or ancestral heritage. Different ethnicities developed over centuries through historical forces, the impact of religious traditions, and other factors. Thousands of years ago, it was more common for ethnic groups to remain in one area with only the occasional interaction with outside groups. In the modern world, different ethnicities interact on a daily, if not hourly, basis, due to better transportation resources and the processes of globalization. For example, in the United States, it is not uncommon for a high school classroom to encompass people of Asian, African, Indian, European, or Native descent. That's not to suggest that all American classrooms have ethnic diversity, but, in general, due to a variety of pull-factors, the United States continues to attract people from all over the world. In less developed parts of the world, travel is limited due to the lack of infrastructure. Consequently, ethnic groups develop in small areas that can differ greatly from other people just a few miles away. For example, on the Balkan Peninsula in southeastern Europe, a variety of different ethnic groups live in close proximity to one another. Croats, Albanians, Serbs, Bosnians, and others all share the same land, but have very different worldviews, traditions, and religious influences. In the case of the Balkan Peninsula, such diversity has not always been a positive characteristic. For example, the First World War began there in 1914 related to a dispute regarding Serbia's national independence. Additionally, Bosnia was the scene of a horrible genocide against Albanians in an "ethnic cleansing" effort that continued throughout the late 20th century.

Linguistics

Linguistics, or the study of language, groups certain languages together according to their commonalities. For example, the Romance Languages—French, Spanish, Italian, Romansh, and

Portuguese—all share language traits from Latin, the language of the former Roman Empire. These languages, also known as *vernaculars*, or more commonly spoken *dialects*, evolved over centuries of physical isolation on the European continent. The Spanish form of Latin emerged into today's Spanish language. In other parts of the world, the same pattern is true. The Bantu people of Africa travelled extensively and spread their language, now called *Swahili*, which is the first Pan-African language. When thinking of the world as a whole, it is important to understand that thousands of languages exist; however, to interconnect the world, it is important to have a means of communication with which everyone is at least somewhat familiar. A *lingua franca* is essentially the language of business. In other words, when executives from multinational corporations need to communicate regarding business, they often communicate in English, which is considered to be the world's lingua franca, due to the economic dominance of the United States.

Religion

Religion has played a tremendous role in creating the world's cultures. Devout Christians crossed the Atlantic in hopes of finding religious freedom in New England, Muslim missionaries and traders travelled to the Spice Islands of the East Indies to teach about the Koran, and Buddhist monks traversed the Himalayan Mountains into Tibet to spread their faith. In some countries, religion helps to shape legal systems. These nations, termed *theocracies*, have no separation of church and state and are more common in Islamic nations such as Saudi Arabia, Iran, and Qatar. In contrast, even though religion has played a tremendous role in the history of the United States, its government remains *secular*, or nonreligious, due to the influence of European Enlightenment philosophy at the time of its inception. Like ethnicity and language, religion is also a primary way that people self-identify. As a result, religious influences can shape a region's laws, architecture, literature, and music. For example, when the Ottoman Turks, who are Muslim, conquered Constantinople, which was once the home of the Eastern Orthodox Christian Church, they replaced Christian places of worship with mosques. Additionally, different forms of Roman architecture were replaced with those influenced by Arabic traditions.

Economics

Economic activity also has a spatial component. For example, nations with few natural resources generally tend to import what they need from nations willing to export raw materials to them. Furthermore, areas that are home to certain raw materials generally tend to alter their environment in order to maintain production of those materials. In the San Joaquin Valley of California, an area known for extreme heat and desert-like conditions, local residents have engineered elaborate drip irrigation systems to adequately water lemon, lime, olive, and orange trees, utilizing the warm temperatures to constantly produce citrus fruits. Additionally, other nations with abundant petroleum reserves build elaborate infrastructures in order to pump, house, refine, and transport their materials to nations who require gasoline, diesel, or natural gas. Essentially, different spatial regions on Earth create jobs, infrastructure, and transportation systems that seek to ensure the continued flow of goods, raw materials, and resources out of their location, so long as financial resources keep flowing into the area.

Patterns of Migration and Settlement

Migration is governed by two primary causes: *push factors*, which are reasons causing someone to leave an area, and *pull factors*, which are factors luring someone to a particular place. These two factors often work in concert with one another. For example, the United States of America has experienced significant *internal migration* from the industrial states in the Northeast (such as New York, New Jersey, Connecticut) to the Southern and Western states. This massive migration, which continues into the present-day, is due to high rents in the northeast, dreadfully cold winters, and lack of adequate retirement housing, all of which are push factors. These push factors lead to migration to the *Sunbelt*, a term geographers use to describe states with warm climates and less intense winters.

In addition to internal migrations within nations or regions, international migration also takes place between countries, continents, and other regions. The United States has long been the world's leading nation in regard to *immigration*, the process of having people come into a nation's boundaries. Conversely, developing nations that suffer from high levels of poverty, pollution, warfare, and other violence all have significant push factors, which cause people to leave and move elsewhere. This process, known as *emigration*, is when people in a particular area leave in order to seek a better life in a different—usually better—location.

The Development and Changing Nature of Agriculture

Agriculture is essential to human existence. The *Neolithic Revolution*, or the use of farming to produce food, had a profound effect on human societies. Rather than foraging and hunting for food, human societies became more stable and were able to grow due to more consistent food supplies. In modern times, farming has changed drastically in order to keep up with the increasing world population.

Until the twentieth century, the vast majority of people on Earth engaged in *subsistence farming*, or the practice of growing only enough food to feed one's self, or one's family. Over time, due to inventions such as the steel plow, the mechanical reaper, and the seed drill, farmers were able to produce more crops on the same amount of land. As food became cheaper and easier to obtain, populations grew, but rather than leading to an increase in farmers, fewer people actually farmed. After the advent of mechanized farming in developed nations, small farms became less common, and many were either abandoned or absorbed by massive commercial farms producing both foodstuffs, staple crops, and cash crops.

In recent years, agricultural practices have undergone further changes in order to keep up with the rapidly growing population. Due in part to the *Green Revolution*, which introduced the widespread use of fertilizers to produce massive amounts of crops, farming techniques and practices continue to evolve. For example, *genetically modified organisms*, or *GMOs*, are plants or animals whose genetic makeup has been modified using different strands of DNA in hopes of producing more resilient strains of staple crops, livestock, and other foodstuffs. This process, which is a form of *biotechnology*, attempts to solve the world's food production problems through the use of genetic engineering. Although these crops are abundant and resistant to pests, drought, or frost, they are also the subject of intense scrutiny. For example, the international food company, Monsanto, has faced an incredible amount of criticism regarding its use of GMOs in its products. Many activists assert that "rewiring" mother nature is inherently problematic and that foods produced through such methods are dangerous to human health. Despite the controversy, GMOs and biotechnologies continue to change the agricultural landscape by changing the world's food supply.

Like Monsanto, other agribusinesses exist throughout the world. Not only do these companies produce food for human consumption, but they also provide farming equipment, fertilizers, agrichemicals, and breeding and slaughtering services for livestock. While these companies are found all over the world, they are generally headquartered near the product they produce. For example, General Mills, a cereal manufacturer, is headquartered in the Midwestern United States, near its supply of wheat and corn—the primary ingredients in its cereals.

Contemporary Patterns and Impacts of Development, Industrialization, and Globalization

As mentioned previously, *developing nations* are nations that are struggling to modernize their economy, infrastructure, and government systems. Many of these nations may struggle to provide basic services to their citizens like clean water, adequate roads, or even police protection. Furthermore, government corruption makes life even more difficult for these countries' citizens. In contrast, *developed nations* are those who have relatively high *Gross Domestic Products (GDP)*, or the total value of all goods and services produced in the nation in a given year. To elucidate, the United States, which is one of the wealthiest nations on Earth when ranked by overall GDP, has nearly a 19 trillion dollar GDP; while Haiti, one of the poorest nations in the Western Hemisphere, has nearly a nine billion dollar GDP. This is a difference of almost seventeen trillion dollars. This is not to disparage Haiti or other developing nations; the comparison is simply used to show that extreme inequities exist in very close proximity to one another, and it may be difficult for developing nations to meet the needs of their citizens and move their economic infrastructure forward toward modernization.

In the modern world, industrialization is the initial key to modernization and development. For developed nations, the process of industrialization took place centuries ago. England, where the *Industrial Revolution* began, actually began to produce products in factories in the early 1700s. Later, the United States and some nations of Western Europe followed suit, using raw materials brought in from their colonies abroad to make finished products. For example, cotton was spun into fabric on elaborate weaving machines that mass-produced textiles. As a result, nations that perfected the textile process were able to sell their products around the world, which produced enormous profits. Over time, those nations were able to accumulate wealth, improve their nation's infrastructure, and provide more services for their citizens. Similar to the events of the eighteenth and nineteenth centuries, nations throughout the world are undergoing the same process in today's world. China exemplifies this concept. In China, agriculture was once the predominant occupation, and although it is true that agriculture is still a dominant sector of the Chinese economy, millions of Chinese citizens are flocking to major cities like Beijing, Shanghai, and Hangzhou, due to the availability of factory jobs that allow its workers a certain element of *social mobility*, or the ability to rise up out of one's socioeconomic situation.

Due to improvements in transportation and communication, the world has become figuratively smaller. For example, university students on the Indian Subcontinent now compete directly with students all over the world to obtain the skills employers desire to move their companies forward. Additionally, many corporations in developed nations have begun to *outsource* labor to nations with high levels of educational achievement but lower wage expectations. The process of opening the marketplace to all nations throughout the world, or *globalization*, has only just started to take hold in the modern economy. As industrial sites shift to the developing world, so does the relative level of opportunity for those nation's citizens. However, due to the massive amounts of pollution produced by factories, the process of globalization also has had significant ecological impacts. The most widely known impact, *climate change*, which most climatologists assert is caused by an increase of carbon dioxide in the atmosphere, remains a serious problem that has posed challenges for developing nations, who need industries in order to raise their standard of living, and developed nations, whose citizens use a tremendous amount of fossil fuels to run their cars, heat their homes, and maintain their ways of life.

Demographic Patterns and Demographic Change

Demography, or the study of human populations, involves a variety of closely related stimuli. First, as has been previously addressed, economic factors play a significant role in the movement of people, as do climate, natural disasters, or internal unrest. For example, in recent years, millions of immigrants from the war-torn country of Syria have moved as far as possible from danger. Although people are constantly moving, some consistencies remain throughout the world. First, people tend to live near reliable sources of food and water, which is why the first human civilizations sprung up in river valleys like the Indus River Valley in India, the Nile River Valley in Egypt, and the Yellow River Valley in Asia. Second, extreme temperatures tend to push people away, which is why the high latitudinal regions near the North and South Poles have such few inhabitants. Third, the vast majority of people tend to live in the Northern Hemisphere, due to the simple fact that more land lies in that part of the Earth. In keeping with these factors, human populations tend to be greater where human necessities are easily accessible, or at least more readily available. In other words, such areas have a greater chance of having a higher population density than places without such characteristics.

Demographic patterns on earth are not always stagnate. In contrast, people move and will continue to move as both push and pull factors fluctuate along with the flow of time. For example, in the 1940s, thousands of Europeans fled their homelands due to the impact of the Second World War. Today, thousands of migrants arrive on European shores each month due to conflicts in the Levant and difficult economic conditions in Northern Africa. Furthermore, as previously discussed, people tend to migrate to places with a greater economic benefit for themselves and their families. As a result, developed nations such as the United States, Germany, Canada, and Australia have a net gain of migrants, while developing nations such as Somalia, Zambia, and Cambodia generally tend to see thousands of their citizens seek better lives elsewhere.

It is important to understand the key variables in changes regarding human population and its composition worldwide. Religion and religious conflict play a role in where people choose to live. For example, the Nation of Israel won its independence in 1948 and has since attracted thousands of people of Jewish descent from all over the world. Additionally, the United States has long attracted people from all over the world, due to its promise of religious freedom inherent within its own Constitution. In contrast, nations like Saudi Arabia and Iran do not typically tolerate different religions, resulting in a decidedly uniform religious—and oftentimes ethnic—composition. Other factors such as economic opportunity, social unrest, and cost of living also play a vital role in demographic composition.

Basic Concepts of Political Geography

Nations, states, and nation-states are all terms with very similar meanings, but knowing the differences aids in a better understanding of geography. A nation is an area with similar cultural, linguistic, and historical experiences. A state is a political unit with sovereignty, or the ability to make its own decision in a particular area; and a nation-state is an entity that combines states into one, singular government system. For example, in the United States, the state of Texas is not an independent nation-state. Instead, it is part of the United States and thus, is subject to its laws. In a similar fashion, the United Kingdom encompasses four member states: England, Wales, Northern Ireland, and Scotland. Although people in those states may consider themselves to be *sovereign*, or self-governing, the reality is that those states cannot make decisions regarding international trade, declarations of war, or other important decisions regarding the rest of the world. Instead, they are *semi-autonomous*, meaning that they can make some decisions regarding how their own state is run, but must yield more major powers to a centralized authority. In the United States, this sort of system is called *Federalism*, or the sharing of power among Local, State, and Federal entities, each of whom is assigned different roles in the overall system of government.

Nation-states, and the boundaries that define where they are, are not always permanent. For example, after the fall of the Soviet Union in 1991, new nations emerged that had once been a part of the larger entity called the Union of Soviet Socialists Republics. These formerly sovereign nations were no longer forced to be a part of a unifying communist government, and as a result, they regained their autonomy and became newly independent nations that were no longer *satellite nations* of the Soviet Union. In a historical sense, the United States can be seen as a prime example of how national boundaries change. After the conclusion of the American Revolution in 1781, the Treaty of Paris defined the United States' western boundary as the Mississippi River; today, after a series of conflicts with Native American groups, the Mexican government, Hawaiian leadership, the Spanish, and the purchase of Alaska from the Russians, the boundaries of the United States have changed drastically. In a similar fashion, nations in Europe, Africa, and Asia have all shifted their boundaries due to warfare, cultural movements, and language barriers.

In the modern world, boundaries continue to change. For example, the Kurds, an ethnic minority in the Middle East, are still fighting for the right to control their people's' right to *self-determination*, but have not yet been successful in establishing a nation for themselves. In contrast, the oil-rich region of South Sudan, which has significant cultural, ethnic, and religious differences from Northern Sudan, successfully won its independence in a bloody civil war, which established the nation's newest independent nation. In recent years, Russia has made the world nervous by aggressively annexing the Crimean Peninsula, an area that has been part of the Ukraine since the end of the Cold War. Even the United Kingdom and Canada have seen their own people nearly vote for their own rights to self-determination. In 1995, the French-speaking Canadian province of Quebec narrowly avoided becoming a sovereign nation through a tightly contested referendum. In a similar fashion, Scotland, which is part of the UK, also voted to remain a part of the Crown, even though many people in that state see themselves as inherently different from those in other regions within the nation.

Political geography is constantly changing. Boundaries on maps from ten years ago are not consistent with those of 2016 and beyond. Simply looking at a map of Africa from 1950 can give one a sense of the level of change that takes place in a lifetime. For example, a map of Africa before 1950 looks completely different than a map of Africa from 2016. There are fewer European nations in the names on the 2016 map. *Decolonization*, or the removal of dependency on colonizers, has altered the political landscape of Africa, allowed more autonomy for the African people, and has forever redefined the boundaries of the entire continent.

Practice Questions

1. Which of the following is the primary problem with map projections?
   a. They are not detailed
   b. They do not include physical features
   c. They distort areas near the poles
   d. They only focus on the Northern Hemisphere

2. Which type of map illustrates the world's climatological regions?
   a. Topographic Map
   b. Conformal Projection
   c. Isoline Map
   d. Thematic Map

3. In which manner is absolute location expressed?
   a. The cardinal directions (north, south, east, and west)
   b. Through latitudinal and longitudinal coordinates
   c. Location nearest to a more well-known location
   d. Hemispherical position on the globe

4. Latitudinal lines are used to measure distance in which direction?
   a. East to west
   b. North to south
   c. Between two sets of coordinates
   d. In an inexact manner

5. Literacy rates are more likely to be higher in which area?
   a. Developing nations
   b. Northern Hemispherical Nations
   c. Developed Nations
   d. Near centers of trade

6. All are true of an area with an extremely high population density EXCEPT which of the following?
   a. Competition for resources is intense
   b. Greater strain on public services exists
   c. Most are found in rural areas
   d. Most are found in urban areas

7. All of the following are negative demographic indicators EXCEPT which of the following?
   a. High Infant Mortality Rates
   b. Low Literacy Rates
   c. High Population Density
   d. Low Life Expectancy

8. Which of the following characteristics best defines a formal region?
   a. Homogeneity
   b. Diversity
   c. Multilingualism
   d. Social Mobility

9. Which of the following is NOT a factor in a location's climate?
    a. Latitudinal position
    b. Elevation
    c. Longitudinal position
    d. Proximity to mountains

10. All but which of the following are true of the Tropics?
    a. They are consistently hit with direct rays of the sun.
    b. They fall between the Tropics of Cancer and Capricorn.
    c. They are nearer the Equator than the Middle Latitudes.
    d. They are always warmer than other parts of the Globe.

11. Which of the following is true regarding the physical process of weathering?
    a. It is the same as erosion.
    b. It involves wind and rain.
    c. It does not involve moving particles.
    d. It is only a problem in cold climates.

12. Which is true of natural hazards?
    a. They generally only affect the tropical regions.
    b. They can occur in all regions of the Earth.
    c. They are more widespread in the Arctic regions.
    d. They have become less prevalent in recent years.

13. A developing nation is more likely to have which of the following?
    a. Complex highway networks
    b. Higher rates of subsistence farmers
    c. Stable government systems
    d. Little economic instability

14. Which best describes ethnic groups?
    a. Subgroups within a population who share a common history, language, or religion.
    b. Divisive groups within a nation's boundaries seeking independence.
    c. People who choose to leave a location.
    d. Any minority group within a nation's boundaries.

15. Which is NOT true of nonrenewable resources?
    a. They tend to be used more frequently than renewables.
    b. They are thought to be responsible for climate change.
    c. They are relied upon heavily in developing economies.
    d. They have slowed industrial growth.

16. Which of the following could be considered a pull factor for a particular area?
    a. High rates of unemployment
    b. Low GDP
    c. Educational opportunity
    d. High population density

17. In recent years, agricultural production has been affected by which of the following?
    a. The prevalence of biotechnology and GMOs
    b. Weaker crop yields due to poor soil
    c. Plagues of pests, which have limited food production
    d. Revolutions in irrigation, which utilize salinated water

18. The process of globalization can best be described as what?
    a. The integration of the world's economic systems into a singular entity
    b. The emergence of powerful nations seeking world dominance
    c. The absence of nation-states who seek to control certain areas
    d. Efforts to establish a singular world government for the world's citizens

19. Which of the following is true of political boundaries?
    a. They have remained static for centuries
    b. They are generally visible on Earth
    c. They are constantly changing
    d. They are never disputed among nations

Answer Explanations

1. C: Map projections, such as the Mercator Projection, are useful for finding positions on the globe, but they attempt to represent a spherical object on a flat surface. As a result, they distort areas nearest the poles, which misrepresent the size of Antarctica, Greenland, and other high latitudinal locations. Map projects can include great detail; some illustrate the physical features in an area, and most include both the northern and southern hemispheres.

2. D: Thematic maps create certain themes in which they attempt to illustrate a certain phenomenon or pattern. The obvious theme of a climate map is the climates in the represented areas. Thematic maps are very extensive and can include thousands of different themes, which makes them quite useful for students of geography. Topographic maps (Choice *A*) are utilized to show physical features, conformal projections (Choice *B*) attempt to illustrate the globe in an undistorted fashion, and isoline maps (Choice *C*) illustrate differences in variables between two points on a map.

3. B: Latitudinal and longitudinal coordinates delineate absolute location. In contrast to relative location, which describes a location as compared to another, better-known place, absolute location provides an exact place on the globe through the latitude and longitude system. Choice A, cardinal directions (north, south, east, west) are used in absolute location, but coordinates must be added in order to have an absolute location. Using other, better known locations to find a location, Choice *C*, is referred to as relative location, and absolute location is far more precise than simply finding hemispherical position on the globe.

4. B: Lines of latitude measure distance north and south. The Equator is zero degrees and the Tropic of Cancer is 23 ½ degrees north of the Equator. The distance between those two lines measures degrees north to south, as with any other two lines of latitude. Longitudinal lines, or meridians, measure distance east and west, even though they run north and south down the Globe. Latitude is not inexact, in that there are set distances between the lines. Furthermore, coordinates can only exist with the use of longitude and latitude.

5. C: Developed Nations have better infrastructural systems, which can include government, transportation, financial, and educational institutions. Consequently, its citizens tend to have higher rates of literacy, due to the sheer availability of educational resources and government sanctioned educational systems. In contrast, developing nations, Choice *A*, struggle to provide educational resources to their citizens. Nations in the Northern Hemisphere, Choice *B*, have no greater availability to educational resources than those in the Southern Hemisphere, and centers of trade, Choice *D*, don't necessarily equate to higher levels of education, as many may exist in poorer nations with fewer resources.

6. C: Population density, which is the total number of people divided by the total land area, generally tends to be much higher in urban areas than rural ones. This is true due to high-rise apartment complexes, sewage and freshwater infrastructure, and complex transportation systems, allowing for easy movement of food from nearby farms. Consequently, competition among citizens for resources is certainly higher in high-density areas, as are greater strains on infrastructure within urban centers.

7. C: Although it can place a strain on some resources, population density is not a negative demographic indicator. For example, New York City, one of the most densely populated places on Earth, enjoys one of the highest standards of living in the world. Other world cities such as Tokyo, Los Angeles, and Sydney also have tremendously high population densities and high standards of living. High infant mortality rates, low literacy rates, and low life expectancies are all poor demographic indicators that suggest a low quality of life for the citizens living in those areas.

8. A: Homogeneity, or the condition of similarity, is the unifying factor in most formal regions. Regions have one or more unifying characteristics such as language, religion, history, or economic similarities, which make the area a cohesive formal region. A good example is the Southern United States. In contrast, diversity and multilingualism, Choices *B* and *C*, are factors that may cause a region to lose homogeneity and be more difficult to classify as a region. Also, social mobility, Choice *D*, is a distractor that refers to one's ability to improve their economic standing in society and is not related to formal regions.

9. C: Longitudinal position, or a place's location either east or west, has no bearing on the place's climate. In contrast, a place's latitudinal position, or its distance away from the direct rays of the sun in the Tropics, greatly affects its climate. Additionally, proximity to mountains, which can block wind patterns, and elevation, which generally lowers temperature by three degrees for every one thousand feet gained, also impacts climate.

10. D: Although nearest the direct rays of the sun, the Tropics are not always warm. In fact, the nations of Ecuador and Peru, which are entirely within the Tropics, are home to the Andes Mountains, which remain snowcapped the entire year. This climatological anomaly is also due to cooler ocean currents and the orographic effect. Choices *A*, *B*, and *C* are all true of the tropics.

11. C: Unlike erosion, which is caused by moving particles from water or wind, weathering occurs due to fluctuations in temperatures, the impact of long-term sun exposure, or exposure to chemicals that break down rocks, trees, or soil. Over time, the effects of freezing temperatures can break down massive rocks or lead to other significant changes in the landscape. Weathering does not involve wind and rain, since those particles are constantly moving to exact change on the earth's surface. Also, weathering takes place in all climates, not just cold ones.

12. B: Although less frequent in some regions of the Earth, natural hazards such as floods, earthquakes, tsunamis, tornadoes, hurricanes, and typhoons can occur anywhere. No region on earth is absolutely safe from natural hazards. Each continent suffers from drought, flooding, earthquakes, and other natural disasters. Although it may seem like they only strike in the tropical or arctic regions, that is not the case. It is also not true that natural disasters have become more intense when compared to previous centuries, although it may seem so when watching the Weather Channel.

13. B: Developing nations tend to have higher levels of impoverished citizens. As a result, many of their citizens must rely on subsistence farming, or producing enough food to feed their families, in order to survive. In contrast, developed nations tend to produce surpluses of food and very few, if any, of its citizens engage in subsistence farming. Developing nations are less likely to have complex highway systems, stable governments, and economic stability due to financial pressures.

14. A: Although some ethnic groups throughout the world do engage in armed conflicts, the vast majority does not. Most ethnic groups tend to live in relative harmony with others with whom they share differences. Ethnic groups are simply a group of people with a religious, cultural, economic, or linguistic commonality. Additionally, ethnic groups don't always choose to leave places. Many have called certain locations home for centuries. Also, some ethnic groups actually make up the majority in some countries and are not always minority groups.

15. D: Most nonrenewable resources are easier to harness and utilize than renewable sources. That may sound counterintuitive, but the reality is that it is harder to develop solar, wind, and geothermal infrastructure than it is to build a coal-fired power plant for the production of electricity. Consequently, developing nations tend to rely on these reliable sources in order to fuel their equally developing economy.

16. C: Pull factors are reasons people immigrate to a particular area. Obviously, educational opportunities attract thousands of people on a global level and on a local level. For example, generally areas with strong schools have higher property values, due to the relative demand for housing in those districts. The same is true for nations with better educational opportunities. Unemployment, low GDP, and incredibly high population densities may serve to deter people from moving to a certain place and can be considered push factors.

17. A: The use of biotechnology and GMOs has increased the total amount of food on Earth. Additionally, it has helped to sustain the earth's growing population; however, many activists assert that scientists are creating crops that, in the long run, will be destructive to human health, even though very little evidence exists to prove such an allegation. Agricultural production has not been affected by poorer soil, plagues of pests, or the use of saline for irrigation purposes.

18. A: Globalization has put students and workers in direct conflict with one another despite their relative level of physical separation. For example, students who excel in mathematics and engineering may be recruited by multinational firms who want the best talent for their business despite where they are educated. Furthermore, products produced in other nations are also in competition with global manufacturers to ensure quality craftsmanship at an affordable price. Globalization does not refer to world domination, an absence of nation-states, or a singular world government.

19. C: Like the boundaries of the United States, political boundaries are constantly changing due to war (South Sudan), religious conflict (India and Pakistan, Israel, East Timor), and differing political ideologies (North and South Korea, Reunification of Germany after the Cold War). The only constant with political boundaries is change. It is not possible to see manmade lines separating countries on Earth, unless they are natural boundaries. Additionally, boundaries are always under dispute and they have not remained static for centuries.

Economics

Economics is the study of human behavior in response to the production, consumption, and distribution of assets or wealth. Economics can help individuals or societies make decisions or plans for themselves or communities, dependent upon their needs, wants, and resources. Economics is divided into two subgroups: microeconomics and macroeconomics.

Microeconomics is the study of individual or small group behaviors and patterns in relationship to such things as earning and spending money. It focuses on particular markets within the economy, and looks at single factors that could potentially affect individuals or small groups. For example, the use of coupons in a grocery store can affect an individual's product choice, quantity purchased, and overall savings that a person may later roll into a different purchase. Microeconomics is the study of scarcity, choice, opportunity costs, economics systems, factors of production, supply and demand, market efficiency, the role of government, distribution of income, and product markets.

Macroeconomics examines a much larger scale of the economy. It focuses on how a society or nation's goods, services, spending habits, and other factors affect the people of that entity. It focuses on aggregate factors such as demand and output. For example, if a national company moves its production overseas to save on costs, how will production, labor, and capital be affected? Macroeconomics analyzes all aggregate indicators and the microeconomic factors that influence the economy. Government and corporations use macroeconomic models to help formulate economic policies and strategies.

Microeconomics

Scarcity
People have different needs and wants, and the question arises, are the resources available to supply those needs and wants? Limited resources and high demand create scarcity. When a product is scarce, there is a short supply of it. For example, when the newest version of a cellphone is released, people line up to buy the phone or put their name on a wait list if the phone is not immediately available. The product, the new cellphone, may become a scarce commodity. In turn, because of the scarcity, companies may raise the cost of the commodity, knowing that if it is immediately available, people may pay more for the instant gratification—and vice versa. If a competing company lowers the cost of the phone but has contingencies, such as extended contracts or hidden fees, the buyer will still have the opportunity to purchase the scarce product. Limited resources and extremely high demand create scarcity and, in turn, cause companies to acquire opportunity costs.

Choice and Opportunity Costs
On a large scale, governments and communities have to assess different opportunity costs when it comes to using taxpayers' money. Should the government or community build a new school, repair roads, or allocate funds to local hospitals are all examples of choices taxpayers may have to review at some point in time. How do they decide which choice is the best, since each one has a trade off? By comparing the opportunity cost of each choice, they may decide what they are willing to live without for the sake of gaining something else.

Economic Systems
Economic systems determine what is being produced, who is producing it, who receives the product, and the money generated by the sale of the product. There are two basic types of economic systems: market economies (including free and competitive markets), and planned or command economies.

- Market Economies are characterized by:

  o Privately owned businesses, groups, or individuals providing goods or services based on demand.

  o The types of goods and services provided (supply) are based on that demand.

  o Two types: competitive market and free market.

Competitive Market	Free Market
Due to the large number of both buyers and sellers, there is no way any one seller or buyer can control the market or price.	Voluntary private trades between buyers and sellers determine markets and prices without government intervention or monopolies.

- Planned or Command Economies:

  o In planned or command economies, the government or central authority determines market prices of goods and services.

  o The government or central authority determines what is being produced as well as the quantity of production.

  o Some advantages to command economies include a large number of shared goods such as public services (transportation, schools, or hospitals).

  o Disadvantages of command economies include wastefulness of resources.

Factors of Production

There are four factors of production:

1. Land: both renewable and nonrenewable resources
2. Labor: effort put forth by people to produce goods and services
3. Capital: the tools used to create goods and services
4. Entrepreneurship: persons who combine land, labor, and capital to create new goods and services

The four factors of production are used to create goods and services to make economic profit. All four factors strongly impact one another.

Supply and Demand

Supply and demand is the most important concept of economics in a market economy. Supply is the amount of a product that a market can offer. Demand is the quantity of a product needed or desired by buyers. The price of a product is directly related to supply and demand. The correlation between the price of a product and the demand necessary to distribute resources to the market go hand in hand in a market economy. For example, when there are a variety of treats at a bakery, certain treats are in higher demand than others. The bakery can raise the cost of the more demanded items as supplies get limited. Conversely, the bakery can sell the less desirable treats by lowering the cost of those items as an incentive for buyers to purchase them.

Market Efficiency and the Role of Government (Taxes, Subsidies, and Price Controls)

Market efficiency is directly affected by supply and demand. The government can help the market stay efficient by either stepping in when the market is inefficient and/or providing the means necessary for markets to run properly. For example, society needs two types of infrastructure: physical (bridges, roads, etc.) and institutional (courts, laws, etc.). The government may impose taxes, subsidies, and price controls to increase revenue, lower prices of goods and services, ensure product availability for the government, and maintain fair prices for goods and services.

The Purpose of Taxes, Subsidies, and Price Controls

Taxes	Subsidies	Price Controls
-Generate government revenue -Discourage purchase or use of "bad" products such as alcohol or cigarettes	-Lower the price of goods and services -Reassure the supply of goods and services -Allow opportunities to compete with overseas vendors	-Act as emergency measures when government intervention is necessary -Set a minimum or maximum price for goods and services

Distribution of Income

Distribution of income refers to how wages are distributed across a society or segments of a society. If everyone made the same amount of money, the distribution of income would be equal. That is not the case in most societies. The wealth of people and companies varies. Income inequality gaps are present in America and many other nations. Taxes provide an option to redistribute income or wealth because they provide revenue to build new infrastructure and provide cash benefits to some of the poorest members in society.

Product Markets

Product markets are marketplaces where goods and services are bought and sold. Product markets provide sellers a place to offer goods and services to consumers, and for consumers to purchase those goods and services. The annual value of goods and services exchanged throughout the year is measured by the Gross Domestic Product (GDP), a monetary measure of goods and services made either quarterly or annually. Department stores, gas stations, grocery stores, and other retail stores are all examples of product markets. However, product markets do not include any raw, scarce, or trade materials.

Theory of the Firm

The behavior of firms is composed of several theories varying between short- and long-term goals. There are four basic firm behaviors: perfect competition, profit maximization, short run, and long run. Each firm follows a pattern, depending on its desired outcome. Theory of the Firm posits that firms, after conducting market research, make decisions that will maximize their profits since they are for-profit entities.

- Perfect competition:
  - In perfect competition, several businesses are selling the same product at the same time.
  - There are so many businesses and consumers that none will directly impact the market.
  - Each business and consumer is aware of the competing businesses and markets.

- Profit maximization:
  - Firms decide the quantity of a product that needs to be produced in order to receive maximum profit gains. Profit is the total amount of revenue made after subtracting costs.
- Short run:
  - A short amount of time where fixed prices cannot be adjusted
  - The quantity of the product depends on the varying amount of labor. Less labor means less product.
- Long run:
  - An amount of time where fixed prices can be adjusted
  - Firms try to maximize production while minimizing labor costs.

Overall, microeconomics operates on a small scale, focusing on how individuals or small groups use and assign resources.

Macroeconomics

Macroeconomics analyzes the economy as a whole. It studies unemployment, interest rates, price levels, and national income, which are all factors that can affect the nation as a whole, and not just individual households. Macroeconomics studies all large factors to determine how, or if, they will affect future trend patterns of production, consumption, and economic growth.

Measures of Economic Performance
It is important to measure economic performance to determine if an economy is growing, stagnant, or deteriorating. To measure the growth and sustainability of an economy, several indicators can be used. Economic indicators provide data that economists can use to determine if there are faulty processes or if some form of intervention is needed.

One of the main indicators to measure economic performance is the growth of the country's Gross Domestic Product (GDP). GDP growth provides important information that can be used to determine fiscal or financial policies. The GDP does not measure income distribution, quality of life, or losses due to natural disasters. For example, if a community lost everything to a hurricane, it would take a long time to rebuild the community and stabilize its economy. That is why there is a need to take into account more balanced performance measures when factoring overall economic performance.

Other indicators used to measure economic performance are unemployment or employment rates, inflation, savings, investments, surpluses and deficits, debt, labor, trade terms, the HDI (Human Development Index), and the HPI (Human Poverty Index).

Unemployment
Unemployment occurs when an individual does not have a job, is actively trying to find employment, and is not getting paid. Official unemployment rates do not factor in the number of people who have stopped looking for work, unlike true unemployment rates that do, causing them to be higher.

There are three types of unemployment: cyclical, frictional, and structural.

Cyclical
The product of a business cycle. This usually occurs during a recession.
Frictional
The difficulty of matching qualified workers for specific jobs. An example would be a person changing careers.
Structural
When a person no longer qualifies for a specific job, or failing out of a retraining course for a job.

Given the nature of a market economy and the fluctuations of the labor market, a 100 percent employment rate is impossible to reach.

Inflation

Inflation is when the cost of goods and services rises over time. Supply, demand, and money reserves all affect inflation. Generally, inflation is measured by the Consumer Price Index (CPI), a tool that tracks price changes of goods and services over time. The CPI measures goods and services such as gasoline, cars, clothing, and food. When the cost of goods and services increase, the quantity of the product may decrease due to lower demand. This decreases the purchasing power of the consumer. Basically, as more money is printed, it holds less and less value in purchasing power. For example, when inflation occurs, consumers in the United States are spending and saving less because the U.S. dollar is worth less, and therefore the consumer cannot buy or save as much money. However, if inflation occurs steadily over time, the people can better plan and prepare for future necessities.

Inflation can vary from year to year, usually never fluctuating more than 2 percent. Central banks try to prevent drastic increases or decreases of inflation to prohibit prices from rising or falling far from the minimum. Inflation can also vary based on different monetary currencies. Although rare, any country's economy may experience hyperinflation (when inflation rates increase to over 50 percent), while other economies may experience deflation (when the cost of goods and services decrease over time). Deflation occurs when the inflation rate drops below zero percent.

Business Cycle

A business cycle is when the Gross Domestic Product (GDP) moves downward and upward over a long-term growth trend. These cycles help determine where the economy currently stands, as well as where the economy could be heading. Business cycles usually occur almost every six years, and have four phases: expansion, peak, contraction, and trough. Here are some characteristics of each phase:

- Expansion:
    - Increased employment rates and economic growth
    - Production and sales increase
    - On a graph, expansion is where the lines climb.
- Peak:
    - Employment rates are at or above full employment and the economy is at maximum productivity.
    - On a graph, the peak is the top of the hill, where expansion has reached its maximum.
- Contraction:
    - When growth starts slowing
    - Unemployment is on the rise.
    - On a graph, contraction is where the graph begins to slide back down or contract.

- Trough:
    - The cycle has hit bottom and is waiting for the next cycle to start again.
    - On a graph, the trough is the bottom of the contraction prior to when it starts to climb back up.

When the economy is expanding or "booming," the business cycle is going from a trough to a peak. When the economy is headed down and toward a recession, the business cycle is going from a peak to a trough.

Four phases of a business cycle:

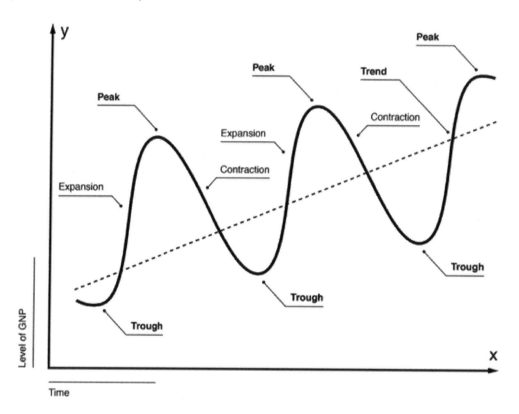

Fiscal Policy
A fiscal policy is when the government is involved in adjusting spending and tax rates to assist the way in which an economy financially functions. Fiscal policies can either increase or decrease tax rates and spending. These policies represent a tricky balancing act, because if the government increases taxes too much, consumer spending and monetary value will decrease. Conversely, if the government lowers taxes, consumers will have more money in their pockets to buy more goods and services, which increases demand and the need for companies to supply those goods and services. Due to the higher demand, suppliers can add jobs to fulfill that demand. While the increase of supply, demand, and jobs are positive for the overall economy, they may result in a devaluation of the dollar and less purchasing power.

Money and Banking
Money is the universal form of currency used throughout goods and services exchanges that holds its value over time. Money provides a convenient way for sellers and consumers to understand the value of

their goods and services. As opposed to bartering (when sellers and consumers exchange goods or services as equal trades), money is quick and easy for both buyers and sellers.

There are three main forms of money: commodity, fiat, and bank. Here are characteristics of each form:

- Commodity money: Money as a valuable good, such as precious metals
- Fiat money: The value of the good set by supply and demand rather than the actual value it represents, such as paper money
- Bank money: Money that is credited by a bank to those who deposit it into bank accounts, such as checking and savings accounts or credit

While price levels within the economy set the demand for money, most countries have central banks that supply the actual money. Essentially, banks buy and sell money. Borrowers can take loans and pay back the bank, with interest, providing the bank with extra capital.

A central bank has control over the printing and distribution of money. Central banks serve three main purposes: manage monetary growth to help steer the direction of the economy, be a backup to commercial banks that are suffering, and provide options and alternatives to government taxation.

The Federal Reserve is the central bank of the United States. The Federal Reserve controls banking systems and determines the value of money in the United States. Basically, the Federal Reserve is the bank for banks.

All Western economies have to keep a minimum amount of protected cash called *required reserve*. Once banks meet those minimums, they can then lend or loan the excess to consumers. The required reserves are used within a fractional reserve banking system (fractional because a small portion is kept separate and safe). Not only do banks reserve, manage, and loan money, but they also help form monetary policies.

Monetary Policy
The central bank and other government committees control the amount of money that is made and distributed. The money supply determines monetary policy. Three main features sustain monetary policy:

1. Assuring the minimum amount held within banks (bank reserves). When banks are required to hold more money in reserve funds, banks are less willing to lend money to help control inflation.
2. Adjusting interest rates. For example, if the value of money is low, companies and consumers buy more (products, employees, stocks) because prices are cheap. Just like an investment, it is risky, but can pay off in the long term.
3. The purchase and sales of bonds (otherwise known as open market operations). When buying bonds to increase money and selling bonds to reduce the supply, the central bank helps control the money supply.

In the United States, the Federal Reserve maintains monetary policy. There are two main types of monetary policy: expansionary monetary policy and contractionary monetary policy.

- Expansionary monetary policy:
    - Increases the money supply
    - Lowers unemployment
    - Increases consumer spending

- o Increases private sector borrowing
- o Possibly decreases interest rates to very low levels, even near zero
- o Decreases reserve requirements and federal funds
- Contractionary monetary policy:
    - o Decreases the money supply
    - o Helps control inflation
    - o Possibly increases unemployment due to slowdowns in economic growth
    - o Decreases consumer spending
    - o Decreases loans and/or borrowing

The Federal Reserve uses monetary policy to try to achieve maximum employment and secure inflation rates. Because the Federal Reserve is the "bank of banks," it truly strives to be the last-resort option for distressed banks. This is because once these kinds of institutions begin to rely on the Federal Reserve for help, all parts of the banking industry—such as those dealing with loans, bonds, interest rates, and mortgages—are affected.

International Trade and Exchange Rates

International trade is when countries import and export goods and services. Countries often want to deal in terms of their own currency. Therefore, when importing or exporting goods or services, consumers and businesses need to enter the market using the same form of currency. For example, if the United States would like to trade with China, the U.S. may have to trade in China's form of currency, the *Yuan*, versus the dollar, depending on the business.

The exchange rate is what one country's currency will exchange for another. The government and the market (supply and demand) determine the exchange rate. There are two forms of exchange rates: fixed and floating. Fixed exchange rates involve government interventions (like central banks) to help keep the exchange rates stable. Floating or "flexible" exchange rates constantly change because they rely on supply and demand needs. While each type of exchange rate has advantages and disadvantages, the rate truly depends on the current state of each country's economy. Therefore, each exchange rate may differ from country to country.

Advantages and Disadvantages of Fixed Versus Floating Exchange Rates			
Fixed Exchange Rate: government intervention to help keep exchange rates stable		Floating or "Flexible" Exchange Rate: Supply and demand determines the exchange rate	
Advantages	*Disadvantages*	*Advantages*	*Disadvantages*
-Stable prices	-Requires a large	-Central bank	-Currency speculation
-Stable foreign	amount of reserve	involvement is not	-Exchange rate risks
exchange rates	funds	needed.	-Inflation increases
-Exports are more	-Possibly mispricing	-Facilitates free trade	
competitive and in turn	currency values		
more profitable	Inflation increases		

While each country may have differing economic statuses and exchange rates, countries rely on one another for goods and services. Prices of imports and exports are affected by the strength of another country's currency. For example, if the United States dollar is at a higher value than another country's currency, imports will be less expensive because the dollar will have more value than that of the country selling its good or service. On the other hand, if the dollar is at a low value compared to the currency of another country, importers will tend to defer away from buying international items from that country. However, U.S. exporters to that country could benefit from the low value of the dollar.

Economic Growth

Economic growth is measured by the increase in the Gross National Product (GNP) or Gross Domestic Product (GDP). The increase of goods and services over time indicates positive movement in economic growth. Keep in mind that the quantity of goods and services produced is not necessarily an indicator of economic growth. The value of the goods and services produced matters more than the quantity.

There are many causes of economic growth, which can be short- or long-term. In the short term, if aggregate demand (the total demand for goods and services produced at a given time) increases, then the overall Gross Domestic Product (GDP) increases as well. Not only will the GDP increase, interest rates may decrease. With reduced interest rates, spending and investing will increase. Consumer and government spending will also increase because there will be more disposable income. Real estate prices will rise, and there will be lower income taxes. All of these short-term factors can stimulate economic growth.

In the long term, if aggregate supply (the total supply of goods or services in a given time period) increases, then there is potential for an increase in capital as well. With more working capital, more infrastructure and jobs can be created. With more jobs, there is an increased employment rate, and education and training for jobs will improve. New technologies will be developed, and new raw materials may be discovered. All of these long-term factors can also stimulate economic growth.

Outside of the short- and long-term causes for economic growth, other factors include low inflation and stability. Lower inflation rates encourage more investing versus higher inflation rates that cause instability in the market. Stability encourages businesses to continue investing. If the market is unstable, investors may question the volatility of the market.

Potential Costs of Economic Growth:

- Inflation: When economic growth occurs, inflation tends to be high. If supply cannot keep up with demand, then the inflation rate may be unmanageable.
- Economic booms and recessions: The economy goes through cycles of booms and recessions. This causes inflation to increase and decrease over time, which puts the economy into a continuous cycle of rising and falling.
- Account inefficiencies: When the economy grows, consumers and businesses increase their import spending. The increase of import spending affects the current account and causes a shortage.
- Environmental costs: When the economy is growing, there is an abundance of output, which may result in more pollutants and a reduction in quality of life.
- Inequalities: Growth occurs differently among members of society. While the wealthy may be getting richer, those living in poverty may just be getting on their feet. So while economic growth is happening, it may happen at two very different rates.

While these potential costs could affect economic growth, if the growth is consistent and stable, then growth can occur without severe inflation swings. Also, as technology improves, new ways of production can reduce negative environmental factors as well.

Practice Test

1. Which of the following is the subgroup of economics that studies large-scale economic issues such as unemployment, interest rates, price levels, and national income?
    a. Microeconomics
    b. Macroeconomics
    c. Scarcity
    d. Supply and demand

2. A homeowner hires a landscape company to mow the grass because they would like to use that time to do something else. The trade-off of paying someone to do a job to make more valuable use of time is an example of what?
    a. Economic systems
    b. Supply and demand
    c. Opportunity cost
    d. Inflation

3. Which kind of market does not involve government interventions or monopolies while trades are made between suppliers and buyers?
    a. Free
    b. Command
    c. Gross
    d. Exchange

4. Which is NOT an indicator of economic growth?
    a. GDP (Gross Domestic Product)
    b. Unemployment
    c. Inflation
    d. Theory of the Firm

5. In a business cycle, a recession occurs between which cycles?
    a. Expansion, peak
    b. Peak, contraction
    c. Contraction, trough
    d. Trough, expansion

6. What is the name of the central bank that controls the value of money in the United States?
    a. Commodity Reserve
    b. Central Reserve
    c. Federal Reserve
    d. Bank Reserve

7. Which option does NOT sustain monetary policies?
    a. Closed market operations
    b. Open market operations
    c. Assuring bank reserves
    d. Adjusting interest rates

8. What determines the exchange rate in a "floating" or "flexible" exchange?
    a. The government
    b. Taxes
    c. The Federal Reserve
    d. The market

9. Which statement is true about inflation and purchasing power?
    a. As inflation decreases, purchasing power increases.
    b. As inflation increases, purchasing power decreases.
    c. As inflation increases, purchasing power increases.
    d. As inflation decreases, purchasing power decreases.

10. Which statement is true about goods and services?
    a. The quantity of goods and services matters more than their value.
    b. The value of goods and services matters more than their quantity.
    c. The quality of goods and services matters more than their production.
    d. The production of goods and services matters more than their quality.

11. Which of the following refers to the value of a good set by supply and demand rather than the actual value it represents?
    a. Commodity money
    b. Fiat money
    c. Bank money
    d. Reserve money

12. Which of the following is not a characteristic of contractionary monetary policy?
    a. Increases the money supply
    b. Possibly increases unemployment due to slowdowns in economic growth
    c. Decreases consumer spending
    d. Decreases loans and/or borrowing

13. Which of the following lists all four phases of the business cycle?
    a. Expansion, crest, peak, trough
    b. Expansion, contraction, peak, trench
    c. Peak, trough, contraction, expansion
    d. Peak, rise, trough, decline

14. Frictional unemployment is best described by which of the following?
    a. When a person is no longer qualified for a job
    b. When a qualified person cannot be matched to a job
    c. When a person is laid off because of the business cycle
    d. When a person is unemployed for longer than six months

15. How is economic growth measured?
    a. By the rise in the inflation of a country
    b. By the amount of reserves that a country holds
    c. By the amount of exports that a country has
    d. By the GDP of a country

16. If a store has a large supply of item *xyz* and they are not selling many of them, what should they do?
    a. Raise the price so that when they do sell one, they will make a large profit.
    b. Lower the price so that hopefully demand will go up and they can get rid of it.
    c. Raise the price so that people will think that it is a limited, high value product and buy it.
    d. Offer the product in a low price bundle with other unrelated products.

17. Who is in control in a command economy?
    a. The consumer
    b. Private businesses
    c. The government
    d. Manufacturers

18. Which of the following correctly lists the factors of production?
    a. Land, labor, material, entrepreneurship
    b. Land, labor, capital, equity
    c. Land, a building, capital, labor
    d. Land, labor, capital, entrepreneurship

19. Which of the following is NOT a purpose of the central bank?
    a. Manage interest rates
    b. Set the tax rate
    c. Backup the commercial banks
    d. Set reserve requirements

Answer Explanations

1. B: Macroeconomics. Macroeconomics studies the economy on a large scale and focuses on issues such as unemployment, interest rates, price levels, and national income. Microeconomics, Choice *A*, studies more individual or small group behaviors such as scarcity or supply and demand. Scarcity, Choice *C*, is not correct because it refers to the availability of goods and services. Supply and demand, Choice *D*, is also incorrect because it refers to the quantity of goods and services that is produced and/or needed.

2. C: Opportunity cost. Opportunity cost can trade time, power, or anything else of value in exchange for something else. Economic systems, Choice *A*, determine what is being produced and by whom. Supply and demand, Choice *B*, refers to the quantity of goods and services that is produced or needed. Finally, inflation, Choice *D*, refers to how the cost of goods and services increases over time.

3. A: Free. A free market does not involve government interventions or monopolies while trading between buyers and suppliers. However, in a command market, the government determines the price of goods and services. Gross and exchange markets refer to situations where brokers and traders make exchanges in the financial realm.

4. D: Theory Of The Firm. Behaviors of firms is not an indicator of economic growth because it refers to the behavior that firms follow to reach their desired outcome. GDP, unemployment, and inflation are all indicators that help determine economic growth.

5. C: Contraction and trough. A recession occurs between the contraction and trough phases of the business cycle. Between expansion and peak phases, employment and productivity are on the rise, causing a "boom." Between the peak and contraction, unemployment rates are starting to fall, but have not yet hit an all-time low. Between trough and expansion phases, the economy is getting back on its feet and starting to increase employment again.

6. C: Federal Reserve. The Federal Reserve is the bank of banks. It is the central bank of the United States and controls the value of money. A commodity is the value of goods such as precious metals. While the Central Reserve and Bank Reserve may sound like good options, the term "bank reserve" refers to the amount of money a bank deposits into a central bank, and the Central Reserve is simply a fictitious name.

7. A: Closed market operations. Monetary policies are sustained by assuring bank reserves, adjusting interest rates, and open market operations. Closed market operations do NOT uphold monetary policies.

8. D: The market. The market, through supply and demand, determines the exchange rate with a "flexible" or "floating" exchange rate. The government, Choice *A*, is not the correct answer because it is involved in "fixed" exchange rates to help keep exchange rates stable. Taxes, Choice *B*, is also incorrect because they create government revenue. The Federal Reserve, Choice *C*, is the bank of banks.

9. B: As inflation increases, purchasing power decreases. As more money is printed, the monetary value of the dollar drops and, in turn, decreases the purchasing power of goods and services. So, as inflation increases, consumers are not spending as much and the value of the dollar is low.

10. B: The value of goods and services matters more than their quantity. For example, in the real estate industry, if a realtor sells ten houses valued at $200,000, their commission would be the same as a realtor who sells one house valued at $2,000,000. Even though one realtor sold more homes, the value of ten houses adds up to the same amount as the single home that the other realtor sold. Therefore, the number of goods and services produced does not determine economic growth—the value of the goods and services does.

11. B: Fiat money. Commodity money, Choice *B*, refers to a good that has value, such as a precious metal. Bank money, Choice *C*, is money that is credited by a bank to those people who have their money deposited there. The term Reserve money, Choice *D*, does not refer to anything.

12. A: In contractionary monetary policy, the money supply is decreased. All of the other choices are characteristics of contractionary monetary policy.

13. C: The four phases of the business cycle are peak, trough, expansion, contraction. The other answer choices include at least one wrong phase.

14. B: Frictional unemployment occurs when a qualified person is unable to find a job. Cyclical unemployment occurs as a product of the business cycle, such as during a time of recession. Structural unemployment occurs when a person is no longer qualified for that particular job.

15. D: The GDP is used to measure an economy's growth. The inflation of a country doesn't tell us anything about their growth. A country may hold a lot of money in reserves but this does not tell us if they are growing or not. The same can be said for having a lot of exports. It does indicate that an economy is necessarily growing.

16. B: As the price of a product is lowered the demand should rise. Raising the price on an already hard to sell item would just make it harder to sell. If you offer it in a bundle of unrelated products then people are unlikely to want to buy those products together.

17. C: In a command economy, the government controls the prices as well as what and how much of a product is produced.

18. D: The factors of production are land, labor, capital, and entrepreneurship. The other choices all include at least one option that is not a factor of production.

19. B: The central bank is responsible for all of these except for setting the tax rate. This is done by the government.

Behavioral Sciences

Behavioral science is the study of human and animal behavior through observation and experimentation. People and animals act and react to their surroundings. Their behaviors differ based on the environment. In this section, the areas covered will be:

- How society, groups, and institutions influence human behavior
- How culture and cultural change, human adaptation, and diversity influence human behavior
- How learning, personal identity, and development affect individual behavior

How Society, Groups, and Institutions Influence Human Behavior

Society refers to the community in which people live together. Human behavior is greatly influenced by society. People may feel pressure to live by certain standards or act in a specific way. Certain societal "norms" influence a person's behavior in both positive and negative ways.

Additionally, groups can influence how people behave. Peer pressure and the pressure to conform to certain group norms are present throughout life. Peer pressure is often greatest during adolescence, where young people seek the approval of those around them and are willing to do nearly whatever it takes to get their peers' approval. Opinions on any topic belonging within a social circle can change drastically with a few dominant personalities. Another concern is peer pressure involving substance abuse. Adolescents may drink alcohol or do drugs because their friends are doing it and they want to be part of the crowd.

While society and groups impact a person's behavior significantly, institutions also influence human behavior. Institutions have formal and informal rules, and an individual must choose whether they comply with the rules. There are five major types of social institutions that can influence human behavior: family, religion, government, education, and economics.

Family
- Regulates sexual behavior (monogamy)
- Creates and provides for new society members
- Socializes new society members

Religion
- Provides explanations for the unexplainable
- Supports societal norms and values
- Provides a means of coping with life situations

Government
- Institutionalizes norms (by creating laws)
- Enforces laws
- Protects members of society
- Provides a means of resolving conflict

Education
- Prepares society members to contribute to the society in specified roles
- Teaches skills necessary to function within the society

Economics
- Produces and distributes goods needed by society members
- Provides services necessary to the society

How Culture and Cultural Change, Human Adaptation, and Diversity Influence Human Behavior

Human behavior is influenced by culture and cultural changes, human adaptation, and diversity. Every person is different. People are born into different types of families, religions, geographic areas, and other circumstances. These differences affect how people act. Respecting differences is key to influencing human behavior.

<u>Culture and Culture Change</u>
Culture derives from the beliefs, values, and behaviors of people in a community. These beliefs, values, and behaviors tend to be passed from one generation to the next. Culture can change over time and from generation to generation.

All people are born into a certain culture, which can be embedded within families, schools, businesses, social classes, and religions. Within these cultural institutions, people learn positive and negative reinforcement, dialect and slang, diet, acceptable and unacceptable practices of society, and many more societal norms.

The social class that people are born into also influences their behavior. A social class is determined by someone's social and economic status and can change over time. Indicators of social class include wealth, education level, job perspectives, marital status, and standard of living. Some living in poverty may strive to attain a higher education level to find a better job and become upwardly mobile. However, others living in poverty may continue to support themselves day to day and use government assistance funds. The culture in which one was raised will influence how a person lives their life. As a person's social class changes, they will adapt their behavior to new situations.

<u>Human Adaptation and Diversity</u>
Over time, the environment in which a person lives changes. Humans adapt their behaviors to fit the needs of their new environment, as well as their own needs. Every person adapts to situations in a unique way simply because everyone is different. Diversity accounts for differences in race, gender, sexual orientation, economic status, and language. Culture creates a set of "norms" to compare what is considered different or diverse within a given culture. In every culture, there is a minority and majority group. The majority of the culture typically sets the "norm" and then influences people's behaviors within the society.

How Learning, Personal Identity, and Development Affect Individual Behavior

Learning is a process in which individuals gain skills or knowledge through experiences, studying, or instruction. Throughout people's lives, human beings are continuously learning and, therefore, the way in which they behave may be affected by new information that is learned. As people learn new things, their behaviors affect how they view their environment, culture, and society. This is also known as a behavioral theory.

Using new technology can affect how people interact with one another. For instance, a new technology allowing people to shop for groceries online and then merely pick up the goods or have them delivered will limit in-store impulse purchases, decrease or eliminate customer service communication, and potentially affect the quality of goods sold if individuals do not personally hand select their own products. Learning processes will constantly change and therefore human behaviors will constantly evolve.

Along with learning, people will continuously adjust their personal identity. Personal identity is a person's own perception of themself throughout their lifespan. Someone's personal identity can relate to where they grew up, race, religion, social class, and many other life experiences. Keep in mind, with new experiences, people learn and may change their viewpoints on topics. Although people may identify with one subgroup or culture now, it does not mean they will agree with that subgroup or culture in the future, or that they have in the past. Personal identity will continue to change an individual's behavior throughout life.

As a person's identity adjusts throughout life, they also develop new skills. Development and learning go hand-in-hand in affecting a person's behavior. Development stems from learning. A person's development progresses through life, and people's behaviors will change many times throughout their lives. New experiences or events, learning something new, identifying with a different group, or natural development in itself will all affect an individual's behaviors.

Practice Questions

1. What is it called when a group uses the majority vote to try to persuade the minority into changing their minds?
    a. Behaviorism
    b. Diversity
    c. Peer pressure
    d. Adaptation

2. Which is NOT a social institution that influences human behavior?
    a. Family
    b. Education
    c. Religion
    d. Transportation

3. Healthcare, taxes, schools, infrastructure, subsidies, unemployment, food stamps, and laws are a part of all people's lives and are influenced by which social institution?
    a. Religion
    b. Economic systems
    c. Family
    d. Government

4. What derives from the beliefs, values, and behaviors of those in a community?
    a. Culture
    b. Diversity
    c. Adaptation
    d. Economic systems

5. Which is NOT an indicator of social class?
    a. Marital status
    b. Wealth
    c. Government
    d. Education

Read the following passage and answer the question.
> "An elderly couple moves from their own residence into an assisted living facility. They no longer have to cook, clean, or plan activities for their day because the assisted living facility has it all prepared for them. At first, the couple gets frustrated about the lack of independence they have, but over time, enjoy the extra help."

6. What is the information in the passage an example of?
    a. Culture
    b. Human adaptation
    c. Diversity
    d. Development

7. A school's parent-teacher meeting had moms from every walk of life: single moms, married moms, religious moms, educated moms, stay-at-home moms, working moms, etc. Which word best describes this group?
    a. Single-minded
    b. Diverse
    c. Conservative
    d. Liberal

8. The values and traits that define who a person is by their own measure is called what?
    a. Personal identity
    b. Development
    c. Human adaptation
    d. Culture

9. Which statement is NOT true about a person's behavior?
    a. Behaviors change over time.
    b. Behaviors are influenced by a person's environment.
    c. A person will always have the same personal identity.
    d. Cultural changes influence a person's behavior.

10. Which group is more likely to succumb to or be influenced by peer pressure?
    a. Adolescents
    b. Senior Women
    c. Middle-aged men
    d. Small children

11. Which of these is NOT a factor in which education can influence behavior?
    a. A school's rules and regulations
    b. Bullying establishing a system of social ranking
    c. School regulated social situations
    d. Grading

12. Which of these is NOT a true statement about culture?
    a. Culture derives from the beliefs, values, and behaviors of people in a community.
    b. All people are born into a certain culture.
    c. Cultures are stagnant and cannot be changed.
    d. Culture can be embedded within families, schools, businesses, social classes, and religions.

13. Differences in race, gender, sexual orientation, economic status, and language can be denoted as what?
    a. Behaviorism
    b. Peer pressure
    c. Adaptation
    d. Diversity

14. Which of the following are indicators of social class?
    a. Wealth
    b. Education level
    c. Standard of living
    d. All of the above

Answer Explanations

1. C: Peer pressure. Peer pressure is when a group uses the majority vote to try to persuade the minority into changing their minds. Choice *A* (behaviorism) is the study of how behavior influences the way human beings interact with their environment. Choice *B* (diversity) refers to how everything and everyone is uniquely different. Finally, Choice *D* (adaptation) is also incorrect because adaptation refers to how a human being adjusts to their surroundings to create a desired outcome. Therefore, Choice *C* (peer pressure) is correct.

2. D: Transportation. While transportation may affect how people live their lives, it is not a social institution that influences human behavior. However, family, education, and religion all influence human behavior.

3. D: Government. Healthcare, taxes, schools, infrastructure, subsidies, unemployment, food stamps, and laws are every part of people's lives and are influenced by government policies and decisions.

4. A: Culture. Culture derives from the beliefs, values, and behaviors of those in a community. These beliefs, values, and behaviors tend to be passed from one generation to the next. Culture can change over time and from generation to generation.

5. C: Government. Government is not an indicator of social class. The social class that people are born into influences their behavior. A social class is determined by someone's social and economic status and can change over time. Indicators of social class include wealth, education level, job perspectives, marital status, and standard of living.

6. B: Human adaptation. Human adaptation is how a person adjusts to change over time throughout their life. While culture (Choice *A*) derives from the beliefs, values, and behaviors of those in a community, it is not the correct choice for this example. Diversity (Choice *C*) is also incorrect because the paragraph does not discuss differences between the population and facilities. Finally, the couple's development (how they grow within their environment) is not a factor in the passage. Therefore, human adaptation is the correct option.

7. B: Diverse. The group of moms is a diverse group because there are many different types of moms represented in the group.

8. A: Personal identity. Personal identity is a person's own perception about themselves throughout life. Someone's personal identity can relate to where they grew up, race, religion, social class, and many more aspects. With new experiences, people learn and may change their viewpoint on a topic. Although they may identify with one subgroup or culture now, this does not mean they will agree with it in the future or that they have in the past. Personal identity will continue to change an individual's behavior throughout their life.

9. C: A person will always have the same personal identity. Even though a person may identify with one subgroup or culture now, does not mean that they will agree with it in the future or that they have in the past. Personal identity will continue to change an individual's behavior throughout life.

10. A: Adolescents are most likely to be influenced by pressure from their peers in making life decisions.

11. B: While bullying may affect a person's life and often happens in schools, it does not establish ranking of any sort, and is not educational or part of the educational system. Choice *A* is correct because the rules established by the school help shape a sense of morals in students, or the lack thereof. Choice C is correct because the social situations foster sharing, patience, teamwork, and respect. Choice D is correct because grades establish a feeling of desire to meet expectations, as well as a fear of failing.

12. C: Each statement about culture is correct except for Choice C. Cultures often will adapt to the settings in which they are found. Some cultures derive from such settings and have continued on adapting to what works best to keep that culture.

13. D: Diversity. Diversity refers to how everything and everyone is uniquely different. Choice A (behaviorism) is the study of how behavior influences the way human beings interact with their environment. Choice B (peer pressure) is when a group uses the majority vote to try to persuade the minority into changing their minds. Finally, Choice C (adaptation) is also incorrect because adaptation refers to how a human being adjusts to their surroundings to create a desired outcome. Therefore, Choice D (diversity) is correct.

14. D: All of the above. Each of these answers is an indicator of social class. Wealth and standard of living are often related as the amount of money you have helps determine your standard of living. Often times if the standard of living in an area is high, the education environment fosters a higher education level, which can cause a higher level of social class. The opposite is true if the standard of living is low.

Dear Praxis II Social Studies Test Taker,

We would like to start by thanking you for purchasing this study guide for your Praxis II Social Studies exam. We hope that we exceeded your expectations.

Our goal in creating this study guide was to cover all of the topics that you will see on the test. We also strove to make our practice questions as similar as possible to what you will encounter on test day. With that being said, if you found something that you feel was not up to your standards, please send us an email and let us know.

We would also like to let you know about other books in our catalog that may interest you.

Praxis II Elementary Education Test

This can be found on Amazon: amazon.com/dp/1628454326

Praxis II English Language Arts

amazon.com/dp/1628454105

Praxis II General Science

amazon.com/dp/1628454385

Praxis II Mathematics

amazon.com/dp/1628454261

Praxis Core Study Guide

amazon.com/dp/1628454946

We have study guides in a wide variety of fields. If the one you are looking for isn't listed above, then try searching for it on Amazon or send us an email.

Thanks Again and Happy Testing!
Product Development Team
info@studyguideteam.com

FREE Test Taking Tips DVD Offer

To help us better serve you, we have developed a Test Taking Tips DVD that we would like to give you for FREE. **This DVD covers world-class test taking tips that you can use to be even more successful when you are taking your test.**

All that we ask is that you email us your feedback about your study guide. Please let us know what you thought about it – whether that is good, bad or indifferent.

To get your **FREE Test Taking Tips DVD**, email freedvd@studyguideteam.com with "FREE DVD" in the subject line and the following information in the body of the email:

    a. The title of your study guide.

    b. Your product rating on a scale of 1-5, with 5 being the highest rating.

    c. Your feedback about the study guide. What did you think of it?

    d. Your full name and shipping address to send your free DVD.

If you have any questions or concerns, please don't hesitate to contact us at freedvd@studyguideteam.com.

Thanks again!

79879051R00102

Made in the USA
Middletown, DE
13 July 2018